Northrop Flying Wings

A History of Jack Northrop's Visionary Aircraft

NORTHROP FLYING WINGS

A History of Jack Northrop's Visionary Aircraft

Garry R. Pape
with John M. Campbell

Schiffer Military/Aviation History
Atglen, PA

ACKNOWLEDGEMENTS

We would like to thank the many people who helped in the research and assisted in the production of this work. A number of past Northrop employees have given invaluable assistance. Among the test pilots are Fred Bretcher, John Myers, Max Stanley, and Chuck Tucker. Insight into the design of these aircraft has been provided by past chief aerodynamicists Herb DeCenzo and Dr. William R. Sears. Roy Wolford, who was chief photographer during the time of the Wings, has graciously opened his photo files to us once again and provided many of the photos in this publication. Past corporate historian, Dr. Ira Chart, PhD. was kind enough to take us under his wing and provided material assistance in the form of photographs and data and provided needed encouragement and guidance in the early days of this effort. John H. Northrop gave of his valuable time in telling of his remembrances and providing historical documentation.

Good friends and fellow Wing enthusiasts Stu Luce and Robert Gerhart also opened their files to us and have given much appreciated assistance in our research efforts. We would also like to thank Terry Clawson and John Amrhein at Northrop Corporation headquarters Public Information and Bill Vas of the Northrop Vintage Aircraft Booster Club for their assistance in obtaining photos and drawings.

Retired Air Force officers Brig. Gen. Robert L. Cardenas and Col. Russ Schleeh who flew the YB-49 and Phil French who was a flight engineer on that aircraft have provided insight into the Air Force's test program as well as data from their own files. Once again Stu Ostler, James Crowder, PhD, Don Klinko, PhD, Laura Casey, at Tinker have provided superb assistance. John Heyer, Mark Copeland, Jerry Czubinski, Wayne Watts, Mike Conners, Gary James, Wayne Walrond, Dorothy Brown, Steven Brown, James Brown, David Brown, Jon Maguire, Ron Willis, Jimmy Root, Mark Bacon, Jeff Ethell, Nick Veronico, Robert Mikesh, A. Kevin Grantham, Marty Isham, James Crow, Bill Davis, Larry Cudd, Richard & Kathy Long, Norm Taylor, Cheryl Gumm, Tom Charmichael, Mandy Humphreys, Tinker AFB Office of History, Office of Air Force Intelligence, National Security Agency, LtCol Kenny Wilkerson of OC/ALC Flight Test Branch at Tinker AFB, Oklahoma City, OK. Steve Wilson, Darrel Moore, Douglas Legg, and Peter Bilan.

Bill Vinson, who worked on the XP-79 project at Avion, shed light on the design and construction of that aircraft. Bill Huffman, who also worked at Avion, has added to the XP-79 story. He also gave his first person account on the smelting of the YB-35s.

Dr. James Young, Fred Johnsen, and Joyce Baker of the Air Force Flight Test Center history office have provided extensive material and research assistance. Jean Harada of the Western Museum of Flight, Tim Wooldridge, Dan Hagedorn, Melissa Keiser, and Larry Wilson at the Smithsonian's National Air & Space Museum's archives division and Ray Wagner at the San Diego Aerospace Museum's archives have also given of their time and have greatly aided us in our research. Tom Lubbesmeyer at The Boeing Company historical archives was of great assistance in locating photos of the 1929 Avion Model I. Garland Gouger and J. Campbell Martin at NASA's Langley Research Center assisted us in obtaining photos and reports of Northrop wind tunnel models tested there in the 1940s. Brenda Pietrowski at the Archives Branch of the Air Force Historical Research Agency, Maxwell AFB, Voncille L. Jones, Chief of the Office of History, Air Force Development Test Center, Eglin AFB, and Dave Menard of the Air Force Museum, Wright Patterson AFB, provided valuable assistance in our quest.

Good friend and fellow aero enthusiast Gerry Balzer was his usual generous self and lent great assistance in our research. And who could forget the support in this project of "Mad" Mike Hill of NODAK Air Force.

By far not last is Peter B. Schiffer who is not only our publisher, but was the instigator of this research project. Likewise, Bob Biondi, Military Editor at Schiffer Publishing, Ltd., has been of much help throughout. Both of the above get a grade of A+ in patience and understanding as this project dragged out and we all went through personal trials and tribulations. Thanks!

As stated in the dedication, one of the trio who started this project is no longer with us – John Campbell's wife, Donna, was of great assistance and support. Barbara Pape, wife of author Garry Pape, put in many hours of grunt work – typing, copying, running to the Post Office, etc. – as well as that very important job of proofreading.

I especially want to thank my mother and father F.D. and Ruth Campbell for all the love and for their eternal support during the dark days, I owe them everything.

Garry R. Pape
Rowland Heights, California

John M. Campbell
Oklahoma City, Oklahoma

DEDICATION

This work is dedicated to the memory of Donna Campbell. She was a true "help meet" to John Campbell – wife, friend, and co-author. Though battling cancer, she gave her all in putting this book together. She passed away in the spring of 1994 but through the legacy of the books she left behind, she will always be with us.

Book Design by Mary Jane M̧ Hannigan

Copyright © 1995 by Garry R. Pape, with John M. Campbell.
Library of Congress Catalog Number: 94-66966

Printed in China
ISBN: 0-88740-689-0

We are interested in hearing from authors with book ideas on related topics.

Published by Schiffer Publishing Ltd.
77 Lower Valley Road
Atglen, PA 19310
Please write for a free catalog.
This book may be purchased from the publisher.
Please include $2.95 postage.
Try your bookstore first.

CONTENTS

Then Maj. Robert L. Cardenas, now Brig. Gen., USAF retired, standing second from the right.

FOREWORD

Mr. Garry Pape has captured the essence of the Wing concept. It is as much about Mr. Northrop as it is about the "clean" aircraft that his vision and perseverance brought about. With great detail he will bring you from Mr. Northrop's youth and his dreams through the many trials and successes, as well as disappointments from which he always rebounded with increased enthusiasm, and finally ending with the triumph which he lived to see in the B-2. Technology had finally caught up with the system that he had conceived some 30 years ahead of its time.

I joined the program in August of 1946 when I was directed to check out in the N-9M at Muroc Air Base. My flights were to prepare me for the Army Air Force Performance Phase II tests on the XB-35 but I was diverted by assignment as operations Officer and pilot of the B-29 being used to explore, with the XS-1, the transonic and eventually exceed MACH ONE which we did in October of 1947. In December, 1947 I returned to the program when Max Stanley the Northrop test pilot checked me and my now Air Force crew out in the YB-49. On January 13, 1948 we took delivery of YB-49 #42-102368 at the Hawthorne Plant and flew it to Muroc AB. On February 19, 1948 the Performance Phase II tests began in earnest. The aircraft demonstrated a high degree of reliability and maintainability producing seven arduous test flights between the 19th and the 26th of February. March and April was planned "downed time" and on 20 and 21 May I checked out Captain Glen Edwards as my replacement since I was to attend USC to finish my Aero- engineering Degree. The rest of my crew remained with captain Edwards.

On June 5, 1948 the wing crashed at Muroc. My school orders were cancelled and I returned on the project to fly the Stability and Control tests on the remaining aircraft #42-102367. The aircraft demonstrated marginal stability about all three axis resulting in rather long bomb runs with less than desirable results. In November of 1948 I was asked to appear before a Board of General Officers at AMC Headquarters in Dayton Ohio to report on my evaluation of the test results. Mr. Northrop was present. I ended my briefing by stating that the mechanical and design deficiencies that I had enumerated were capable of being corrected but that the system had exceeded the human sensory and electronic response system thereby requiring some form of stability augmentation device.

I could not state at that time what it was since the age of microelectronics and "chips" with the attendant computers had not yet arrived on the scene. The B-2 has such a system today along with a crew ejection system for emergencies which were not available during the days of the YB-49. All the deficiencies of the YB-49 have been corrected and Mr. Northrop has been vindicated. He is up there looking down and smiling. I feel honored and humble to have known him.

Robert L. Cardenas
Brigadier General USAF ret.
San Diego, CA   04/13/95

INTRODUCTION

Flying wings and tailless aircraft design has become synonymous with John K. "Jack" Northrop and his passion for a clean design.

The following pages contain an in-depth look at both the man and his designs. He got into aviation in its infancy just prior to the First World War. Soon the first inkling of an airplane with reduced drag came in the form of the Loughead S-1 Sportplane.

With a glut of war surplus aircraft on the market, the Loughead brothers closed up shop in Santa Barbara, California, and Jack Northrop and the rest of their employees were looking for jobs. After a short interlude from the aviation industry, Jack Northrop found employment with the Douglas Aircraft Company. Here he and kindred spirit Tony Stadlman hit upon the idea of a Flying Wing as a most efficient aircraft – low parasitic drag and high lift.

A smaller step had to be taken which required Northrop to leave Douglas and help start up another Lockheed company. What Jack came up with was a beautiful cantilevered wing aircraft which became the Lockheed Vega. This plane was so successful that there didn't seem to be any time to advance his idea of a Flying Wing. Once again he left his job, but this time it was to form his own company. With Ken Jay, whom be befriended at Lockheed, the Avion Corporation was formed. Their first design, the Avion Model I, was about the closest thing to a flying wing that could be without going all the way. With engine, cockpit, and landing gear housed in a wing, only minuscule booms protruded from the back of this craft to support a tail unit. It did seem to prove that a flying wing was feasible, but most of all through its design Jack Northrop came up with multicellular stressed skin construction.

The Great Depression of 1929 hit the aviation industry hard. Late that year William Boeing, interested in Northrop's new aircraft construction method, was instrumental in buying out Avion. It became the Northrop Aircraft Corporation, a division of United Aircraft and Transportation Corporation. When the Northrop division was merged with the Stearman division in Wichita in 1930 and the operations moved to this Kansas city, Northrop and many of his people elected to leave the firm and stay in southern California.

Another stint with Douglas, including a division carrying the Northrop name, saw a number of Northrop designs produced for the Douglas Aircraft Company through 1937. As successful as these "conventional" aircraft were, Jack Northrop once again found little time to pursue the ultimate design. Effective January 1, 1938, he left Douglas and once again went about forming his own company. Jack Northrop formed Northrop Aircraft, Incorporated in early 1939. Through this company his dream of a clean aircraft would come to fruition. To Jack Northrop, the wing, with its reduced drag and increased lift, seemed to be "the" flying machine. The first effort, project N-1 – a true flying wing, would prove the wing could fly. Within a few years Jack's dream seemed to be on the verge of fulfillment when his company was awarded the contract for the large B-35 flying wing bomber project. Design, supply, and personnel problems would delay the project. Once airborne, the problems continued. The jet era had arrived and the engineers at Northrop readily converted the flying wing bomber into the jet-propelled YB-49. Once again Jack Northrop's dream seemed on the verge of being realized. But there were other technical problems. A rapid downsizing of the American air force, along with a greatly reduced national defense budget at the conclusion of World War II, was being felt at Northrop.

In the late 1940s and on, speed was of the essence in bombers. The Flying Wing was not built for speed. With two YB-49s destroyed by accident, the project was soon cancelled and Jack Northrop left the aircraft industry. It would take years, but technology and the inherent attributes of a large flying wing bomber would converge in the late 1970s. Jack Northrop would be vindicated and he would live long enough to learn of this fact – much sooner than most of the rest of the world. To the memory of John K. Northrop, this book is commemorated.

A beautiful Northrop Alpha is caught frolicking through the clouds. The Alpha would start what would become known as Northrop's "Greek" series of aircraft. (Northrop)

Chapter 1
AN IDEA IS BORNE
Evolution of John K. Northrop's Early Designs

"Go west young man" is what Charles Northrop and his family did. After intermediate stops in Chicago, Illinois, and Lincoln, Nebraska, they arrived in the beautiful seaside town of Santa Barbara, California, in 1904. Their son John (Helen Northrop had two older sons by an earlier marriage), now nine years old, would find fascination in the California skies.

The Wright brothers had made their historic flight the year before the Northrops settled in California. As the next five years passed, both John K. "Jack" Northrop and the aeroplane grew up. As he entered his high school years, Jack Northrop's interests were in the sciences, excelling in math, chemistry, physics, and geometry. When he saw French aviator Didier Masson gliding through the clear blue skies, his fate was sealed – not as an aviator, but a designer.

During his high school days and for a while afterwards, Jack Northrop honed his technical skills by working as a garage mechanic and for his father, a building contractor, as a draftsman and for an architect in performing stress and structural integrity analyses. It was quite fortuitous when Allan and Malcolm Loughead moved their fledgling aircraft manufacturing company down from San Francisco and set up operations in the rear of the garage where Jack was then working as a mechanic. Jack's interest was perked, and he spent time helping the Loughead brothers when he could, getting rides in their seaplane as a benefit. The Loughead's recognized the technical talent inherent in Jack and initially hired him as a draftsman. As Jack Northrop would put it some years later:

> I made a nuisance of myself until they gave me a job. I had a little experience as a garage mechanic, and I worked for a year as a draftsman for an architect, and I worked for my father who was in the building business and this sort of qualified me to design airplanes, you can understand . . . in those days.

The Loughead's brought Czech-borne, ex-barnstormer Anthony (Tony) Stadlman down from San Francisco to take care of the manufacturing operations. Stadlman would be a major influence in shaping the course Northrop's life interests would take.

Jack Northrop was soon a full fledged engineer. His first assignment was on the Loughead F-1 seaplane. Then the Loughead's were awarded a contract by the U.S. Navy to construct two Curtiss HS-2L flying boats. This project was completed in 1919.

By this time Jack had become aware of the penalties of parasitic drag. This led to the Loughead company's next project, the S-1 Sportplane – a joint effort between Northrop, Stadlman, and the Lougheads. Jack designed a sleek little cigar-shaped airplane. The fuselage, unlike the then prevalent fabric covered wood and wire construction, was of monocoque design built up of layers of thin veneer. This type of construction provided strength from the outer skin rather than internal components. Tony Stadlman was instrumental in devising the concrete mold used in forming and gluing together the plywood layers, though all four men shared in the patent rights. Unfortunately, the $2,500 price tag made it non-competitive with the many World War I surplus airplanes hitting the market for only a few hundred dollars.

The Loughead brothers first aircraft, the Model G hydroaeroplane, was built and test flown in the San Francisco Bay area in 1913. When the brothers moved to Santa Barbara in 1916, they obtained some of their operating capital by giving rides to Santa Barbara residents and visitors in this craft. (Western Museum of Flight)

With the lack of a market for their new S-1, the Loughead brothers closed up shop in 1920. The aviation business was in a slump so Jack went back to work with his father assisting in the design and construction of new homes. But by the time 1923 rolled around, the housing industry was in a downturn, and Jack Northrop was in the job market again. It was suggested to Jack that he see Donald Douglas, who had an aircraft manufacturing company in the southern California community of Santa Monica. Tony Stadlman, who had returned to San Francisco after leaving the Lougheads in Santa Barbara, had made his way to Douglas some time earlier. With recommendations from both Tony and Allan Lockheed (the spelling of the name had been changed by this time to reflect the proper pronunciation), Jack was hired in the carpentry shop where he helped build wooden ribs for the Douglas World Cruisers. This work lasted for just a short while before a drafting job opened up, and he was in engineering again.

As with most very talented people, Jack Northrop was driven towards new and better designs. He would put in a full day at Dou-

Loughead Aircraft Manufacturing Company of Santa Barbara, California, first aircraft, the Model F-1. It was as this plane was being designed that John Northrop entered the world of aircraft designing. (Lockheed/Western Museum of Flight)

glas and then go home and work on his own ideas. He was ever aware of the severe penalties imposed by drag. To eliminate drag, protruding surfaces which did not add to lift needed to be eliminated. His investigations into this started in Santa Barbara while working for the Lougheads where he studied the plentiful sea gulls. In his quest for a cleaner design, Northrop found an ally in Stadlman, whose nickname at the time was "Tailless Tony." He agreed with his friend that the ideal concept was the perfect wing – the flying wing. Tradition has it that this occurred in 1923. This concept intrigued Jack, but his initial efforts would be towards streamlining the standard airplane structure.

By 1926 Jack had come up with a very streamlined airplane consisting of a monocoque fuselage and cantilevered wing – no drag inducing bracing. The molded veneer fuselage would use the patented techniques and processes which had been developed earlier in Santa Barbara for the S-1 Sportplane. Jack approached Allan Lockheed with the idea of starting up a company to build this airplane and other advanced designs. Allan Lockheed liked the design, but they needed financing for this new venture. Lockheed took the idea to an acquaintance of his, Los Angeles industrialist Fred Keller. Also brought in on the project was a bookkeeper of Keller's, William Kenneth (Ken) Jay, who had been a flying instructor during World War I and had kept his enthusiasm for aviation over the

The F-1 was touted as the world's largest seaplane at the time of its construction in 1918. It was 47 feet long and had a wing span of 74 feet. (Lockheed/Western Museum of Flight)

years. Like Lockheed, Jay liked what he saw in the new Northrop design. Thus the Vega was borne, and Lockheed was back in the aviation business.

Jack Northrop explained the impetus behind his then latest design advancement in the aeronautical sciences:

> The whole objective was to build as clean an airplane as we could possibly conceive in those days. The average airplane had struts or wires or fuselage forms that weren't as smooth or streamlined – with as low a drag as possible. It was pretty obvious, it seemed to me, that a full cantilever wing neatly faired to the fuselage on a perfectly streamlined fuselage would take less power to do the job than some other types. So it was a breakthrough in that we went wholeheartedly into, for the time and at the time, to conceive as clean an airplane as we could. Fortunately, the work in Santa Barbara some years previously had already developed the technique for building a fuselage. It was then just the necessity of designing a full cantilever wing.

As with the Model G, the F-1 was also used to give rides as a means of bringing income into the company's coffers. (Western Museum of Flight)

Jack became chief engineer, for a time the only engineer, and Tony Stadlman joined the new company as factory superintendent. Within the first six months of 1927, the first Vega was built and soon thereafter Edward A. (Eddie) Bellande performed the initial flight. Jack's stay with Lockheed was relatively short. He had found very little time to work on a number of advanced concepts, including an all-wing aircraft. There was little support within Lockheed for Jack's tailless airplane theories. The last straw was when Ray Acker was brought in from Chicago. Acker was quite critical of Jack Northrop's designs, which apparently hastened Northrop's departure. Jack did find a supporter in Ken Jay for his flying wing concepts.

Like so many other Americans, John K. Northrop was called by his country to serve in the Great War. But shortly after his induction into the Army, the Lougheads received a contract to build two Curtiss HS-2L flying boats. Not only were they going to build these craft, but some engineering improvements were to be made. They needed Jack Northrop, and he was soon back at the drafting board.(Northrop/Western Museum of Flight)

Jack Northrop's First Company

Jack Northrop and Ken Jay resigned from Lockheed in June 1928 and formed the Avion Corporation. To finance this new company, Jay and Northrop approached newspaper publisher George Hearst of San Francisco, California. They had become acquainted with the Hearst family when George, the eldest son of William Randolph Hearst, bought one of the Northrop-designed Lockheed Vegas. Apparently George Hearst liked Jack Northrop's ideas, as he and his mother-in-law, Ada Wilbur of Los Angeles, provided the capital to start up the Avion Corporation. Operations were set up in rented shop space in the San Fernando Valley of Los Angeles.

The company's first airplane, the Avion Model I, was Jack Northrop's next step toward the ultimate "clean" airplane. Robert S. Catlin, who joined Northrop in 1929, recalled:

Jack wasted no time incorporating many of his advanced design concepts in a single airplane. It had an all-metal wing, a tail boom, and a conventional empennage; there was no fuselage. Although it was not tailless, it was called the Northrop "Flying Wing." Both the pilot and powerplant were submerged in the center section. The first of the many flying wings to follow it had a wing span of 30 feet and was 20 feet long from nose to tail and was completed in 1929.

The original model had a pusher propeller and the engine was later changed to a tractor configuration. Both versions flew successfully, verifying the inherent stability of the design. Once again, Eddie Bellande was the first to fly the new design at Muroc Dry Lake, which is now Edwards. Eddie reported the flight characteristics to be nor-

mal in every respect. Many flights were made, providing conclusive evidence that the increased performance resulted from greatly reduced drag.

The wing utilized Northrop's smooth stressed skin all metal construction, which proved much stronger than other structural forms of equal weight. In test to destruction, it was found that the structure yielded gradually by bending and did not fracture suddenly. In many ways, one of Jack Northrop's most important designs was this first all metal "Flying Wing" which made important contributions to the progress of aviation.

Jack was a "hands on" person. If a shop worker would exclaim, "We can't make this," Jack Northrop would step in and show them how to do it. There wasn't much known about the forming of metals in those days as aluminum alloys strong enough for structural members were just coming into existence. Very frequently Jack could be seen out in the shop working with the production people, showing them how to make the tools needed to form the material, in particular, those in the tempered state.

Jack Northrop later reflected on what had led him to this point:

A steady program of development and refinement has been under way for the past twenty years until we have at present [1930] a number of carefully designed and comparatively efficient planes embodying streamline fuselages, carefully cowled engines, and 'clean' landing gears with superfluous struts, wires and fittings suppressed to an absolute minimum. It seems quite apparent that our best designs are close to the limit of practical efficiency; yet we find that their maximum over-all L/D (lift-drag) ratio is only about 10, whereas the L/D ratio of the active supporting surfaces of an airplane is normally double this amount.

An analysis of the items adding to parasite drag in the normal design shows that landing gear, power plant, fuselage, interference and bracing, and control surfaces are the major contributors to parasite power loss; the item of control surfaces being by far the smallest. Individual examination of the various units show that nearly all possible improvement has been made in existing designs.

Many years later he would add:

"We didn't dare to go the whole way and eliminate the tail."

It was hoped that Jack Northrop's Avion Model I was only the starting point for larger flying wing craft. Envisioned was a 12 passenger transport which could reach a speed of approximately 200 mph. Passenger seating arrangement would consist of three rows of four seats in each wing so each passenger could get a good view looking forward and sideways. The aircrew were to be situated in a streamlined cupola in the leading edge and have 360 degrees of vision. This airplane would be powered by two engines, either in pusher or tractor arrangement.

It was obvious that the ideal flying wing was impractical or impossible to construct except in very large sizes. The airplane can not justify its existence unless it has capacity to carry a comparatively bulky cargo. With conventional wing thicknesses it was impossible, even with very large wing taper, to build a flying Wing in sizes of less than 150 or 200 foot span.

The typical Biplane with its basic design, in 1919, was not very aerodynamically efficient. The struts, wires and braces all added to its parasitic drag.

At last Jack Northrop was in the environment he had been longing for over many years. Previously, at both Douglas and Lockheed, he started out with the feeling that he would be able to push into new frontiers. But in both cases, once the new designs entered production and were profitable, Northrop felt that his drive for further advancement was stifled.

The design of Avion's first aircraft was very advanced and was completed in late 1928. To a great extent, it proved much of Jack Northrop's flying wing concept. It was built to reduce drag and increase lift. The inverted air-cooled engine was carried entirely within the wing which constituted the major portion of this craft. Only the engine air intake in the center of the leading edge and a small propeller shaft housing projecting to the trailing edge of the wing disturbed the smooth lines of the wing. Construction of the wing set new standards for aeronautical design, standards which would be used for many years.

The material used to construct this flying laboratory was the new alclad, or duralumin, sheets in lieu of the common fabric covering. This all-metal wing was constructed of deep U-shaped channels lying on their sides and nesting together. The sides of the light, span-wise members became the airfoil. This stressed skin, multicellular construction invented by Northrop would become an industry standard.

Two cockpits were included in the wing to the right and left of the center line where the engine was installed. The tail group was carried on two cantilever outrigger booms which extended to the rear of the wing and were considerably above the wing. This was accomplished to provide ground clearance for the tail group and to place the tail control surfaces above the wing wash and propeller blast.

It would seem that Northrop hadn't started out to build an all-metal aircraft. Up to this point in time the aluminum alloys available were not strong enough to carry loads. It seemed to Northrop a good idea to make the horizontal stabilizer out of some of the stronger aluminum alloys then becoming available. He related some years later:

In those days, if you analyzed the load that a thin sheet [of metal] would carry without buckling, it was negligible, and just appeared impossible to use the sheet covering for any structural members. We had a problem of designing a horizontal tail surface that was a perfectly rectangular piece. It wasn't heavily loaded and it occurred to us to build a little test section and see what it would do, just to check the buckling, stress analysis and so forth. Well, this particular experiment came out so well I think the part held some ten times as much as it was supposed to. It also held a high percentage of the bending load as

Now with a good bit of engineering experience, Jack Northrop felt that a "cleaner" airplane, one with less parasitic drag, could be built. He, the Lougheads, and Tony Stadlman came up with the S-1. (Western Museum of Flight)

it had started to buckle. This was a pure happenstance, and a lucky happenstance that enabled us to proceed with the monocoque metal structure that came into use so well after that.

Menasco Motors, Inc. of Los Angeles, California, was also involved in the production of this plane. The original configuration of the engine for this craft was as a pusher. A Menasco modified Mark III Cirrus engine, specially inverted by Northrop's friend Al Menasco for this project, was installed. A tubular steel drive shaft ran from the engine to the propeller. The aft end of the shaft, nearly seven feet long, ran in a large ball bearing which was housed in a fin-like structure over the trailing edge of the wing. In early 1930 a Menasco A-4 air-cooled, four cylinder, in-line inverted engine drove a tractor propeller. In both cases the cooling was provided by air passing through a large tunnel extending entirely through the wing. Initially the plane's reversed tricycle landing gear was retractable. The retraction mechanism was of Jack Northrop's design and the components were manufactured by Menasco. The retraction mechanism proved troublesome from the start and fixed gear was soon attached to the aircraft.

Construction was completed in the spring of 1929 and registration was approved on May 31st of that year.

Initial taxi runs were undertaken at Mines Field (now Los Angeles International Airport) on July 30th. Test pilot Eddie Bellande apparently broke ground a couple of times as his log shows two "hops" for a total time of two minutes. He reportedly found the craft nearly uncontrollable. It would seem that it was at this time that the vertical stabilizers had a half moon extension added to their trailing edges, and the horizontal stabilizer stubs that extended outboard of the vertical stabilizers were removed. The plane was then trucked to Muroc in California's Mojave Desert where Bellande once again flew the Northrop design on its "official" maiden flight on September 26. Two flights were accomplished that day for a total flight time of five minutes; three days later Bellande flew the little plane for the last time at Muroc; this time he stayed aloft for five minutes on a single flight. Jack Northrop would describe its performance as:

Flight tests have now been conducted over a period of months and during many hours in the air the plane has shown remarkable maneuverability and performance, and although beset with most of the troubles common to new types, the plane as designed has proved eminently satisfactory.

It was found that the plane's maximum speed was approximately 25 percent faster than contemporary designs of equivalent power and capacity.

Northrop and Tony Stadlman had been friends and kindred spirits for many years. They had worked together at the Loughead Aircraft Manufacturing Company in Santa Barbara, then with Douglas in Santa Monica, and finally again at Lockheed on the Vega. Both were interested in optimizing aircraft design by reducing drag and increasing lift. It seems that the idea of a pure wing was possibly first conceived by Stadlman, but both men worked together in brainstorming sessions particularly during their Douglas tenure. They had even been working on a joint project to build such a craft. But by the time Avion Corp. was established the two were not talking. In a 1930 article Northrop gave Ken Jay credit in the flying wing development, but Stadlman was not mentioned. "Tailless Tony" left Lockheed about a year after Northrop and Jay departed to form Avion. Stadlman hoped to find his own place in wing history. At the time of the Avion "Flying Wing," Tony had his own

Northrop and the Lougheads had high hopes for their sporty little biplane. The growing aviation-minded public was sure to buy it. (Western Museum of Flight)

Tony Stadlman designed the concrete mold in which wooden monocoque fuselage shells would be created. (Northrop/Western Museum of Flight)

First successful molded shell. This process would later be used on the Northrop-designed Lockheed Vega. (Northrop/Western Museum of Flight)

scale model quite similar to Avion's. The principal difference was the use of a single vertical stabilizer. Though Stadlman would find success in other endeavors, he would never find it in his beloved wing. Northrop and Stadlman would reconcile most of their differences in their later years.

As 1929 was approaching autumn, both Avion and the United States were beginning to experience fiscal problems. For the nation a depression was starting. For Avion, the Flying Wing project had consumed most of its capital. Flight testing would have to be greatly scaled back, if not discontinued, if additional financing could not be obtained. A new commercial venture, the Alpha, had to be stopped. This new brainchild of Jack Northrop's would add another first in aeronautics. It was to be an all-metal, stressed-skin monoplane to embody multicellular wing structure.

Earlier that year a conglomerate called United Aircraft and Transport Corp. was formed, which included such entities as Boeing, Pratt & Whitney, Standard Steel Propeller, and others. William E. Boeing, of Boeing Airplane Company, visited Jack Northrop at Avion, being quite interested in Jack's new all-metal designed aircraft and production processes. At the time Boeing Airplane Company was constructing their planes out of metal tubing with fabric covering. Agreements were struck and United Aircraft bought out Hearst and Wilbur and the new Northrop Aircraft Corporation, a division of United Aircraft and Transportation Corp was born.

Though the Avion assets were sold to United Aircraft & Transport Corporation in October 1929, the new Northrop Aircraft Corporation was not inaugurated until January 1, 1930. The needed funds were provided and operations were transferred from Avion's

Jack Northrop designed the wings so they could be folded, facilitating storage (in your own garage if you wanted) and ease of towing to the closest airfield. The bottom wing also pivoted to give the little plane STOL-type features. (Northrop/Western Museum of Flight)

The plane performed as its designers planned, but its price and the large surplus of Curtiss Jennies, spelled the end of the S-1 and the Lougheads in Santa Barbara. (Northrop/Western Museum of Flight)

Alger Street location in Los Angeles to a hangar at United Air Terminal in Burbank, California sometime between the October consummation of the buyout and early November.

From their new facilities, Northrop Aircraft Corp. put the Alpha into production. The Flying Wing flight test operations were moved from Muroc to United Air Terminal; the first flight from United took place on November 18th.

On February 10th, the Flying Wing was first shown to the public. With the success of the Wing, discussions ensued of a much larger passenger carrying version, but the depression would soon silence that idea. Economic realities struck home and Northrop informed the Civil Aeronautics Authority on September 22, 1930 that flight testing of the Wing would be suspended. With a sense of finality, Jack Northrop dismantled the craft. It would be nearly ten years before Jack Northrop would be able to pursue his dream again. Jack Northrop said of this plane, "The design, when completed, turned out to be about as queer a looking machine as we could wish to see."

The Northrop Aircraft Corporation, as a unit of United Aircraft and Transport Corporation, became one of the many casualties of the Great Depression. Contraction and consolidation of operations were being undertaken by most companies of any size. United Aircraft and Transportation decided to combine its Northrop unit with its Stearman unit in Wichita, Kansas. Jack Northrop, along with many of the other Northrop Aircraft employees, stayed in California. It was September 1931, a year after Jack Northrop concluded research of his first "flying wing," that once again he was looking for employment.

The Second Northrop Company

Even in a depression, talent is appreciated. Jack Northrop went to his friend Donald W. Douglas, Sr. and soon the new Northrop Corporation, a division of Douglas Aircraft, was formed. On January 1, 1932, the new Northrop organization went into operation in the old Moreland Aircraft building in Inglewood, California. Following Northrop from the previous company were Ken Jay, as vice

The key players in getting the new Lockheed company going and building Jack Northrop's Vega. Standing, left to right: Jack Northrop, Ken Jay, and Allan Lockheed. To the left of the aircraft is Tony Stadlman and to the right the shareholders' attorney, Ben Hunter; engineer Gerard Vultee kneels inside the Vega fuselage. (Northrop/Western Museum of Flight)

president and general manager, and Donovan R. Berlin, as chief engineer, as well as engineers Walt J. Cerny and Thomas H. Quayle. A Douglas engineer by the name of Edward H. Heinemann transferred into the new division from the Santa Monica plant.

Jack Northrop's new company designed a number of famous aircraft, but Jack would have no time to devote to his dream of a flying wing. The one exception would be in 1937 when he and Ed Heinemann developed a delta shaped flying wing which consisted of a fuselage flared into the wing in such a manner that the two

Vegas under construction at Lockheed. (Western Museum of Flight)

seemed to be one. With the company designation of Model 25, a wind tunnel model was produced. The tests indicated that a tail was necessary. With a lack of support and funding for the project, the scheme was dropped. Ed Heinemann never became a proponent of the flying wing, but would gain much fame for his own designs, especially the beautiful little delta wing A-4. Heinemann would remark many years later: "Jack Northrop, from whom I learned an enormous amount, became an industrial giant . . . I am deeply indebted to this grand and innovative man for all the knowledge he imparted to me." Both men did much for the advancement of aviation.

In 1937 Douglas, who owned 51 percent of the Northrop Corporation stock, purchased the remaining 49 percent. The company, which had moved to El Segundo, became the El Segundo Division of Douglas Aircraft. Because of labor strife and very little opportunity to work on such advanced designs as the flying wing, John K. Northrop resigned from Douglas Aircraft as of January 1, 1938.

Opposite top:
The first Vega, built in 1927, was purchased by newspaper tycoon George Hearst. Jack Northrop would later use his Hearst family connections in starting his own company. Hearst's Vega, named the Golden Eagle, is pictured in Oakland, California after Eddie Bellande's (second from the left) flight from the Lockheed factory in Burbank. Pictured with Bellande: to his left, race pilot Jack Frost; and to his right, Jack Northrop, Allan Lockheed, and Ken Jay. Frost was to fly it in the Dole California to Honolulu race (the aircraft was subsequently lost in the race). (Northrop)

Opposite bottom:
If the S-1 was Jack Northrop's first step in designing a "cleaner" airplane, the Vega has to be his second step. With its cantilever wing design, Northrop eliminated all the typical struts and bracing so common on biplanes. The Vega was a sure thing to break records. One who helped write history with the Vega was Wiley Post, pictured here with his Winnie Mae (the Winnie Mae of Oklahoma, to be exact). (Northrop)

Right:
Jack Northrop and George Hearst at the Hearst Castle, near San Simeon, California. With Hearst's financial assistance, Northrop would start his Avion Corporation. (Western Museum of Flight)

Below:
Construction of the Avion Model I takes place in a small shop on Alger Street in southern California's San Fernando Valley. Shown here, looking rearward, the spar which forms one side of the grid in multicellular construction. (The Boeing Company Archives)

Jack Northrop load testing his "nested channel," later to be referred to as multicellular construction. (The Boeing Company Archives)

Nearing completion, the Northrop designed and patented retractable landing gear is clearly shown. Northrop's friend, Al Menasco, fabricated many of the components for the landing gear. (The Boeing Company Archives)

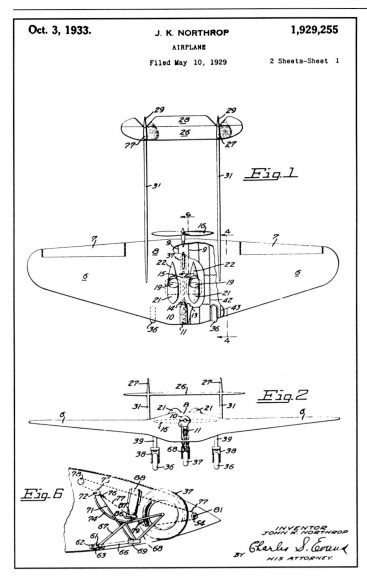

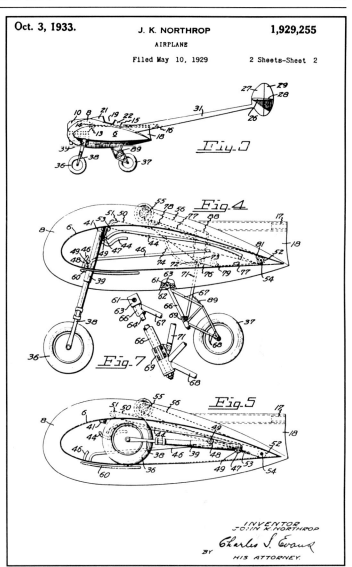

Original Configuration of Avion Model I (Drawings from Patent)

The Avion Model I at Mines Field near El Segundo and Inglewood, California. Eddie Bellande was called upon to test the experimental craft. On July 30, 1929, while making high speed taxi tests, the plane lifted off the ground on two occasions. Bellande logged a total time of two minutes in the air. (The Boeing Company Archives)

Jack Northrop and Bellande confer prior to a test hop. (Western Museum of Flight)

Edward Bellande was amassing quite a reputation as a pilot. He would even make the honored position on the back of a box of Wheaties cereal. (Western Museum of Flight)

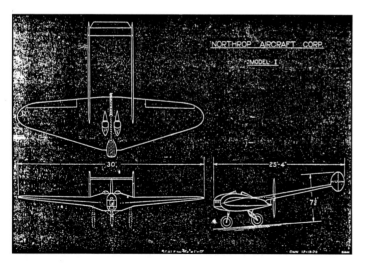

Final Configuration of Model I with Pusher Engine
(Note: All dimensions do not agree with data released to the public; no explanation has been found for this.)

Jack Northrop's first attempt at eliminating (reducing) an airplane's tail flies over an uncluttered southern California. He would later say that he "didn't dare to go all the way." (San Diego Aerospace Museum)

Above and below:
The photo above shows the Model I as it was first produced. Bellande found its handling characteristics unacceptable and a number of modifications were made, mostly around the tail. The portion of the horizontal stabilizer that projected outboard of the vertical was removed and an extension piece was added to the trailing edge of the vertical stabilizer. Somewhat later fixed gear, as shown in the photo below, replaced the retractable gear because of operating problems that persisted. (The Boeing Company Archives and Northrop)

Jack Northrop and Eddie Bellande (in the cockpit) pose with the Model I at the company's Burbank facility. The propeller and shaft installation as well as other details can be clearly seen in this closeup shot. (Northrop)

After Bellande's trial runs at Mines Field, the flight testing moved to the dry lakes in the Mojave Desert near Muroc. When Avion was bought by United Aircraft, operations were moved to Union Terminal near Burbank, California. (Western Museum of Flight)

Preparing for a test flight. (San Diego Aerospace Museum)

Jack Northrop always saw the value of publicity. Here he is caught in the process of being interviewed. (San Diego Aerospace Museum)

Preparing for flight? Here the Model 1 has become the Model 1-A with an engine change and the propeller installed in the more standard tractor arrangement. (Northrop)

The modification on the rear half of the wing is clearly shown where the propeller shaft and housing were removed as part of the changeover to the tractor arrangement. (The Boeing Company Archives)

Most spectators found the Model I quite odd looking, but its performance gave Jack Northrop encouragement that he was heading in the right direction. (San Diego Aerospace Museum)

Left to right: Jack Northrop, Eddie Bellande, and Ken Jay pose for the camera. Details of the propeller in the tractor installation can be seen in the photos above and below. (Western Museum of Flight)

The Model 1 was constructed with a passenger cockpit, as shown in this photograph, on the left side of the engine installation. Quite often this cockpit was covered over during test flights. (San Diego Aerospace Museum)

Relations between Jack Northrop and Tony Stadlman soured and the two men went their own ways. Here Stadlman, in 1929, shows his version of a flying wing. (Western Museum of Flight)

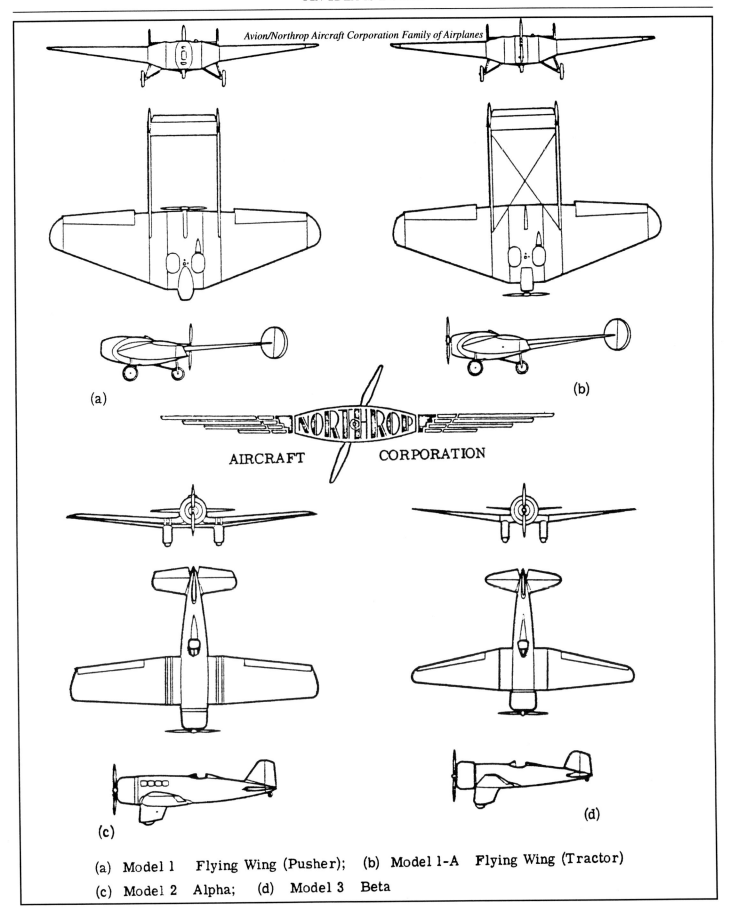

Avion/Northrop Aircraft Corporation Family of Airplanes

(a)

(b)

(c)

(d)

(a) Model 1   Flying Wing (Pusher);   (b) Model 1-A   Flying Wing (Tractor)
(c) Model 2 Alpha;   (d) Model 3 Beta

The economy was heading for a depression and Northrop was once again forced to design more conventional aircraft. But his experimentation was not to be wasted. His next aircraft, designated as the Avion Model II, would be called the Alpha, and was constructed out of aluminum using Northrop's multicellular construction technique. The wing of an Alpha is being constructed with the Model I shown in the background. (Northrop)

With the depression, United Aircraft combined the Northrop operations with their Stearman division in Wichita, Kansas. Jack Northrop and many of the others of the old Northrop Aircraft Corporation elected to stay in California. Soon a deal was struck where Northrop Corporation, as a subsidiary of Douglas Aircraft Company, would design and build aircraft in an El Segundo, California, facility. Here a XA-16 sits outside of that facility. (Northrop)

Many military aircraft were designed and built in Northrop's El Segundo plant. One of the most noted was the A-17 series. (Northrop)

The N-1M's flight test program concluded in early 1943. It was put in storage for a few months, given a fresh coat of paint and turned over to the Army for future display. In this September 22, 1943 photo most of those associated with the N-1M "Jeep" pose with the little craft. Some people of interest are: test pilot Moye Stephens in front of the nose wheel, Jack Northrop is on Moye's right, and immediately to his left are Dr. Theodore von Karman and Walt Cerny. (Northrop)

Chapter 2

FIRST WING
The N-1M Jeep

Jack had entered his arrangement with Douglas in the early 1930s with the idea that his company, the Northrop Corporation, would emphasize research and development. This type of work takes money, and with a depression still affecting the economy, production soon took up most of the activity of the firm; Jack Northrop would have to start over again.

1939 was going to be the year that Jack Northrop would have his way. With a few kindred spirits, they started formulating both the organization that would become Northrop Aircraft, Inc., and the first steps towards the all-wing airplane that Northrop knew would be the airplane of the future. By August 1st of that year, the new company showed six employees on the payroll (there were also a number of consultants involved in their design efforts), and a total floor space of only 9,000 sq. ft. It was a beginning.

It would be different the next time! With the help of a couple of pilots, Eddie Bellande and Moye W. Stephens, that Jack Northrop had worked with over the years as well as others, plans were formulated and financing obtained for yet another company. This time Jack would have it his way. Long time Northrop employee Jack Mannion recalled these events some years ago:

On March 7, 1939 John K. Northrop's third company, Northrop Aircraft, Incorporated, was incorporated. The next step was to locate facilities, hire personnel, and get contracts. (Western Museum of Flight)

Northrop Corp. [as part of Douglas] had been originally conceived as an organization that would devote itself largely to aeronautical research and development activity. However, demands for many of the Northrop designs had been so great that the company moved hurriedly into aircraft manufacturing. Primarily because of the increased impetus on production, Jack resigned intending to form a new company staffed with the best engineers he could find. His intent was to keep it small enough to develop advanced designs without the inertia and organizational complications imposed by a large company.

While discussions concerning the new company were going on, his long time colleague, Eddie Bellande, got in touch with La Motte T. Cohu, a TWA director who was in California on business. In 1939, the probability of war in Europe was increasing and Cohu was quick to see the early role of the United States as the arsenal of the allied nations. He proposed a new approach: that Jack's new company manufacture aircraft as well as design them. This was agreed to and Northrop Aircraft, Inc. was incorporated on March 7th 1939. By July what would become the company's first project was started.

In August 1939 the organization was being staffed. A number of people that Jack Northrop had been associated with over the years were soon with him in his new venture. Jack Northrop was president and chief engineer, La Motte T. Cohu became general manager and chairman of the board. Moye Stephens, as a board member, was secretary of the company as well as flight chief; Eddie Bellande was also a member of the board. Gage H. Irving came over from Douglas and became vice president and assistant general manager, besides becoming a board member.

Another Douglas associate, Vladimir H. Pavlecka, was approached by Jack to join him in a most clandestine way:

I don't know whether you know this, but Northrop started in what used to be a bawdy house. Hawthorne used to be a community of oil well workers. And they had this big house full of girls, and that was the social center; and we had offices right in that house.

Northrop sent a messenger in a round-about way to me; he couldn't directly, of course. He invited me to see him, which I did. I knew him before. He said he would like very much for me to come with him to continue this work on magnesium structures. He really was interested in it. I did not expect this; I was sort of taken aback. I said, 'Well look, you are a very far sighted enterprising man. I will come right away if you promise me that you will develop or see to it that the jet engine is developed.' He is a blessed avenger! I said, 'I don't want it right now, but in due course. I will persist on you. I have a lecture on it. It is about 80 slides; I will give it to you. I will show you what it is all about; what it can do.' Which I still have. He said, 'Well, maybe some time in the future.' 'All right,' I said, 'that's good enough for me; I'll come.' And I went with him, on magnesium alloy structures essentially.

With operations set up in Hotel Hawthorne, they searched for a suitable site for permanent operations. Not far from their temporary location they found 72 acres that was suitably located and at the right price. It was purchased and on September 30, 1939 a ground breaking ceremony for what would be a 122,500 sq. ft. plant took place with such dignitaries as Hawthorne Mayor Fred Hauser, Los Angeles Mayor Fletcher Bowron, and Los Angeles County Sheriff Eugene Biscailuz.

By this time the firm's employment had risen to 26 and their first design, the N-1M flying laboratory, was starting to take shape in the minds of these intrepid designers.

The new plant and adjoining air strip would not be occupied until February 1940. From their rooms in Hotel Hawthorne, often referred to as the "Yellow Peril" because of its yellow painted exterior, the engineering staff of John Northrop, Walt Cerny, Tom Quayle, Francis Johnson, and Ray Gaskell initiated design studies on the company's first project. Not surprisingly, the first Northrop design project, N-1, was a twin-engined flying wing. Though not intended to be the ultimate design by far, this project was to be a flying laboratory to prove Northrop's long held belief that the flying wing would provide maximum aerodynamic efficiency. Walt Cerny reminisced on those early days and Jack Northrop's introduction of this project to him:

> When I first joined the present company after leaving Douglas El Segundo in August 1939, Jack sat down with me and made a rough sketch of a very unusual airplane without a tail and very peculiar wing tips drooping down. He explained to me that there had been early attempts at the so-called tailless or flying wings by some in Germany, like [Alexander] Lippisch, and in England, by [G. T. R.] Hill, which had very poor directional stability. He [Jack] hoped that by introducing these drooped [wing] tips this [directional stability problem] would be overcome. He also suggested that these drooped tips be adjusted so that eventually we could try it with the tips straight. He also pointed out that we should try to attempt to make it so we could vary the CG. The airplane was to have a 38 foot wing span and was to have a 14 foot chord in the center, and I think the landing gear tread was nine feet and roughly four and a half or five feet high.

Herb DeCenzo, who hired on at the new Northrop company on October 2, 1939, was put on the N-1M project early on. Some years ago Mr. DeCenzo has recalled those days at Northrop:

> My first introduction to Walt Cerny, who was chief of design, was laying out the big steel fittings for the wing tips for the N-1M. This tip could be both increased in angle downwards as a cathedral as well as increasing or decreasing the angle of attack so that the washout could be studied as natural flight.
>
> Now, the N-1M: the first thing I had to do was to double check, well, I won't say double check, because there was nothing for me to use, I just simply had to pick up some layouts they already had and aerodynamically make a complete analysis of everything. Apparently

Initially temporary quarters were found in the Hotel Hawthorne. Its reputation as an ex-house of pleasure would be a topic of conversation for decades to come. (Northrop/Western Museum of Flight)

because no one else had, or if they had it was not firmly done, because I certainly had nothing to check over or work from. In any event, I made a thorough aerodynamic analysis for performance and stability. Now, please understand, we never made stability analysis in those days that included dynamic stability, it was always, in a sense, static. Dynamic stability, why, that was beyond the knowledge of quite a few of us, number one. Number two, it would have taken real good computers to have made such calculations accurately and within a given period of time that they were worthwhile.

During this initial analysis, one thing I never did learn was: whoever made the initial layout or anything else. Just went in there, and whatever meager information, and it was meager, that there was, I just simply took and in essence made my analysis. By then, you might say, some of the layouts were pretty well firmed up and the design set in concrete. I'd like to mention here that at no time was any mention ever made that "I'm the designer" by anybody nor was anybody that I know of the project man, unless it was Mr. Northrop himself. Another thing that was quite nice was that everybody was so friendly and everything was informal, but we had control of everything. Don't get the impression that things were not under control, they were at all times. Very informally, but things were done well done right. And of course this was in the old Hawthorne Hotel, which we called Yellow Peril, and believe me, everything was just jammed in place. Nobody had any fancy desks or drawing boards or anything because there wasn't any room for them, and I don't think at that time much money for it either. It was a happy place, a very nice place and of course, such loyalty, everybody gave to Jack Northrop, I'll never forget. The loyalty there was unbelievable, it was great.

First engineers hired by the new Northrop Aircraft, Inc. in August 1939. Left to right are Walt Cerny, Francis Johnson, Ray Gaskell, and Tom Quayle. (Northrop)

Expert Help

Jack Northrop felt that because of his lack of formal education and the small staff then at his disposal he needed assistance from experts. He wanted the best. Edward Zap, known for his Zap wing and Zap flaps, had his offices in Hollywood, California. His services were obtained originally for a joint Northrop/Navy/National Advisory Committee for Aeronautics (NACA) project. Working with Zap was Northrop's first aerodynamicist, Herb DeCenzo. DeCenzo recalled several years ago some of the pioneering work in flight controls that was later applied to the flying wing projects.

Prior to the P-61 a lot of work was being done in this country for the NACA which, of course, was the forerunner of NASA. A lot of work was being done on high lift flaps for them under contract by Mr. Edward Zap. Zap, if you recall, had one of the first initial flaps ever used on aircraft. I believe again, the Northrop Delta, the old single engine Delta, was one of the first. It was a simple split flap and it was called a Zap flap at that time; although later on it just traded on the designation of a split flap.

Zap came to Northrop [as a consultant much like Dr. von Karman] and it was there that we worked very closely with him. I became his consultant, with Northrop's approval. That is, I actually wore two hats. I worked for Ed monitoring a lot of tests and doing the work that he had to do. Northrop had the contract to design and build this high lift wing for the Fairchild Model 22 for the NACA using this newly developed Zap flap. In turn, when those tests were completed on models, the actual design work to build a wing for the old Fairchild Model 22 [began]. The wing, for that purpose, was designed and built by Keith Rider and myself working as Northrop employees.

This was very unique in a sense and different than the others [flaps] and naturally that was one reason why NACA wanted this wing built and tested in the Full Scale Wind Tunnel, initially, and then later on flight tested on this Fairchild Model 22. This wing was a simple wing but a beautiful wing in that it was all wood. The success of the wooden Schoenfelt Firecracker [which Keith Rider was associated with], which of course is finished like a Grand Piano, gave Burk the idea to make this test wing also of plywood, so everything could be nice and smooth and flush just like your regular wind tunnel models. So, aside from your regular fittings and flap tracks, the entire wing, including the flap, was of nice smooth plywood. This wing was built and shipped back east [to NACA's Langley facility] and the tests were very, very successful and of course we got all the test data. We were probably one of the first actually to get the test data from the NACA.

Follow on to this effort was a NACA/Northrop program in which a Vought-Sikorsky OS2U-2 Kingfisher was modified with Zap flaps and spoiler-type ailerons. The spoiler-type ailerons were used on all P-61 Black Widow variants and were considered for the XB-35 in the early stages of the program.

But for the flying wing, the services of Dr. Theodore von Karman, then Director of California Institute of Technology's Daniel Guggenheim School of Aeronautics, was needed. Von Karman, the world's leading aerodynamicist, found the wing fascinating. It was

---

EXECUTIVES AND SUPERVISORS

LaMotte T. Cohu
Chairman of the Board and General Manager

Gage H. Irving	**Ted C. Coleman**	**M. W. Stephens**	**Claude N. Monson**
Vice-Pres., Asst. Gen. Mgr.	*Vice-Pres., Sales Mgr.*	*Secretary*	*Treasurer*
George Gore	**Thomas Quayle**	**Ted Hawkins**	**Al Morgan**
Asst. Secretary, Legal	*Washington Representative*	*Comptroller*	*Contract Administrator*
Philip I. Chase	**Walter T. Gage**	**B. G. Reed**	
Materiel Director	*Personnel Director*	*Plant Engineer*	

John K. Northrop
President and Chief of Design and Engineering

Walter Cerny	**V. H. Pavlecka**	**Dr. T. Von Karman**	**R. A. Dutton**
Asst. Chief of Design	*Chief of Research*	*Consulting Engineer*	*Engineering Supervisor*
T. E. Piper	**Dr. W. L. Sears**	**A. M. Schwartz**	
Process Engineer	*Aerodynamics Engineer*	*Design Co-ordinator*	

F. J. Baum, W. Knieriem, S. J. Waters
Project Engineers

Glen M. Aron .... *Standards*	E. W. Jones .... *Handbooks*	R. A. Smith .... *Electrical and Radio*
C. W. Bibb .... *Instruments*	I. A. Lusk .... *Power Plant*	G. J. Zilz .... *Liaison Engineer*
R. Ehringer .... *Systems*	F. J. Meyer .... *Weights*	S. E. Weaver .... *Stress*
T. A. Feeney .... *Controls*	H. R. Peterson .... *Fuselage*	R. L. Wolford .... *Photo Laboratory*
E. A. Gardner .... *Test Engineer*	B. A. Provost .... *Wing and Empennage*	J. O. York .... *Armament*
N. R. Graham .... *Parts List*	Alton Royer .... *Chief Checker*	M. S. Harmer .... *Librarian*
R. Irwin .... *Landing Gear, Hydraulics*	D. B. Smith .... *Preliminary Design*	

Paul V. Buckner
Factory Manager

Ernest H. Lawson	**Robert S. Catlin**	**Richard Nolan**	**F. M. Johnson**
Production Superintendent	*Experimental Superintendent*	*Tool Superintendent*	*Assistant Superintendent*
C. B. Spencer	**George F. West**	**Al Carr**	**Mel Abbott**
Night Superintendent	*Night Asst. Superintendent*	*Night Asst. Superintendent*	*Industrial Engineer*

M. L. Chappell, D. W. Phillips, J. O. Potts, L. C. Strong
Project Supervisors

SUPERVISORS	NIGHT SUPERVISORS	C. B. Sturtevant .... *Police Lieut.*
A. R. Frank .... *Tool and Machine*	J. A. Richardson .... *Tool and Machine*	R. Lindstrum .... *Police Sergeant*
M. A. Seeley .... *Sheet Metal and*	O. J. Gause .... *Sheet Metal*	F. S. Faulkner .... *Police Sergeant*
Cowls, Tanks and Fairings		W. Gee .... *Police Sergeant*
W. A. Boyes .... *Sub-Assembly*	DAY FOREMEN	W. Caldwell .... *Police Sergeant*
D. B. Fish .... *Anodic, Paint, Upholstery*	C. Leidtke .... *Machine Shop*	G. J. Voyer .... *Production Control*
R. C. Joyce .... *Nacelle Assembly*	G. Hard .... *Welding*	A. L. Swanholm .... *Prod. Stockrooms*
P. A. Cribby .... *Wood Shop*	W. Jones .... *Sheet Metal*	J. Daley .... *Elec., Radio, Plumb.*
H. S. Thompson .... *Final Assembly*	D. Kraybill .... *Sheet Metal*	L. Lee .... *Shop Liaison*
D. Leland .... *Production Engineer*	L. C. Fosholt .... *Wings, Empennage*	
Tom Freeman .... *Jig Construction*	G. C. Thomas .... *Fuselage*	NIGHT FOREMEN
T. Ruble .... *Field Service*	C. W. Drury .... *Jig Construction*	A. A. Hadsell .... *Welding, Met. Fit.*
F. M. Gibian .... *Loft and Template*	M. F. Sayan .... *Cowls, Tanks, etc.*	E. Raferty .... *Sheet Metal*
R. E. Strong *Raw Stock and Shipping*	E. L. Crumm .... *Experimental*	J. M. Weidner .... *Sheet Metal*
R. W. Gaskell .... *Inspection*	C. Hoffman .... *Final Assembly*	R. E. DuPriest .... *Sub-Assembly*
J. T. Foote .... *Production Planning*	J. Powell .... *Inspection*	C. M. Zeller . *Wings and Empennage*
C. D. Freshwater .... *Employment*	F. Haller .... *Production Planning*	H. E. Brunner .... *Anodic, Paint*
E. F. Burke .... *Plant Protection*	C. Raker .... *Electrical Maintenance*	O. L. Crawford .... *Wood Shop*
C. H. Slaughter .... *Cost Estimating*	J. Hinrichs .... *General Maintenance*	J. R. McFall .... *Cowls, Tanks, Etc.*
T. H. Schlosser .... *Material Control*	F. J. Butler .... *Personnel Service*	E. O. Bennett .... *Inspection*
E. C. Harris .... *Production Control*	J. Miljus .... *Athletic Coordinator*	C. J. Myler .... *Production Planning*
	J. B. Clark .... *Program Coordinator*	J. S. Breneman .... *Elec. and Main.*

Early Northrop Aircraft, Incorporated Organization

The engineering department at Hotel Hawthorne. In August 1939 the company had a total of six employees and 9,000 square feet of working space at the hotel. (Northrop/Western Museum of Flight)

not surprising that Jack Northrop went to von Karman for assistance. All the aircraft companies in southern California had been using Cal Tech's wind tunnel for years. It was the only one to be found on the west coast. So von Karman and Northrop had crossed paths on many occasions. The initial arrangement was for him to spend two days a week in Hawthorne working with Northrop and his engineers. Soon one of von Karman's assistant, and ex-student, Dr. William R. Sears, would join the effort. Dr. Sears would become a full time Northrop employee in February 1941.

An Australian friend of Northrop's sent him a Zanonia seed. Walt Cerny was there at the time. "The seed looked just like a flying wing. It had a large seed bag with almost transparent wings, and the seed was right in the nose. And we use to fly it across the room and it would dive down and pick up speed and glide as gracefully as can be. We, in fact, tried to tumble it, and it would right itself and continue gliding down.

Herb DeCenzo worked with Jack Northrop and Dr. von Karman in verifying the N-1M's design.

I made numerous calculations to get the spanwise load on the wing to be sure that we would not get into anything like a tip stall. Because with the wing, and no vertical, fin, tip stall and spinning could be a serious problem. Calculation after calculation was made by the slide rule. At that time we didn't have more than two tiny Monroe calculators in the house, that is, for engineering anyway; and it stayed that way until the day I left. I didn't have one that's for sure. A slide rule was adequate because we could get the information down to at least three numbers, and that was accurate enough because you were talking about one, two or three percent, which is as good as our theory.

We made some calculations based the hard way; what you would call the accurate way. It would take three or four days to do one particular angle of attack of the basic airplane. Then in turn there was a new technical report out by the NACA on span loading of tapered wings. They ran actual wind tunnel tests in their big tunnel for different wings of different planforms and different aspect ratios. I'd say maybe about six different types. Then in turn worked out some theo-

ries of their own as to spanwise distribution and chordwise based on results of these tests. This information was most welcome, not only to check the information we had, but it also gave us real short method of computing spanwise distribution and the possibilities of tip stall. Well, we made quite a few calculations and were quite satisfied with everything. We still wanted to make more calculations because now we were doing some work on the big bombers that Mr. Northrop was interested in. So we tried to shorten even that method of calculating and that's where Dr. von Karman, who was our consultant, came into play.

I recall quite vividly being present when he went to this blackboard, I think it was at Cal Tech where I happened to be with him, and he proceeds to write out the different equations. It just came right out of his mind, I was astounded. He didn't have any notes, no book, no nothing. He just had that stogie in his mouth and his crayon [chalk] and away he would start to write things down. Boy, he would put this equation down which had everything in it; and it must have been about, oh, I dare say at least 10 to 15 feet long on the blackboard, nice and neat. He would walk up and down and mutter to himself. Ashes from his stogie would just fall onto his vest. He would say 'Cross out this because this is not too important', and so on. Kept muttering and working on it, and then he would lay out the equation all over again and study it and look at it and study it, and then make a few more changes and some more cancellations. Well, after about an hour and a half I'll be dog gone if he didn't have that thing shortened to where we were doing the same kind of a job in about an hour and a half that used to take two or three days the hard way and about a day with the new NACA short method. And, of course, I made a test plot of a

Ground breaking for the new Northrop plant near Hawthorne, California, took place in late September 1939. Dignitaries attending the ceremony were, left to right: Los Angeles County Sheriff Eugene Biscailuz, Hawthorne Mayor Fred Houser, John K. Northrop, and Los Angeles Mayor Fletcher Bowron. (Northrop)

As 1939 closed, the Northrop staff grew steadily. It went from 26 in late September to 73 by year's end. Here the enlarged engineering department pose in their Hotel Hawthorne quarters. (Northrop/Western Museum of Flight)

given wing and I was dumbfounded to see where the variations between the three methods, between the most accurate and, of course, the quicker one of von Karman's was almost like zero. A little bit more than the width of the pencil line on our graphs. That was a very interesting experience.

Funding was needed to sustain the company's flying wing, project one (N-1). To accomplish this, subcontract work which required minimal engineering effort was desired. In rapid succession contracts were obtained to construct elements of Consolidated's PBY Catalina and Boeing's B-17 Flying Fortress as well as the construction of Vultee's V-72 Vengeance for both the Royal Air Force and U.S. Army Air Corps. But soon Northrop had two more design projects but, unlike the wing, these were under contract. Northrop project two (N-2) was for a radical approach to a single engine fighter to be developed for the Air Corps. This would become the XP-56, which will be discussed in a later chapter. The third project (N-3) was for the design and production of 24 single engine patrol bomber seaplanes for the Norwegians; these aircraft would carry the Northrop designation of N-3PB.

Design Development

With the help of Walt Cerny, Herb DeCenzo, and the others of his small staff, along with the assistance of Dr. von Karman, rough sketches of the N-1 became engineering drawings. Tedious hand calculations for angle of attack, span-wise loading, and such were undertaken. Paper models were made and flown in various configurations. Balsa wood and paper models were made and tests flown, the earliest in nearby Pasadena's Civic Auditorium. Flight testing of models was also part of Herb DeCenzo's realm:

> Don Smith, who was head of the electrical group, took over on making a small scale model out of balsa wood and paper for spin tests. This model was roughly about 14 inches in span, and accurately made and balanced. We took this model, that is, Mr. Northrop, von Karman, and myself, to the Pasadena Civic Auditorium, which in reality was a dance hall. It had a very high ceiling, probably at least two

stories plus a copula, which opened into the sky. So Mr. Northrop would sit on the edge of the copula up there and try to spin this model down to the floor below where von Karman and I would observe the spinning. Of course Mr. Northrop would do his best to make it spin by giving it a high angle of attack and putting it into a spiral. But the model seemed to just refuse to really spin. It would go into a spiral but it always would recover long before it would start hitting the floor of the dance hall. We would do our best to evaluate the results of these tests. There must have been about 10 drops, if you want to call them that. We were pretty well satisfied with the fact that the model was not too prone to spinning.

> Also, at the same time, the wood shop was busy making a small model of about that same size of 14 inches span, of white pine, for tests to be conducted at the Pasadena Junior College wind tunnel, since we were unable to get into the GALCIT tunnel at Cat Tech. This was the only wind tunnel available to us in the area, so beggars weren't choosers. We took this little model and put it in that little tiny tunnel, which was a simple blow type tunnel, not much better than the one

On February 20, 1940 the main plant, consisting of 122,500 square feet of floor space, was ready for occupancy. (Northrop)

An early contract that the New Northrop company obtained with the National Advisory Committee for Aeronautics (NACA) was to design and flight test various control surfaces. This Vought-Sikorsky OS2U-1 was bailed to Northrop by the Navy to flight test the surfaces. (Northrop)

the Wright brothers had, frankly, not much bigger either. All the tests were conducted by Professor Merrill of PJC [Pasadena Junior College]. Tests were conducted early mornings, up until about 10 o'clock, at which time we would knock it off until about four. That enabled Merrill to get his rest because he was in his 80's then, in very good physical condition. He wasn't dottering at all, but he needed rest; and we'd conduct more tests from about four o'clock on to about six. During those rest hours, I'd take the data and reduce it, plot it, and so forth, and from there plan any additional tests that we would be doing. We conducted these tests for a period of about two weeks, and there would be visits by Dr. von Karman from nearby Cal Tech. Specifically, I do not recall that he would study them in great depth and all that. He would walk over; he would review the data and we might ask or he might suggest some added tests, what have you. Simply would nod his head that he liked what he saw and that was about it.

At the conclusion of these tests, we conducted tests at the NACA spin tunnel. Because, in the meantime, Don Smith had made a model for the NACA spin test tunnel, which was very similar to the model we had built for the spin tests at the Pasadena auditorium. Now this model, of course was built to specifications that required a little bit of a ratcheting or time mechanism in there so that if the model did spin, you could then ratchet some of your controls to try to overcome or neutralize the spin. The model was beautifully built and very successful in the sense that we did get it to NACA. I flew out there...and went to work at the wind tunnel with them [NACA people]. The tunnel was a vertical tunnel and, of course, the air blew from the bottom on up, so that you would throw the model in there, and try to spin it. The velocity of the air would keep it up at your level. If it didn't spin, it would go into a dive down into the protective netting, that is a netting to protect the wind tunnel's propeller. As I recall these tests, these experts in the spin tunnel, and they were experts, couldn't get that model to spin more that a quarter of half a turn. This little rascal would come right out. So it pretty well established that the N-1M would be fairly safe with regard to not being spun in. That was a real problem in those

days with different aircraft. Finally wind tunnel models were fabricated. As part of the new Northrop plant, a wind tunnel was being constructed. The design was under the oversight of Dr. von Karman, but the Northrop wind tunnel would not be completed until December 1940. With von Karman's assistance, the Cal Tech wind tunnel was used.

Jack Northrop envisioned a flying wing with a wing span of at least 70 feet with a maximum thickness of six feet. Such an airplane could carry cargo or passengers, or possibly as a medium range patrol plane or bomber. As an intermediate step from the wind tunnel model to the full size plane, a one-third to one-half scale flying mockup was produced, thus the flying mockup for Northrop project number 1, the N-1M.

It was intended that this craft would be constructed in such a fashion that changes in its configuration could be accomplished with relative ease. The skin was basically mahogany with spruce and mahogany structural members; metal was used only as required. It was constructed in three major components, two outer wing panels and a center section. At the break point between the outer panels and the center section, the outer panels could be modified to change wing sweep and dihedral. Though this true flying wing was built without a standard tail group, the wing tips were drooped to act as rudders. These tips were adjusted on the ground, and after a number of flights at various angles, Northrop and his engineers decided that this droop was unnecessary. The airplane spent the remainder of its life with the tips in the straight wing tip configuration.

The control surfaces on this prehistoric looking bird were also unusual. Instead of the standard elevator and aileron, Northrop combined their function into a single control surface, the "elevon." This technique was also being used in Europe by many flying wing designers, like the Horten brothers. At the end of the drooping wing tips were clamshells which gave directional control. When operated, they produced drag.

To power the N-1M were two 65 horsepower Lycoming (apparent Continental engines were contemplated) O-145 four-cylinder air-cooled engines driving two-bladed pusher propellers at the end of 10-foot shafts. The two engines were submerged within the wing with a shroud encircling them which routed the cooling air for the engines and their accessories.

Flight Test

By the end of June 1940, Jack Northrop's first true "flying wing" was completed. Black Sunday, as Walt J. Cerny, Northrop's assistant chief of design, called it, was a day of horror. The N-1M was to be trucked to the desert early in the coming week, but there was one remaining task to be performed that day at the Northrop plant in Hawthorne. The aircraft had to be weighed, and it had to be determined if the cg was where they expected it to be. Cerny recalled that fateful weekend.

After weighing the airplane, we found that the cg was so far forward that the airplane wouldn't take off [it was also about 200 lbs. over weight]. In spite of this condition, the airplane was moved early Monday morning to [Baker] Dry Lake anyway. In the morning, I went in to face the music. Everything turned out all right. In fact, we fabricated a nose wheel extension on the strut so it would give the airplane more of an angle of attack. On Tuesday at [Baker], the airplane was taxiing on this, and that's the way things used to work.

Along with Walt Cerny and other Norcrafters was Herb DeCenzo.

It wasn't long before we had the N-1M taken out to Muroc, the old dry lake, which was the place where all the hot rodders from Los Angeles County would test out their cars. We went to what you might call the little base which was run by some of the fellows that were doing time from March Field. There were about eight of them there, That area consisted solely of about two or three tents, one wood shack,

From left to right: Walter Cerny, Thomas Quayle, and Jack Northrop pose in this 1940 photo over a drawing of a land-based version of the company's third design, the N-3. Cerny would serve as assistant chief of design through most of his long career with Northrop Aircraft, Inc. Quayle, who started out in engineering, soon became the company's Washington, D.C. representative. (Northrop/Stu Luce)

Important players in the Northrop designed wings and tailless craft of the 1940s. Second from left is Cal Tech's Dr. Theodore von Karman who acted as a consultant to Northrop and had much to do with the designs in their early phases. His ex-student and associate, and soon to join Northrop, is Dr. William Sears on the far right. Chairman of the Northrop Board of Directors La Motte T. Cohu is on the far left with John K. Northrop, President and Chief Engineer, second from the right. (Northrop)

and one water tower that stood about 10 feet up into the air. Maybe it was about five feet in diameter and five feet tall. Just where they got the water, I don't know. I remember the tower because everybody, during any relief period, wanted to sit in the shade of that tower, it was the only shade in the entire area. And so on the appointed day Vance Breese, who was a test pilot by contract, didn't work for the company, started making initial test runs, if you even want to call them flights. To my horror, and I guess to everybody else's, the airplane could not get off the ground--it was overweight. That's when I learned that the airplane was overweight by something like 200 lbs. So there we are and the airplane was some 200 odd lbs. overweight. The poor airplane would get off the ground and fly straight, had a high angle of attack, but as soon as Vance Breese would try to put it into a really true climb, all the ship could do with the throttle to the wall was get off the ground about two feet or so and that was about it. No way could he lower the nose to pick up speed and go into a climb or anything else. So numerous tests were made in straight and level flights in that kind of a condition. We tried to learn as much as we could. We even tried changing the pitch angle on the adjustable blades of the propellers but that didn't buy us anything.

After being trucked to Baker Dry Lake, test pilot Vance Breese would perform the taxi tests, first flight, and about a dozen subsequent flights.

It is of interest to note that most reports of the first flight refer to it as an accidental flight where the N-1M, now nicknamed the "Jeep," hit a bump and bounced into the air to an altitude of about ten feet off the ground and flew for several hundred yards and then settled back down to earth. This seems to be about all that plane could do at the time. The Lycomings were greatly underpowered for this 4,000 lb. wing. Breese would make about a dozen flights, all in a straight line at a maximum altitude of 10 feet above the

desert for relatively short durations.

Succeeding Breese as test pilot on the Jeep was Northrop's Moye Stephens. During one of Stephens' test flights, the aircraft got too close to the desert floor and about one foot of propeller was knocked off. Stephens managed to get the extremely vibrating plane down to a safe landing. Subsequent inspection also found that it had suffered a broken rear spar. Testing was interrupted for some time as the plane had to be trucked back to Hawthorne for repairs, a lengthy process, and then trucked back to the desert. Besides the problem of being underpowered, the test pilots found that there were control difficulties – an elevator dead area. Dr. von Karman was put to work and shortly discovered that, because of the thickness of the wing, airflow separation was occurring and the flow was not coming together until it proceeded beyond the trailing edge of the wing. The answer to this was adding extensions to the elevons.

The Lycomings were replaced with 117 hp Franklin 6AC264F2 engines driving three-bladed propellers in early 1941. Though these engines enabled the plane to get to a maximum altitude of about 4,000 feet, they had to be run at settings beyond normal operating limits. This created a problem of constant overheating. Northrop would contemplate replacing the engines again, but this apparently never occurred. Possibly the development of the N-9M and the XB-35 bomber overrode the necessity of upgrading the N-1M.

From mid-1940 through mid-1941 Moye Stephens flew the wing about two dozen times. Significant time was lost in trucking the plane back to the Northrop plant for alterations to be made on this flying laboratory. Between January and early March 1941 the flight test program was put on hold while Stephens and his crew were flight testing the N-3PB patrol bomber at Lake Elsinore, California.

In May 1941, Jack Northrop wrote his friend General H.H. "Hap" Arnold, Chief of the Air Corps, concerning their progress to date:

> You have requested that you be kept informed as to the progress of the flying mockup, and I wish to report at this time that we have completed a number of flights of 10 to 15 minutes duration with the landing gear retracted, which have proven thoroughly the practicability of this airplane. At the present time, due to the warmer weather in the desert, we are having some difficulty with engine cooling, and therefore have to operate at reduced throttle after take-off. However, the stability of the airplane about all three axes has again been confirmed, and we now have very satisfactory controllability directionally as well as laterally and longitudinally.
>
> We have made no attempt at this time to reduce control forces to an absolute minimum, or perfectly synchronize the controls, but the airplane is in such condition that any competent pilot could fly it at any time with no difficulty whatsoever. Both Vance Breese, who did the initial testing for us, and our own pilot, Moye Stephens, have reported the airplane is absolutely normal in every respect. It feels and flies just like any other airplane, and in some respects has better characteristics than the average plane. We have not as yet endeavored to spin the plane or maneuver it violently, but spin tests made at NACA on a model of the XP-56 indicate entirely satisfactory spin characteristics for this type of airplane. And in some respects has better characteristics than the average plane.
>
> We plan for the immediate future further tests to improve the engine cooling and then a series of routine flights during which we

will establish acceptable cg positions for various degrees of dihedral, sweepback and wing tip deflection.

Through the flight tests, they varied the sweep of the wing. With minimum sweepback, Stephens found the plane to be longitudinally unstable. With the outer panels of the wing at maximum degree of sweepback, the plane exhibited quite good characteristics. In varying the droop of the wing tips, it was found that the tip droop had very little impact on directional stability (the initial reason for drooping them). It was found that when in the drooped configuration they lessened lift. The plane was flying with no droop in the tips from 1942 on. Engine overheating, a problem with all embedded air-cooled engine designs, would continue throughout the program. Northrop and his engineers would believe that it was the fins on the engine's cylinders and its installation or the internal design of the engine that was the cause. Being underpowered would always hamper the test program, but much was learned and incorporated into the N-9M and XB-35 projects.

Jack Northrop had envisioned his flying mockup to be a scaled down version of a larger transport or medium bomber. With war in Europe seeming eminent, he pursued the design of the medium bomber. To protect his new radical designs, Northrop had prepared the necessary drawings and documents to submit to the US Patent Office. The first of these was for the XP-56 fighter which was applied for on May 10, 1940, followed with an application for his medium bomber on November 20th of that year. Looking much like an N-1M with defensive turrets, this twin engine medium bomber had a wing span of 85 feet and carried a crew of five. But by May 1941, Jack Northrop queried General Arnold on how this matter should be handled from both a security and publicity perspective.

In consideration of the present satisfactorily advanced status of the project [the N-1M flight tests], several questions have come up which I feel only you can answer definitely. We have recently been informed, through our patent attorneys, by the Chief of the Legal Di-

N-1M wind tunnel model. (Northrop/G. H. Balzer Historical Archives)

The Northrop plant was put into operation as soon as it became available. Construction of the N-1M was started almost immediately and a contract was obtained in late January 1940 from Consolidated Aircraft Corp. in San Diego for PBY-5 empennages, cowlings and seats. Here Jack Northrop sits in the mockup of the N-3. (Northrop/Western Museum of Flight)

The first production line for a complete aircraft at Northrop Aircraft. Here N-3PB fuselage assemblies start to take shape. (Northrop/Stu Luce)

In their permanent quarters the Northrop engineering department expands rapidly in 1940. (Northrop/Western Museum of Flight)

vision of the Air Corps at Washington, D.C., that the subject matter of two design patents filed by this company, one covering the design of the XP-56 Tailless Pursuit, the other the design of a medium bomber following the configuration of the flying mockup, have been determined issuable. This means that very shortly these designs will become public knowledge; and in view of the fact that it has been rumored for some time that we are working on some secret project, I feel it probable that some bright aeronautical editor may pick up the subject, and a certain amount of publicity will result therefrom.

I believe that the successful flight demonstration of the first real flying wing airplane in which every portion of the machine contributes to lift, and in which power plant, crew, and all appurtenances are completely enclosed in the wing, is an accomplishment which deserves careful handling from the publicity angle, and I would hate to have one or two half-baked stories published as a result of patent disclosures, which would probably have the effect of limiting the news value of the announcement as and when we care to make it. You have asked that this development be maintained on a confidential status and we have therefore done our best to keep it so to date. If you are willing that this status be changed from now on, I think we can secure some dignified and valuable publicity for the Air Corps as well as this company, without disclosing any appreciable amount of technical detail covering the manner in which our results have been accomplished.

Northrop went on in some detail concerning his medium bomber size flying wing:

Several months ago we made a study of a twin engine medium bomber around the now non-existent X-1800 Pratt & Whitney engine which appeared to be capable of meeting all the desired characteristics of the latest medium bomber specification No. XC-219, and exceeding the desired maximum speed by 25 miles per hour, and the minimum maximum speed in the specification by 125 miles per hour.

Just what Jack Northrop attempted to prevent, happened. Soon after, the patent and the wing drawing appeared in the U.S. Patent Office's "Official Gazette," an artist rendering and story showed up in the Los Angeles Times newspaper. From here speculation on the wing (also called a manta ray and pterodactyl) spread to aviation publications with much conjecture to its being a 500 mph fighter among other things. The Army and Northrop had to do something. With no mention of it being a design of a medium bomber, "vanilla" information and a photo of the N-1M were released with a promise that the news media would soon have a personal look at the N-1M. Overseas publications soon carried the story of Northrop's wing, which helped strengthen the Horten brothers efforts in Germany. The media event that all anticipated came, and the cameras rolled in the California desert as the yellow wing taxied by for the cameras and then took to the sky and performed for the media. It was Thursday, December 4, 1941. That following Sunday the nation had much more on its mind, and the public paid little attention to the wing story.

As the flight tests continued, Jack Northrop saw much more than what the little N-1M was doing; he saw what could be done. In November 1941 Northrop was proclaiming that the Jeep had reached an altitude of 7,500 feet, had sustained flight in excess of an hour, and had made a total of 200 flights to date. According to Moye Stephens' records, a total of slightly under 50 had actually been

Moye Stephens, to the right, looks on at the N-1M as construction nears completion. Stephens will fly the little wing during most of its flight test program. (Northrop/Wolford Collection)

The N-1M as it looked when it first flew. Here it is being weighed in preparations for its taxi tests in the summer of 1940. (Northrop/Wolford Collection)

accomplished by Vance Breese and himself at this time. Also, the underpowered wing found it very difficult to go much above 4,000 feet.

In May 1942, Jack wanted to bring the little wing back to the airfield at the Northrop plant to continue its flight testing, possibly because the hot summer air in the desert aggravated the engine overheating problem. Moye Stephens felt that the city of Hawthorne was too close in proximity to the field and that a disaster was waiting to happen. Northrop, who shied away from debates, took Stephens off the flight test program. Vance Breese was hired to fly the plane back to Mines Field. Because the plane had a limited ceiling, an Army C-47 had to tow it over the mountains dividing the desert from the Los Angeles area. From Mines Field, newly arrived Northrop test pilot John Myers took over the flight test duties in June.

The plane was back at the desert sporadically as time went on. On one occasion, as the plane was towed back to Hawthorne once again by a C-47, John Myers cut loose from the tow cable. But instead of just making a normal landing at Northrop Field, he put the plane into a spin, recovered, and brought it in for a beautiful landing. Myers last flight in the N-1M was in mid-January 1943.

Breese, Stephens, and Myers were not the only ones to flight test the N-1M. Northrop test pilot Richard H. Ranaldi had one flight in the plane, as did two Army pilots from Wright Field, Col. F. R. Dent (who flew the C-47 that towed the N-1M on some occasions) and Col. Marshall S. Roth (who was project engineer on Northrop's XP-56 and P-61 Black Widow projects).

Not much is known of the N-1M's history beyond January 1943. By October 1943, the plane had been repainted and turned over to the Army. It was kept in storage at Northrop Field for quite a while. In early June 1946 it was part of the Army Air Forces collection at Freeman Field in Indiana for a short while before going to the Museum Storage Depot at Park Ridge, Illinois. It has been restored and is on display at the Paul E. Garber Facility of the National Air and Space Museum in Maryland.

First flight of the N-1M occurred on July 3, 1940 with veteran contract test pilot Vance Breese at the controls. Its initial flights were less than spectacular, getting only a few feet off the ground; the Lycoming's just didn't have the power required. (Northrop/Wolford Collection)

Taking over from Vance Breese after the first few flights was corporate secretary, and the sole company test pilot, Moye Stephens. (Northrop/Wolford Collection)

This June 1940 photo shows the N-1M as it was first constructed. The original engines were Lycoming O-145s with two-bladed propellers. The texture of the wood grain can also be seen in this photo. (Northrop/G. H. Balzer Historical Archives)

This rare shot shows that the N-1M originally had a front windscreen which curved down to the leading edge of the craft. Also note the flush engine air intakes; a lower lip would be added later to give better air flow into the engines. (Northrop/G. H. Balzer Historical Archives)

The flight tests in 1940, and for most of the program, took place over the southern end of California's Mojave Desert near the little town of Muroc. There were two dry lakes, Rogers and Rosamond (quite often referred to as Muroc Dry Lake), which provided safe havens to carry out the experimental flights. (Northrop/Wolford Collection)

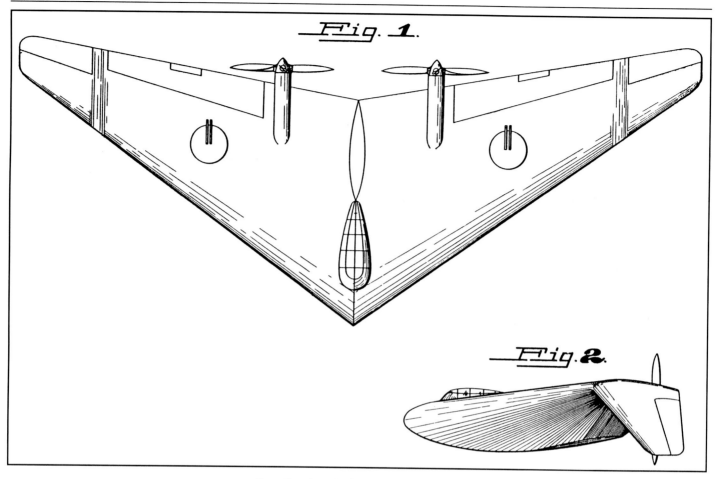

Patent Drawing of Medium Bomber Flying Wing

The N-1M was modified soon after the initial flights. The Lycoming engines were replaced by a pair of Franklins. A lip was added below the engine air intake to give better air flow, and the canopy windscreen was modified so that it ended well behind the leading edge. (Northrop/Wolford Collection)

The N-1M was a flying laboratory. Much of it could be changed on the ground in order to test flying characteristics in different configurations. Wing tip droop, sweepback, and dihedral could be changed, and different configurations of the flight control surfaces were also tried. (Northrop/Wolford Collection)

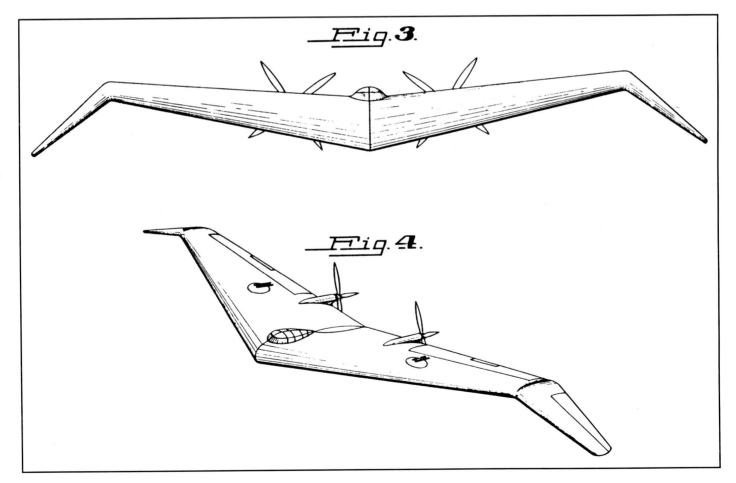

Patent Drawing of Medium Bomber Flying Wing

There were a number of lengthy periods where flight testing could not be carried out. The engine change and rework of the engine cooling ducts as well as repair of the rear spar after an accident all grounded the plane. Between late December 1940 and early March 1941 test pilot Moye Stephens and his flight test crew had to discontinue their N-1M flight test activities in order to test the N-3PB seaplanes then coming off Northrop's production lines for the Norwegian government. Here one of the N-3PBs is seen at Northrop's flight test facility at Lake Elsinore, California. (Northrop)

The 117 h.p. Franklin engines were an improvement over the 65 h.p. Lycomings but the N-1M was limited to a maximum altitude of about 4,000 feet according to test pilot Moye Stephens. (Northrop/Wolford Collection)

The Muroc crew. From left to right: Walt Cerny, Moye Stephens, Dr. William Sears, Tom Ruble, Harold Pedersen, Ed Lesnick, Earl Paton, and Ralph Winiger.
(Northrop/Wolford collection)

Army Air Corps chief, General H. H. "Hap" Arnold, on the right, was a strong supporter of Jack Northrop and his flying wing and tailless aircraft projects. (Northrop)

The N-1M is on truck scales being weighed on the desert floor near Muroc, California. (Northrop/Wolford Collection)

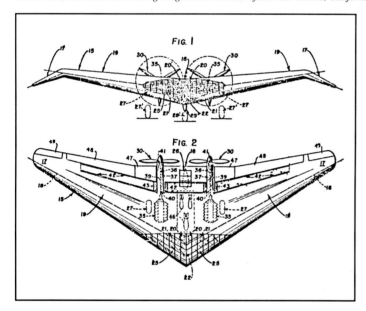

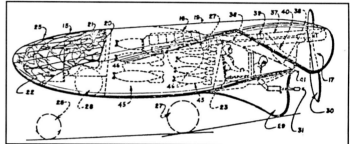

Left and above:
Patent Drawing of Medium Bomber Flying Wing

Because of its altitude limitation, the nearly 4,000 pound craft could not make it over the mountains separating the desert from the greater Los Angeles area. Early on, Northrop trucked the little craft which took a good bit of effort and time. Later it was towed by C-47. (Northrop/Wolford Collection)

Northrop photographer Roy Wolford leans out of the cargo door of the C-47 to get this spectacular view of the N-1M in tow. (Northrop/Wolford Collection)

A bird's eye view of the C-47 towing the tiny N-1M with the rugged mountainous background. (Northrop/Wolford Collection)

After the patent drawings of Northrop's twin engine medium bomber appeared in aviation publications in both the U.S. and Europe in mid-1941, the press put pressure on Northrop to see his flying wing. With the Army's permission, Photo Day was held on the dry lake near Muroc on December 4, 1941. Here Moye Stephens, in the cockpit, and Jack Northrop pose for the photographers. (Northrop/Wolford Collection)

Reporters as well as still and newsreel photographers are poised for the N-1M's flight demonstration. (Northrop/Wolford Collection)

Above and Below: With motion picture cameras rolling and still cameras snapping, the N-1M puts on an impressive demonstration for its spellbound audience in the Mojave Desert on that fine Thursday. Three days later the Japanese attack on Pearl Harbor would give the American public much more to think about. (Northrop/Wolford Collection)

The N-1M performance, though not outstanding, did prove Jack Northrop's flying wing theory. Much was learned from its flight testing which was later incorporated in the N-9M. The N-9M was built as part of the development process of the B-35 heavy bomber project. (Northrop/Wolford Collection)

Left: A couple of still shots printed from N-1M flight test film. As shown in these photos, the Northrop engineers found that the straight wing configuration was the best design through the N-1M's flight tests. (Northrop)

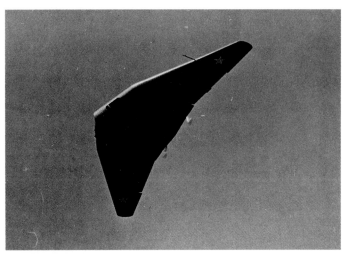

Shortly after the breakout of hostilities with Japan, the civilian registration was removed from the N-1M and the National insignia was applied. (Northrop/G. H. Balzer Historical Archives)

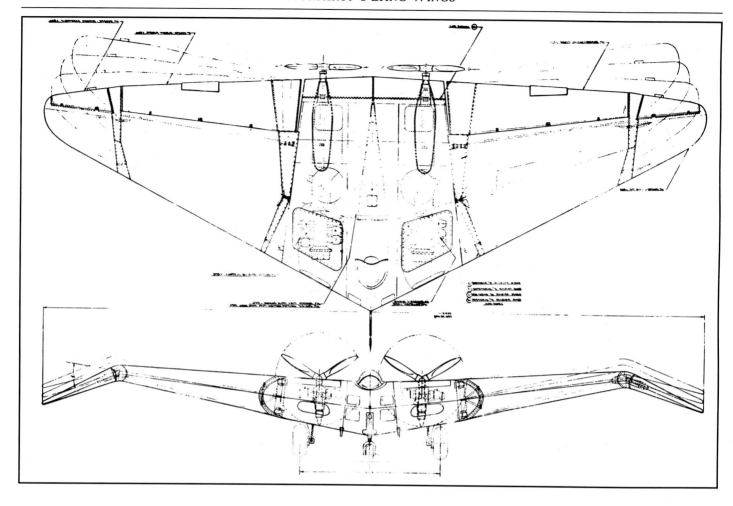

N-1M Three View

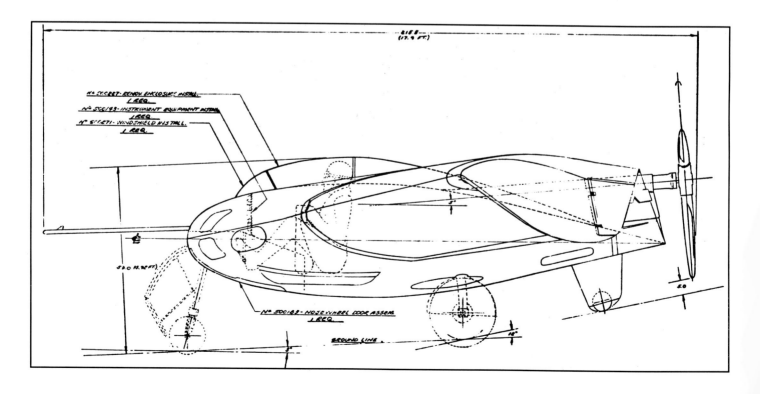

U.S. Senator Walgren poses in the cockpit of the N-1M. With the right engine cover removed, some detail of the engine installation can be seen. This photo was taken during one of the times the N-1M was back at the Northrop plant for repairs and/or modifications. (Northrop)

The first XP-56, sporting a three tone paint scheme, performs engine runs in May 1943. A special cooling system was required for the Pratt & Whitney R-2800 Double Wasp engine buried within the fuselage. (Northrop/Wolford Collection)

Chapter 3
RADICAL FIGHTER DESIGN
Development of the XP-56 Tailless Fighter

In early 1939, Jack Northrop, an acknowledged talented aeronautical engineer, was unemployed. It was for a good reason; he had a dream to fulfill and he had just recently resigned from Douglas to once again pursue that dream. The U.S. War Department was also examining their plans for the future. Their paths would soon cross.

In March 1939 a special Air Board was appointed within the War Department. Headed by General Hap Arnold, the board's task was to define the Air Corps' role in national policy and what it needed to enable it to fulfill that mission. The Board issued its report on September 15th in which it stressed the need for a strong

research and development program in order to keep ahead of the enemy. In May, General Arnold appointed an Air Corps board which was headed by Brig. Gen. Walter G. Kilner and included Lt. Col. Carl Spaatz, who would shortly become one of the air force's outstanding war time leaders, and Charles A. Lindbergh. On June 28th, the Kilner Board presented a comprehensive list of characteristics for aircraft and other requirements for the next five years.

As the result of the Kilner Board's action, the Assistant Secretary of War approved a plan calling for a new fighter design capable of flying at 525 mph at 15,000 feet. At least two companies were to design competing models – each company to construct two

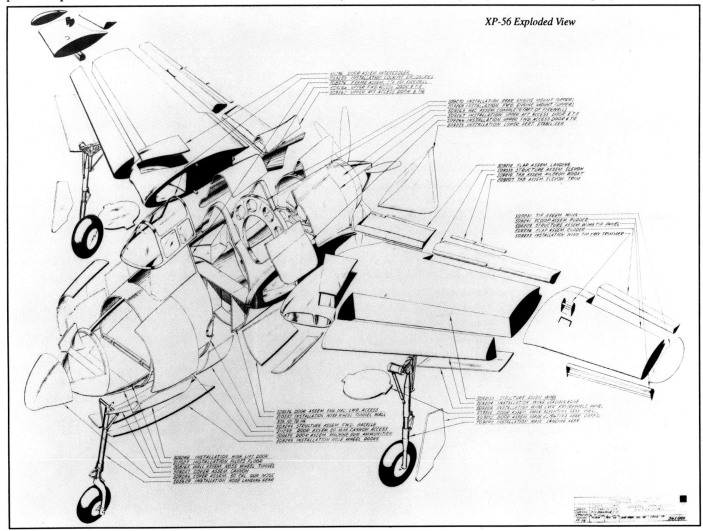

XP-56 Exploded View

55

The XP-56's cockpit arrangement. (Edwards AFB History Office)

examples. Of the two aircraft to be constructed by each company, the first was to be a flying mockup while the second would be a prototype for the production model.

Herb DeCenzo was in on the early conceptual designs that eventually lead to the XP-56.

> Keith Rider had been hired by Northrop Aircraft, and he joined us when we moved into the new building [from the Hawthorne Hotel]. He was, supposedly, just in design, but all of a sudden, why, he was in preliminary design and I worked both with Keith and another fellow they had in preliminary design. Mr. Northrop had some projects he wanted us to do and most of them were all on fighters. They would be, of course, all wing fighters. You might say, 'Well, what's the big deal there?' Well, the big deal was that all the engine manufacturers were all of a sudden turning out bigger and better engines and naturally that demanded, bigger and better fighters. And so, there we were. We were drawing one configuration after another. Most of them, however, were still basically the same. You might say they were pretty much like the XP-56 that was built. I might add that I know we laid that one out. I guess it must have been based on one of the layouts and reports that Keith and I put together on the XP-56 which had a big radial engine in it.

> Keith could really lay down the lines. We designed almost every time with the full approval of Mr. Northrop. Keith used to design racing airplanes and of course there isn't a heck of a lot of difference between a good fighter and a good racer. They have to be clean and they have to look good. If they don't look good, they're dogs. And, of course, they have to be practical. So Keith, having quite a bit of experience designing aircraft from scratch, building them from scratch, and going through all the hardships of racing them, knew what could be sone and what could not be done...

We also had to make a report to go along with these different designs. After all, they were not pretty pictures; they had to be something that was realistic and could be sold. I know we made about six to eight of them. Keith would make the designs, make all the different installations, get the configurations right, and we would have to figure out how much fuel we would need for a given engine for whatever endurance and range were required. And in turn Keith had other problems that weren't mine, such as installation of the different types of armament that might be required, including cannons. With the powerplant in the rear, of course, it was natural to put the cannons and other machine guns up in the nose of the airplane instead of having to put them out in the wings or anything of that nature. So Keith Rider had his hands full trying to install that cannon, in fact we would always say why put in one when we could put in two. And there was another problem, whether is was a cannon of a 50 cal. gun up front, or even 30 cal., it would eject the shells like crazy and you had to catch them. You couldn't let them go into the wind stream like a regular airplane because you had the propellers in the tail of the airplane. So you had to put in bags and what have you to catch all that stuff. In fact, nothing could be ejected on that airplane, you had to be very careful.

The Air Corps' specification for this new pursuit ship was completed on November 27th with an informal design competition started on December 18th; a formal Request for Data (R-40C) was issued in February 1940. Thirteen contractors were invited to bid, including the new Northrop Aircraft, Inc. Seven of the contractors submitted a total of eight designs which were subsequently reviewed by a board of officers. The designs submitted by Vultee, Curtiss, and Northrop, in that order, were selected. All of the chosen designs had the engines in the pusher configuration. It was rationalized that this would produce aircraft of greater aerodynamic "cleanness" and would enable them to take greater advantage of the clear nose area for armament. Northrop's Model N-2 was assigned classified project number MX-14 and the military designation XP-56. On June 22, 1940 the young Northrop Aircraft, Inc. received an $11,000 contract (W535 ac-15021) calling for engineering data and wind tunnel models, with an option for one experimental airplane.

New Materials for Radical Designs

Though all three manufacturers would produce quite distinctive designs, the Northrop product would be the most unique. An acquaintance from Jack Northrop's Douglas days, Vladimir Pavlecka, would strongly influence the construction of the XP-56 and later the XP-79 designs. Unlike anything seen before, the XP-56 would be made of magnesium and a Northrop process developed by Pavlecka called Heliarc welding would be used. This was a fortunate time for Pavlecka. The government was quite concerned that aluminum production could not keep up with war-time needs. Non-critical materials were being required and such materials as duramold, steel, and magnesium were being contemplated. The development of the magnesium welding process would turn out to be a much greater success story than that of the XP-56. Pavlecka recalled the development of Heliarc welding some years ago:

> Magnesium welding we did first of all with boron flux. With this you always had a porous weld; you could never succeed in making a good weld. In most cases the flux did not purge out, inside the joint it

corroded, and the weld was only a fraction of the metal's strength. With the magnesium we had all kinds of problems. One problem was that we could get magnesium only in a very wavy form. We couldn't get from Dow Chemical, which was the only producer of magnesium then, a flat sheet. They just couldn't succeed in doing it. I didn't believe we couldn't do it. So I took the sheets we got from them to National Steel Corp. in Torrance [California], and I got these steel people interested in flattening them out for us. They went at it with gusto. They put these sheets through rollers that they used to straighten out steel sheets and the sheets came out worst than before. You would have to laugh and at the same time have tears for the people who were doing it because they were so frustrated. They knew they could do it with steel. We tried to stretch it; we tried to roll it, and we didn't succeed. So we took it as it was and heated it on forms, and once it had that form, which was curvature, it stayed put and didn't wave any more.

Then came the welding, and the welding was hopeless. I had experience in gases; I used to be in dirigible engineering. I handled the helium and was always interested in the five inert gases. I went to [Jack] Northrop and said we ought to go to General Electric because they had done work on arc-atomic welding; that is a weld in which you disassociate the hydrogen molecules into hydrogen atoms, and then an association back into the molecule which releases a vast amount of heat. So we tried this, but it was too hot for us. Amazingly enough, which we should have foreseen, the hydrogen made corrosive agents with the magnesium, and we didn't solve the problem of purity at all.

We needed an inert gas. At this time I wrote a letter to General Electric in Schnectady [New York] asking them about their study into gas presence at electric arc, if they have any record of helium being used. Helium was most likely because the other inert gases are unsuitable for this. For instance, neon doesn't have a good specific heat; argon is like air almost; helium has a very high specific heat, which would be a coolant, which we needed for magnesium. We didn't get an answer from them for about three months. Finally there came an elderly gentleman from GE who said it was not workable for this purpose. I briefed him on what we needed and he took copious notes. He said he would go to GE and he would find out just what they knew. Several months elapsed again, and this time six people came from the lab. We all sat around a conference table and they said they had correspondence, and they showed it to me. GE declared that they had nothing like it, that they had never done any work with helium in an arc, and that they knew nothing about it. So we discussed the problem at some length. They departed and that was the last time I ever saw them.

So I went to Northrop and said, 'Jack, we either have to give this up or we may try helium ourselves.' He said, 'Try, go ahead with it.' Here's where I encountered the big obstacle. The welder's union insisted that they weld; I cannot weld. We didn't have enough power for a welding laboratory; we didn't have enough means for it. So the boss of the welding department appointed a welder to work with me. I told him what to do and he would do it. Well, this just didn't work. Every time I would come to the welder he would say he was too busy with production. And when he did it, and it wouldn't work and I said, 'What have you done?' And he said, 'Well I don't know; I just did what you told me.' I said, 'It doesn't look like what I told you. And you didn't use the tool I told you to use.' We just didn't get anywhere. So a new welder [was assigned to the project]; this man was just as bad as the first one.

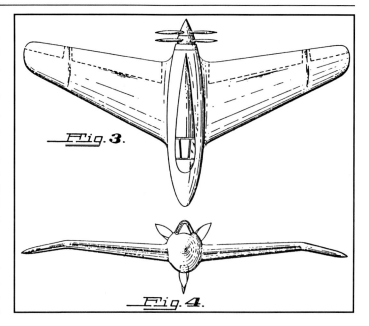

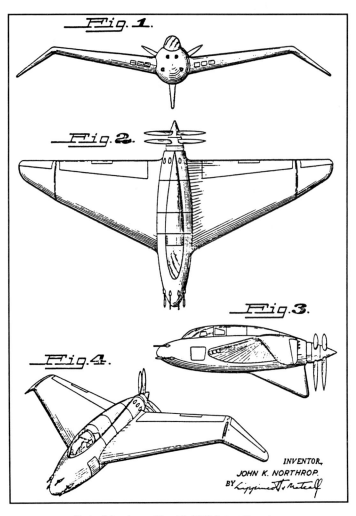

Both of the above : May 10, 1940 Patent Drawings

High speed taxi tests performed by XP-56 number 1 at Hawthorne Field. These stills were made from flight test movie film. (Northrop)

We were getting nowhere very slowly. We did, however, succeed in welding about an inch long seam in magnesium. It was so beautiful. But each time we welded about an inch, the electrode, which was a magnesium wire, got heated, broke off and fell into the seam that we had just laid out. So we were welding inches, leave, weld inches. Well, that was no good.

So then I went back to arc-atomic welding which uses tungsten wire rods. The thought was why don't we use tungsten arc weld here, surrounded by a helium stream and then feed a metal electrode into it separately. I ordered tungsten electrodes, and they wouldn't come for several weeks. I wrote for them again from General Electric, and finally they promised they were being sent. One morning (my office was next to Northrop's) I came in and Northrop was there already, and he called me in. And as early as it was, the office was full of people – there was the controller, plant manager, vice president, chairman Cohu and a couple of others. The welding boss was there. Northrop told me, 'Pavi, these people tell me we should drop this trying to weld with helium because it doesn't work.' I said, 'No, I disagree. It works, but we just can't do it continuously. We hope to do it continuously with these electrodes from General Electric. They should be here before the next weekend.' Northrop turned around in his chair and looked out of the window and said, 'What day is today?' It was March 1940. He turned around and said, 'How much have we spent on this?' The controller said we had spent about 3,200 hours already, which was the salaries of the welding boss and the wage of the welder. Later on I found out they were charging me for their own faults and mistakes. Well, I didn't object to it. It was a large sum for that day. Northrop said, 'Let's continue to the end of the month; and if at the end of the month you cannot weld, let's stop.' Well, the electrodes came and we were able to weld with them almost immediately. Beautiful seams. We welded thick magnesium bars, we welded thin ones, we welded anything.

Then came Senator Truman, who was with Senator Mead, a greenhorn from Washington. He was on the oversight committee over expenditures in the government. He came to Northrop to see what was going on. And it happened by accident that I was the highest ranking member of the company, everybody was gone somewhere, so I took him around. Before he left he loaded his pockets with my samples until he was bulging. He liked them all so much; they were so beautiful.

At this time we, of course, applied for patents. We were able to weld at last; we welded magnesium just like nothing to it – with purity and consistency. Then came an answer from the Patent Office, and the answer was, 'You cannot get basic patents because General Electric has it all patented already.' This was a shock. They denied they had anything. I investigated the situation; we got all the records from the Patent Office.

Sometime in the 1920s there were two men at General Electric in Schnectady – Hobart and Deberet. These two men worked on electric arc in gases. They tried argon, neon; they tried them all, and they had covered them all in the patent. So we couldn't get any patents on basic principles, but we did get patents on the torch. General Electric was sitting on it, doing nothing with it. I found that this was not the only firm that does that. Corporations do it as a matter of policy all the time. I have many other examples since then, some relating to my own work by the way. Northrop then sold it to Lindy, and Lindy made an agreement with Air Corp., which was owned by General Electric, and they shared the profits. In 1949 Fortune magazine came out with an article on heliarc welding which stated that by that year the inert gas welding industry had reached gross product of one billion dollars a year.

The Tailless Fighter

By August 1940, the Air Corps' Materiel Division liked the XP 56 engineering data to the extent that the option under the contract calling for a flight test article was exercised. On September 26 Change Order Number One calling for a mockup within 120 days and the first XP-56 to be completed within a year was approved for which Northrop Aircraft received $393,380. Armament was to consist of four .50 cal. machine guns with 400 rounds per gun and two 20mm cannon with 100 rounds each – all in the nose.

A story that has become all too familiar impacted two of the three aircraft in this advanced fighter competition – one was Northrop's XP-56. The promised advancement in power plant did not materialize. Pratt & Whitney's liquid-cooled X-1800 was an engine the Air Corps had great hopes for, but by mid-1940 all was not going well. It seemed that the time required to develop the engine to its potential would be quite a bit longer than anticipated (a change in Pratt & Whitney's engineering staff seems to have compounded the problem). In September 1940 the director of War Production issued a directive terminating the X-1800-AG3 engine "so that the company could devote full time to production problems and other more important development work." For Northrop, they reluctantly chose the air-cooled R-2800 as an alternative power plant. Change Order Number Two dated March 21, 1941 authorized this change at no cost to the government.

Both Pratt & Whitney and Northrop had extensive work to do to make this new matchup work. Pratt & Whitney had to develop a version of the R-2800 Double Wasp which had concentric drive shafts. Also, with the XP-56's engine being of the pusher configuration, the propeller had to be jettisoned for pilot safety in case it was necessary to bail out. To jettison the counter rotating propeller, an explosive cord was wrapped around the engine gearbox. In an emergency the pilot would detonate the explosive, blowing the propellers and a portion of the airplane's aft end away, thus making it safe for the pilot to egress. This model of the Double Wasp was designated the R-2800-29.

Northrop was not too pleased with the substitution. They felt that turbo-supercharging was needed but did not prevail on this request. Structurally, Northrop had to redesign the engine bay and central wing area in order to replace the sleeker liquid-cooled engine first envisioned with the bulkier radial, plus there was the need to incorporate a fan and discharge system for the new air-cooled engine. It was estimated that this redirection caused a five and a half month delay in program development, not to mention a 2,000 pound increase in weight and a 14 mph decrease in high speed at critical altitude.

There were problems for Northrop at the wind tunnel also. A special model had been providing quite satisfactory data until one day when it unfortunately came loose from its fixture in the tunnel and was severely damaged. Compensating somewhat for this loss, flight test data from Northrop's N-1M flying mockup supplemented the wind tunnel data already obtained. The wing layout for the XP-56 resembled that of the N-1M. A similar elevon system in place of

This September 1943 photo shows the first XP-56 with a coat of silver paint. Flights number one and two took place on September 6, 1943. The nose blisters cover two of the planes six gun ports. (Northrop/Edwards AFB History Office)

the conventional aileron and elevator control surfaces were used and the outer portion of the wings was sloped at an anhedral, though the degree of slope was changed as a result of N-1M experience.

The mockup was completed in July and the Air Corps' mockup committee consisting of representatives from Wright Field's Aircraft, Armament, and Equipment Laboratories, Major Marshall S. Roth of the Aircraft Projects Section (who was associated with a number of Northrop projects for Materiel Division), and three civilian technical advisors from the Power Plant, Photo, and Equipment Laboratories. Major Thayes S. Olds acted as technical advisor for General Headquarters.

Three major changes were required by the committee. They felt that the design presented would cause the plane to "flop" on to the nose wheel when the main gear touched the ground on landing. To remedy this potential problem, the main gear was to be moved forward. Northrop had designed the fuselage in a circular shape. The committee felt that an elliptical configuration would improve the armament installation. And last, they requested the pilot's canopy be redesigned to give it greater rigidity and to provide the pilot with better visibility.

The design and construction of the plane would drag out over the next year and a half. A major cause for the delay was the shortage of engineers and the constant demands on the limited engineering resources by the many projects Northrop had undertaken, particularly the XB-35, which had a higher priority. Pratt & Whitney was having difficulties with the engine and associated gear box which resulted in a late delivery of these items. Other required government furnished equipment was also late in arrival. Compounding this, Northrop was having its own problems in perfecting magnesium welding.

There was concern within the Air Corps that the loss of the sole XP-56 would not only impede that program, but the need to replace the lost aircraft would also have a detrimental effect on the XB-35 project because of limited engineering manpower and manufacturing space at Northrop. The Air Corps proposed the construc-

tion of a second article to Jack Northrop and he replied in October 1941:

It is estimated that little difference in engineering is involved, whether one or two airplanes are constructed. It would be impossible to undertake the second airplane if it involved appreciable additional engineering time, as the Engineering Department is definitely overloaded at present and is the critical spot in our organization with regard to the completion of the XP-56 and Project MX-140 [XB-35]. It is believed, however, that two experimental airplanes could be built from the same engineering drawings as one experimental airplane, and that outside of a very small amount of liaison engineering, which is handled by a separate department, no additional burden would be involved. The addition of the necessary shop time is a very small proportion of our total shop load and would have a hardly measurable effect on our total rate of production.

But manpower and shop space were not the only concerns at the Northrop plant. Northrop also stated in his letter to the Air Corps that under the arrangement he had with his bank in which he had obtained working capital it was stipulated that the company could not accept any additional fixed price contracts as the first XP-56 was under. The only alternative was for the Air Corps to renegotiate the first XP-56 in a package that included a second article. This was acceptable to all and a cost-plus fixed-fee contract was arrived at under which the original cost of the first remained as agreed upon. The total package came to $600,000. The contract was approved on February 13, 1942.

By early March 1943, the first XP-56 was completed. Personnel from Air Technical Service Command conducted vibration tests on the XP-56 at the Northrop plant. This was followed by the first engine runs later that same month. In subsequent engine runs engine roughness was experienced. Investigation proved the problem to be a faulty ignition harness. The next step leading to first flight were the taxi tests. On April 12th Northrop test pilot John Myers powered up the XP-56 and took it out for its preliminary taxi tests with generally good results. By early May all seemed ready and the plane was prepared for shipment by truck to Muroc for its final taxi tests and first flight. But an incident thousands of miles away stopped all this.

Pratt & Whitney had been running a R-2800-29 engine in a test stand at its Connecticut facility when one of the propeller blades was torn loose. This was the same engine that powered Northrop's bullet shape fighter-interceptor of the future. It was decided to run further vibration tests on the plane before any further thought of flying it. Complete engine, gear box, and propeller vibration tests were undertaken. During the tests, an engine failure was experienced. Investigation proved the cause of the problem to be movement of the gear box brought about by vibration. The movement of the gear box had forced the extension shaft forward into the engine. The XP-56 project had to be put on hold for a while because Pratt & Whitney could not supply a replacement engine until early August because of their own work load. At the same time, Pratt & Whitney was also to install a new gear box with more rigid mountings.

Test Operations

In early September, the XP-56 was finally trucked to Muroc where Myers performed the last taxi runs leading up to first flight. On September 6th Myers took the XP-56 into the air for the first time in a conservative trial in which he flew the craft in a straight line for about a mile at an altitude of four feet. This short 140 mph dash seemed successful enough, so a second flight was undertaken that day. In the second flight John Myers took the craft to an altitude of 25 to 50 feet and doubled the endurance while increasing the speed to 170 mph. In this flight the plane showed some unwanted directional tendencies and the post flight analysis indicated that the dorsal fin area needed to be increased by about four square feet.

With the modification completed, pilot and plane were back at Muroc taxiing around the desert floor. On October 8th Myers and

the XP-56 took to the air for their third flight. Like the first flights it was in a straight line for a short duration with an altitude of somewhere between 10 and 15 feet. Upon touch down, Myers performed a high speed taxi run and then immediately lifted into the air again. This second flight was a repeat of the first and upon landing Myers proceeded to commence another high speed taxi run. As the craft sped across the desert at 130 mph, the left main tire blew and the plane immediately started to yaw to the left. It rotated about 90 degrees and started skidding sideways and eventually slightly backwards. After traveling for about 250 yards the tail skid hit, then the propeller about ten yards later and after about another ten yards the right wing tip struck the ground. From this latter act, the airplane started tumbling backwards, making two and a half revolutions before coming to rest on its back. Fortunately for test pilot Myers, he and the seat came out after the first revolution. The final impact of the back of the plane into the desert floor would have pushed his head very unnaturally into his body, if not ripping it off. Myers' major injuries were a ruptured vertebrae in his back, a broken ankle, and assorted cuts and bruises – all of which he would recover from and be back on flying status within six months. (By April of the next year, Myers would start his sojourn to the Pacific combat theater to check out the Army Air Forces' night fighters in the P-61 Black Widow.)

The subsequent accident investigation found no fault on the pilot's part, the aircraft, or in the tires. The investigators found bits of glass and broken bottles along the runway. They felt that it was possible that some of the glass might have been imbedded in the tire thus causing the blow out. In their recommendations they stated that tires with nylon cord construction (the XP-56's tires were of an older design) be used on all experimental aircraft until a full study could be made of their takeoff and landing characteristics. They also recommended that a "tire expert" be consulted in selecting the appropriate type of tire for experimental airplanes.

Concern for what made the first XP-56 flip, led to the conclusion that it was the geometry of the landing gear, but to redesign the second XP-56 would be costly and time consuming. As an alternative, the center of gravity was moved forward by reballasting the second plane. To forestall the ventral fin from possibly digging into

A rear view as test pilot John Myers runs up the XP-56's engine on one of southern California's dry lakes. (Northrop/Edwards AFB History Office)

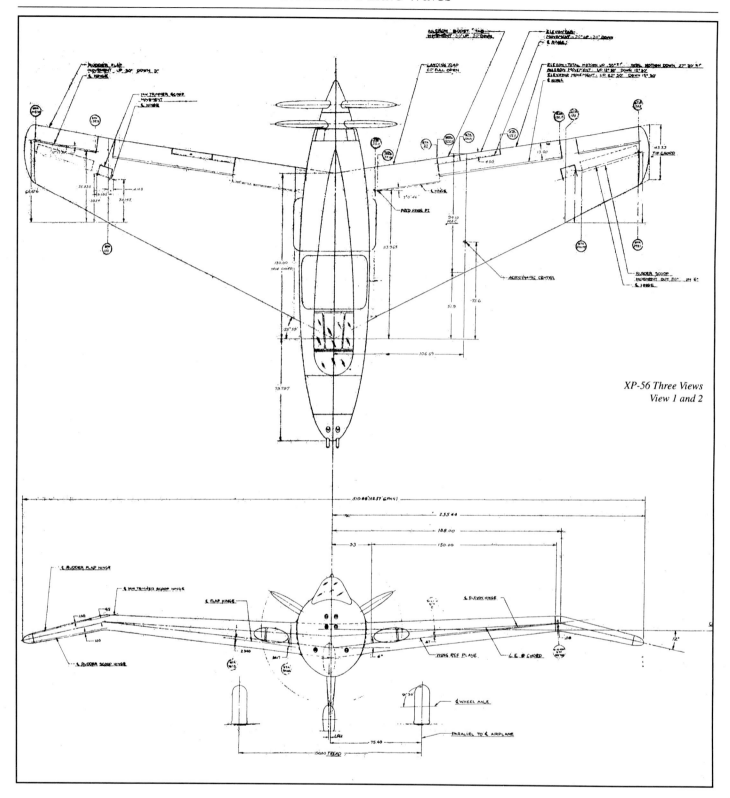

XP-56 Three Views
View 1 and 2

the ground, a wheel was installed in lieu of the bumper used on the first plane. It was thought that this would allow it to roll over the ground in the event of contact rather than digging in.

Myers felt that there was still some stability problem with the first aircraft. To improve rudder action, the original control linkage was disconnected from the air brakes, which provided rudder con-

trol and were connected to air valves in the venturi ducts that had been constructed in the wing tips of the second plane.

This system was operated by depressing the rudder pedals. When the pedal was depressed, the valve operation would shut off the air flow through the duct and redirect it to a bellows which in turn opened the air brake and caused the plane to turn. Thus by depressing the right rudder pedal, the right air brake would be activated and the plane would turn in the desired direction.

The required modifications took precious time and the second XP-56, sporting the enlarged dorsal fin as had been scabbed onto the first plane, was ready for engine runs in early January 1944. Replacing the injured Myers for flight test duties on the second plane was Northrop test pilot Harry Crosby.

Initial taxi runs were conducted at Northrop Field shortly after the successful completion of the engine tests. Before first flight, a high speed taxi test was to be made. But for safety, special ten ply nylon cord virgin rubber tires were installed as insurance against a blow out such as had ended the career of the first plane. A run at 110 mph was successfully accomplished. The plan was to take the plane to Muroc for final taxi tests and flight testing, but a wet winter had caused the "dry" lakes to flood.

Flight test was on hold while the winter rains persisted. The first dry spot to become available was Roach Dry Lake in Nevada. Shop facilities had to be arranged, and a special ground radio station was required. On March 23rd Harry Crosby took the second XP-56 into the air for a short seven minute flight in which Crosby reached an altitude of 2,500 feet. During this flight he experienced nose heaviness, which he could not correct by trim tab action alone, and extreme rudder sensitivity.

The second flight, and most successful for the XP-56 program, took place on March 31st. With the relocation of the center of gravity, the nose heaviness was now correctable with the trim tabs alone. Crosby put the plane through simple maneuvers in which it performed satisfactorily and attained an air speed of 250 mph at 7,800 feet. A reasonably low speed was attained during approach and landing without the use of the flaps (longitudinal instability was experienced during flap usage). Flights three through six were conducted at Roach Dry Lake. By this time, May 1944, the California Dry Lakes, which had much better facilities, were dry and Northrop got Materiel Command's permission to move flight test operations. On May 12th flight number seven was flown in which operations were moved to Harpers Lake. During the flight to Harpers', Crosby varied the speed at which he was flying and conducted a number of stability checks. During these, he experienced wing heaviness, which at times was not correctable with the trim tabs. Upon landing, Crosby reported he had experienced lateral instability and control reversal at slow speed. The plane was grounded and an investigation was conducted though a definite cause for the instability phenomenon could not be found.

Northrop was concerned over both the stability and control problems that persisted and the inability of the XP-56 to get to the guaranteed high speed of 465 mph at 25,000 feet. NACA's Ames Laboratory at Moffett Field south of San Francisco was contacted in late May. The initial proposal was for Ames personnel to instrument the XP-56, Northrop personnel to fly and support the plane, and the Ames personnel to assist in data reduction. But due to further instability problems experienced with the aircraft in flight tests that were occurring as the plan with NACA was being negotiated, Wright Field engineering personnel decided it would be too dangerous to fly the plane to Moffett Field. The new plan was to truck it to Moffett where it was to be installed in the Ames full scale wind tunnel.

By this time the XP-56 had a fairly low priority and had to wait for an available time slot in the Ames wind tunnel schedule. While waiting, flight number 10, which would be its last, occurred on August 11, 1944. Extreme tail heaviness was encountered while

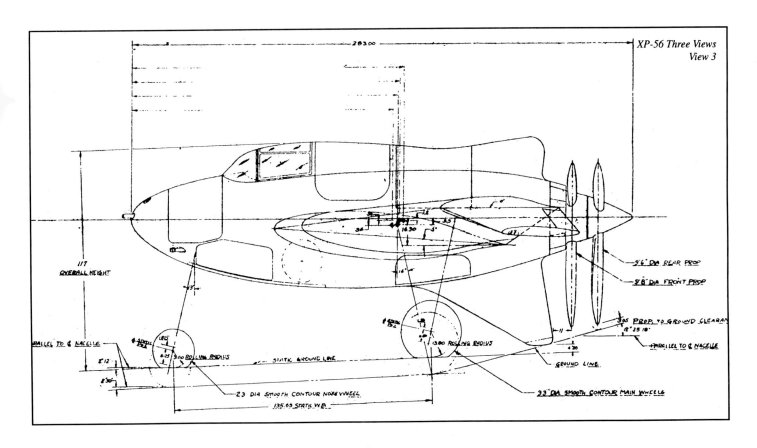

XP-56 Three Views
View 3

on the ground; in flight full power could not be obtained and fuel consumption was deemed excessive. It was decided that the plane should be put into storage at Muroc and trucked to Moffett Field when the wind tunnel was available. A year later it was still in storage at Muroc.

In December 1945, Wright Field felt that this design had nothing further to offer and wind tunnel testing was canceled. On January 31, 1946, Air Technical Service Command requested the XP-56 be returned to the Northrop plant. The local AAF plant representative accepted the plane, and the XP-56 was sent to Freeman Field in Indiana for display purposes. It is presently in the Smithsonian Institution's Silver Hill, Maryland, storage facility awaiting restoration.

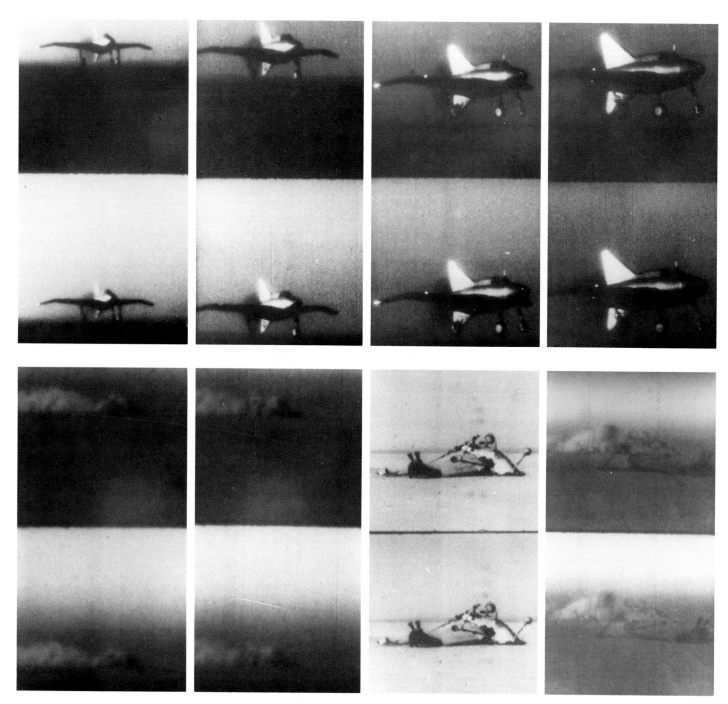

Above and above opposite: October 8, 1943 flights number three and four were flown. The following series of prints from flight test film show the XP-56 landing following flight four and consequences of the left main tire blowing out during the high speed taxi performed after landing. Also evident is the fact that an extended dorsal fin, as the second XP-56 would have, had been added to the first XP-56 also. (Northrop)

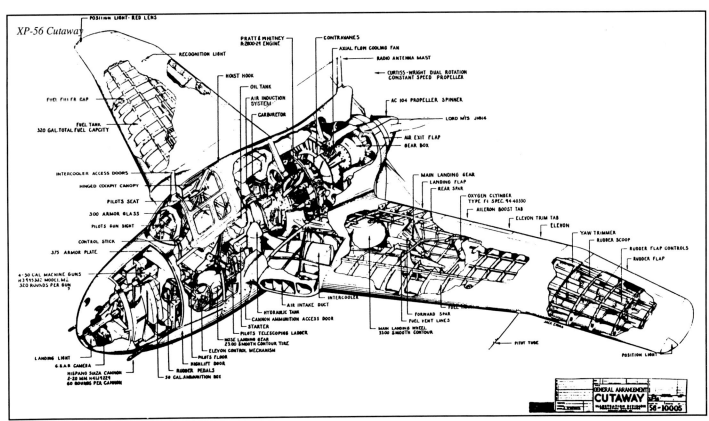

XP-56 Cutaway

A bevy of onlookers at Northrop Field watch as the second XP-56 performs engine runs. The wing tip openings on this example are to allow ram air to go into a venturi through which the air could be redirected by the pilot; the pilot would actuate a valve which would redirect the airflow to a bellows which would assist in operating the wing tip split flap rudders. (Northrop\Wolford Collection)

The second XP-56 had a slightly greater wing span because of the redesigned wing tips. A wheel was added to the ventral fin in lieu of the first aircraft's skid. This was to prevent the fin from digging into the ground in a tail low position. (San Diego Aerospace Museum)

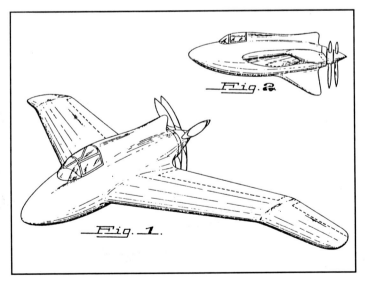

Dec. 3, 1941 Patent Drawings

Operations at Roach Dry Lake in March 1944. Operations were moved to this Nevada site when the California dry lakes were flooded during the rainy season. Here maintenance is being performed in quite primitive conditions. (Northrop/ Wolford Collection)

Somewhat like the original paint scheme of the first XP-56, the second version was painted olive drab over gray with yellow fin tips. The gun blisters are absent from this second variant. (Northrop)

This rear view shows the exhaust ports around the aft portion of the fuselage as well as the propeller installation. (Northrop/Edwards AFB History Office)

In the air, this sleek looking fighter looks as if it were a "real performer." Unfortunately, it never achieved the performance originally estimated. A lack of stability as well as performance caused the Army Air Forces to lose interest in this aircraft as it was recognized that the jet-powered fighter was the future. (Northrop/Wolford Collection)

The stars and stripes are raised above the new Northrop plant on Saturday, September 28, 1940. When the facilities were first occupied in February of that year Northrop had some 122,500 square feet of floor space and 109 employees. At the time of the flag raising, floor space had increased to 196,780 and employment swelled to 994. (Northrop)

Chapter 4

AN IDEA REALIZED
XB-35 Contract is Won

In the 1930s the bomber held precedence in Air Corps thinking. Performance-wise, the sleek little Martin B-10 was out performing the pursuits of the day. Bomber aviation was the keystone in the airborne element of American defense policy. Aircraft that could fly higher and farther at increased speeds and with greater bomb loads was desired. Two projects were initiated in the early 1930s in an effort to push the frontiers of aeronautics.

Project A became the Boeing XB-15 and the later Project D became the Douglas XB-19. Both of these massive aircraft would suffer from the unavailability of engines equal to the task of propelling their large airframes through the atmosphere as their designers envisioned. But they did prove to be worthwhile flying laboratories which aided in the development of future bombers.

The Air Corps Kilner Board was convened as the war clouds were getting blacker and blacker over the European skies. The Board's report in June 1939 urged the development of bombers of greater range than those then currently on the drawing boards. At that time the new B-17B, sporting a top speed of about 268 mph and a combat range of 2,400 miles, was entering the Air Corps' inventory. The next generation bomber, the B-29, was on Boeing's drawing boards (the B-29B of 1945 would have a top speed of almost 400 mph and a combat range of about 4,200 miles).

Northrop Aircraft, Inc. in September 1940. Plans were already in the works to more than double floor space. It was needed and even more. They would soon receive an order from the British Purchasing Commission worth some $17 million to produce Vultee V-72 Vengeance dive bombers. (Northrop)

The decimation of the Polish army in September 1939 by the German war machine set in motion the Second World War. As the Wehrmacht was marching into the Low Countries in the spring of 1940, US Army Air Corps' General Hap Arnold was bringing together another board, this time headed by Maj. Gen. Delos C. Emmons. With the assistance of Wright Field engineers, the Emmons Board report of June 1940 included the requirement for a long range bomber. The need of a long range bomber, soon to be referred to as an intercontinental bomber, was reinforced by reports coming from Europe. From London, Maj. Gen. James E. Chaney, who commanded the Army's Special Observer Group there, saw the need of a bomber capable of flying from the US to Berlin and back in the event that Great Britain should fall. With the deterioration of the European situation, Brig. Gen. Carl A. "Tooey" Spaatz, Assistant Chief of the Air Corps, directed the Air War Plans Division on January 1, 1941, to pursue the development of a bomber capable of flying from Point Barrow to Berlin and back.

XB-35 Contract

On April 11, 1941, the Air Corps invited Boeing Aircraft Company and Consolidated Aircraft Corporation to bid on a bomber with a top speed of 450 mph (at 25,000 feet), cruising speed of 275 mph, an overall range of 12,000 miles (flying at 25,000 feet), and a service ceiling of 45,000 feet. Somewhat later both Douglas Aircraft Company and the Glenn L. Martin Company were invited into the competition by the Air Corps. Martin declined due to the scarcity of engineers.

All that was going on at Materiel Division and their interest in a new bomber was not lost on Jack Northrop. From practically the inception of his new company in 1939, he had kept in contact with his friend Hap Arnold at Air Corps headquarters and had made numerous trips to Wright Field to discuss his flying wing development with Materiel Command.

About a month after Materiel Division distributed its invitation to bid on the new intercontinental bomber to Boeing and Consolidated, Jack Northrop wrote General Arnold. In Northrop's May 13th letter he gave Arnold an update on the N-1M flying mockup and then addressed the possibility of a flying wing bomber:

> With regard to the importance of the development and its possible future effect on airplane design, it is my belief at this time that we can build transport or bomber aircraft of any size over 25,000 pounds gross weight, which will do the same job as a similar airplane

Heading up the multiple design efforts that Northrop had on its books were Dr. William R. Sears, chief aerodynamicist; Walter J. Cerny, assistant chief of design; and John K. Northrop, chief of design and engineering. (Northrop)

of conventional design, and have a high speed of from 75 to 100 miles an hour greater. Put another way, I think we can obtain the same high speeds as attained with conventional aircraft with, roughly, half the amount of power. Several months ago we made a study of a twin engine medium bomber around the now non-existent X-1800 Pratt & Whitney engine which appeared to be capable of meeting all the desired characteristics of the latest medium bomber specification No. XC-219, and exceeded the desired maximum speed by 25 miles per hour, and the minimum maximum speed in the specification by 125 miles per hour.

He went on to state:

Even if there were no aerodynamic advantages, the simplicity of the straight line structure, the large amount of space available for the housing of retractable landing gears, fuel tanks, bomb bays, etc., and the ease with which airplanes of this configuration can be armed, render them of great military significance, in my humble opinion.

A few days later Thomas H. Quayle, Northrop's Washington representative, made a follow-up call on General Arnold.

As with General Arnold, Jack Northrop had developed a relationship with a Col. Howard Z. Bogert, Materiel Division's Technical Staff Chief at Wright Field. In a letter to Col. Bogert about a week later he states:

On several occasions you have mentioned your interest in having us study the possibility of a long range airplane based on the flying wing principle. Within the last thirty days, as you have no doubt already learned from my official letter to Materiel Division on the status of the project [the N-1M], we have made very successful and encouraging flights of the flying mockup, and I believe the time is here when we can seriously consider the possibility of building bomber aircraft to this design. Yesterday, the project was further accentuated by a visit of Mr. Robert A. Lovett, who I believe is now Assistant Secretary of War for Air. He had previously heard of our flying wing development and was much interested in the progress made, so we took the liberty of showing him the flight test pictures which show

the airplane [N-1M] really flying and are pretty good sales propaganda in their present form.

Assistant Secretary Lovett must have been impressed as he asked how soon the Northrop team could present a design. He also inquired of Jack Northrop as to what he expected the performance of such a design might be. Jack Northrop thought that a preliminary study could be put together in five or six weeks; actually, Col. Bogert of Wright Field had requested a similar study several months earlier. As to performance, Jack estimated that the flying wing bomber would be some 75 to 100 mph faster than a similar bomber of conventional design. Lovett's reaction was to instruct Northrop to proceed with the study. In this study the Secretary wanted a bomber that was considered capable of carrying a bomb load of 16,000 pounds, had a maximum speed of 400 mph and margins in design would go towards extending the bomber's range.

Maj. Gen. Oliver P. Echols, chief of the Materiel Division, who had heard of Northrop's work from Secretary Lovett, paid Northrop a visit on May 22nd. After a replay of the briefing given earlier to Lovett, General Echols and Northrop discussed the requirements of the flying wing bomber study. The next day Jack Northrop sent another letter to Col. Bogert in which he stated that they had calculated that a flying wing bomber with a gross weight of approximately 100,000 pounds could carry a bomb load of between 10,000 and 15,000 pounds and would have a range of about 5,000 miles. As in earlier letters, Northrop asked Bogert if he could provide any additional insight as to the specific requirements being looked for by the Air Corps.

On the 27th Materiel Division sent Northrop a letter that must have thrilled Jack Northrop and his associates.

The Air Corps contemplates initiating, in the near future, a project that may involve the design and construction of one or more experimental Heavy Bombardment Type Aircraft or flying scale models thereof. Prior to crystallizing ideas as to the exact military and technical requirements for such an airplane, the Materiel Division desires to solicit design studies and engineering data from several qualified manufacturers with a view of exploring the aeronautical art to determine what may be technically possible of accomplishment in the field of large airplanes within the next three or four years. It is desired to solicit design studies from your company of a flying wing type of bomber.

Based on a design with turbosupercharged engines of 2,300 to 3,000 hp, the bomber was to have a high speed of 400 to 450 mph at 25,000 feet. Also, flying at this same altitude, the plane would be capable of flying from 5,333 to 8,000 miles with a ton of bombs while flying at an average speed of between 250 and 300 mph.

A flap of sorts came about in the summer of 1941 as Northrop was in the throes of selling his wing idea to the AAC. From the start, the Air Corps desired that Northrop keep information concerning the development of the flying wing, in all forms, as restricted as possible. Northrop agreed with their concerns, though the Air Corps' thinking was along the lines of military secrecy, while Jack Northrop's line of reasoning was more on the publicity angle. In May of that year, Northrop wrote his friend General Arnold concerning the release of flying wing information. Patent information concerning the design was expected to become public knowledge soon. Arnold saw no problem in this. But when Assistant Secretary Lovett was at the Northrop plant in late May, the subject came up again. With the probability of the wing becoming a bomber, Lovett felt that military secrecy was needed, even the information concerning the N-1M. Lovett also advised Northrop that the Air Corps would assist in having the patents placed in a secret classification. Lovett reiterated the agreement in a letter to Northrop on June 11th.

The Air Corps was quite shocked when on June 18th Frank A. Tichenor, publisher of *Aero Digest*, brought to the Air Corps' Intelligence Division offices in Washington, D.C., a request for permission to publish an article concerning the Northrop flying wing. It seems that late in May, after Lovett's meeting with Northrop, Tichenor and one of his writers also made a visit to the Northrop plant. While there they received information on the N-1M and photographs, with the understanding that the material would not be published without the permission of the Air Corps.

The fact that Northrop gave any information out concerning the wing agitated military security. Because of the potential application of the wing, all information, including the N-1M which had been flying for some time, was classified and Northrop was informed that no information was to be disseminated. In a letter dated July 7th, Lt. Col. Franklin O. Carroll, Chief of the Experimental Engineering Section, Materiel Division, at Wright Field wrote

Above and below: California Institute of Technology's wind tunnel in Pasadena, California was the only major wind tunnel on the west coast. To alleviate the problem of Cal Tech's nearly constant backlog of work, Northrop built its own tunnel. (Northrop)

Northrop: ". . . information pertaining to this project be withheld from the public, it is requested that you consider all phases of this project as 'Confidential.'"

On July 2nd Northrop went to Wright Field to meet with the Materiel Division personnel to go over the preliminary design. The design seemed technically feasible to the Division evaluators, and agreement was reached on contractual requirements for design investigation including wind tunnel and flying models, mockup, and such. To Northrop's flying wing bomber design study effort the AAF assigned Classified Project No. MX-140.

On the 13th of that month Materiel Division started the contractual path leading to an official Air Corps contract. The effort was to be in three phases. Phase I called for engineering data which would be used to evaluate the design and subsequent release for development. The second phase called for tests of models and submittal of reports covering the N-1M's flight test. The last phase called for the construction and test of a flying mockup that would be three-tenths to four-tenths scale of the full-scale article. Delivery of this latter mockup was scheduled for 360 days after contract award. Following this mid-July research agreement, negotiations for one full-size airplane were initiated on August 6th.

Germany's military advances through the summer of 1941 made the fall of Great Britain seem to transition from the realm of the possible to the probable. The development of the intercontinental bomber needed to be accelerated. To accomplish this, a high level meeting was held in the Washington office of Materiel Division on August 19th. Present at the meeting were Brig. Gen. Oliver P. Echols, Division Chief; Lovett; and Chief of the Air Corps, Maj. Gen. George H. Brett; along with Wright Field representatives and staff officers. They decided that in order to accelerate the bomber's development the specifications that were originally given to Boeing and Consolidated on April 11th needed to be relaxed.

The revised requirements were apparently passed to the aircraft manufacturers in short order the following day as Walt Cerny, Northrop's Assistant Chief of Design, received a phone call from the Chief of the Experimental Engineering Section at Wright Field, Lt. Col. Franklin O. Carroll. Col. Carroll started the conversation:

We have just had a very important meeting in Washington. This is highly confidential. We are going ahead with a big airplane from Northrop of the type you are working on. Are you the project engineer on the Bomber study also?

An airfoil section installed in the throat of Northrop's wind tunnel. This wind tunnel's throat had a 10 foot diameter. (Northrop)

After an affirmative from Cerny, Col. Carroll asked him to take some figures down. He then described the attributes of the new flying wing bomber. It was to have a range of 10,000 miles, a cruising speed of 240 mph to 300 mph, a high speed of 350 to 450 mph, critical altitude of about 35,000 ft., service ceiling of 40,000 feet (with two-thirds of its fuel on board), two engine performance called for a service ceiling of 15,000 feet (with half of its fuel on board and no bombs) and takeoff distance between 4,000 and 5,000 feet. Armament was a tall order also. It was to consist of at least six 37 mm cannons with 300 rounds each and eight .50 cal. machine guns with 1,000 rounds each. These were to be contained in at least five turrets and two of the cannon to be in a tail stinger. A hundred and fifty pounds of armor plate was to be provided for the protection of each aircrew member and another 150 pounds for each engine and its vital installations (blower section and critical points in the fuel system). The crew area was to be pressurized and the fuel tanks were to be leak-proof.

Carroll went on to explain:

Now I know that is a terrific job. They blew us right out of our chairs with it, but we have practically decided that we are going ahead with Northrop and buy these airplanes – one of them or more, so I would like to have you make some studies and talk to Jack as soon as you can.

You tell Jack this is probably first national priority and tell him that we are going ahead with an airplane and he has been elected to build one, so we just have to do it some way. As soon as you have some preliminary studies, we would like to have you and Mr. Northrop come in and we will cook up a specification here and preliminaries on a contract. There is a contract being prepared on this other study [the effort laid out on July 2nd].

They hadn't received it, so the Colonel continued:

I was going to suggest that you go ahead and sign it, and as soon as we go over the specification together we will issue an Engineering Order or Change Order on that and let it go right ahead.

Cerny's reply was:

I see. As I see it from these figures, the armament will be the hard part of it.

Carroll:

Yes, that is the minimum. You go ahead and make studies. That is what we would like to have if we could absolutely get it. In fact they want more than that but we talked them down to that as a minimum.

We don't know how you are going to do it, but we have got to do it.

Cerny concluded, "We will try it and do our best."

Events in Europe continued to shape American military thinking. The 1930s theory of bomber invincibility was being disproved in the skies over Europe, and the AAF was now rationalizing the theory that the best defense would be a variant of each type of new bomber, with additional armament, flying with formations of standard bombers of like design. To implement this, the AAF added the requirement that simultaneous development of an escort variant be included in new bomber contracts by issuing Materiel Division Confidential Technical Instruction 310 dated August 23, 1941. CTI-310 had the long title of "Studies Covering Development and Procurement of Long Range (10,000) Bombardment Aircraft and Concurrent Studies as to Feasibility of Escort Fighter Types."

Air Corps' General Hap Arnold was a frequent visitor to the Northrop plant and followed Northrop's flying wing efforts quite closely. (Northrop/Western Museum of Flight)

On September 9th a meeting was conducted in General Echols' office which included Jack Northrop and Bill Sears, representing Northrop Aircraft, along with representatives from Pratt & Whitney. The requirements of CTI-310 were discussed, variations of Northrop's Model N-9 flying wing, and Pratt & Whitney's Tornado and X-Wasp engines. Northrop presented versions of Model N-9 with gross weights ranging from 125,000 lbs. to 185,000 lbs. Northrop promised a plane 24 months after contract award (Echols felt that the minimum would be 30 months). To power this intercontinental flying wing, Northrop and Materiel Division representatives felt the X-Wasp engine with dual rotating two-speed gearing was required. The Pratt & Whitney representatives felt it would take them at least 28 months to develop and produce the X-Wasp engine, extension shaft, and dual rotating two-speed gearing. After further discussion, the Pratt & Whitney reps reduced their quote to 24 months without the two-speed gearing. They said that they would make every effort to include the two-speed gearing to meet the schedule.

Northrop's preliminary design designated N-9E, an 140,000 lbs. gross weight variant, was selected. With Northrop's data, General Echols and Colonel Carroll presented the results of that meeting to General Arnold that same day. Arnold agreed with Materiel Division's recommendations and directed them to proceed with the procurement of one experimental flying wing.

Classified project MX-140, the Northrop flying wing bomber, was now moving along two paths. The September meeting would result in an XB-35 mockup and one experimental article being purchased under contract W535 ac-21920, which Secretary of War Henry L. Stimson would approve on November 22, 1941. At the same time as the negotiations for the experimental article were underway, the three-phase research effort agreed upon in July was also in negotiations.

In the three-phase agreement, Northrop would provide engineering data, wind tunnel models, reports on the N-1M project, and construct a flying mockup similar to the N-1M which would simulate the larger flying wing bomber. On August 26th Northrop provided a cost estimate of $314,187.50 to accomplish these tasks, initially covered by Purchase Order 42-2552. The Secretary of War approved the effort on October 3rd. This effort finally came under contract W535 ac-21341 which was signed on October 30th.

Northrop's first complete airplane manufactured, an N-3PB, came off the production line in December 1940. This was no little feat as Northrop received the contract for 24 of these aircraft just that past April. (Northrop)

Visible along the wing's trailing edge are the various control surfaces. Starting from the outside and going toward the center are the wing tip rudder, pitch control flaps, elevons, and landing flaps. The outboard wing sections also contain retractable airerudder scoops on the upper surface and retractable rudder scoops on the lower surface. (Northrop)

Chapter 5

A FLYING LABORATORY
N-9M Development and Testing

Like the N-1M, the XB-35's flying mockup would take on a similar designation. As the flying bomber was designated as the Northrop Model N-9, the flying mockup (covered by Northrop Specification No. 99 (NS-99)) received the designation of N-9M. The N-9M was the 1/3rd scale flying mockup of the XB-35. Bill Sears, Northrop's Chief Aerodynamicist, remembers: "Now it only had the two propellers. There were not four little engines available and four little propellers to make this a more accurate scale model. So those propellers were located so that their asymmetrical thrust, with one engine out, would represent the XB-35 with two engines out on one side. It had a wing span of 60 feet."

In a little over a month after contract award for the design and construction of the N-9M, the Japanese attacked Hawaii and the world was at war. Not surprisingly, priorities changed and engineers were soon in short supply. The little Northrop company of Hawthorne, California, found itself overtaxed in a number of directions. They were producing A-31 Vengeance dive bombers and had subcontract orders from Boeing and Consolidated in which they were making components for B-17 Flying Fortress bombers and PBY Catalina patrol planes. The Northrop engineering department had more work than they could handle with XP-56 experimental fighter, P-61 night fighter, and now the XB-35 flying wing bomber with its associated N-9M flying mockup. Then the Air Corps' Western District Supervisor notified Northrop that they were to suspend shop work on the contract containing the N-9M in order to expedite production deliveries of the A-31 and Boeing and Consolidated subcontract orders. All this would eventually push out the contract requirement for the N-9M to fly within 360 days by about three months.

The purpose of the flying mockup was to provide maneuverability, controllability, and performance data to augment wind tunnel results as part of the XB-35 design process. To keep cost down, used Menasco C6S-4 inline, air-cooled engines were obtained. Construction was of welded steel tubing covered with wood and aluminum and was quite similar to the N-1M. Along the trailing edge were most of the craft's controls – landing flaps, elevons, and pitch control flaps. Somewhat unusual controls were incorporated in the craft's wing tips called split flap drag rudders, or clamshells.

This approximately one-third scale representation of the XB-35 had a span of 60 feet, was 17.79 feet in length, and the top of the canopy stood some 79 inches off the ground. It weighed in at 5,451 lbs., with a calculated gross weight of 6,325 lbs. With its 260 hp Menasco engines, it was expected to hit a high speed of 257 mph at 7,000 feet and cruising speed (60% of power) of 208 mph. An ab-

solute ceiling of 26,800 feet and a service ceiling of 19,500 feet were anticipated. It had a fuel capacity of 100 gal. which was expected to give it an endurance of 3.2 hours.

On September 10, 1942, Change Order No. 3 against contract W535 ac-21920 was received, calling for two additional N-9Ms at a cost of $213,841. The first aircraft, designated N-9M-2, was to be delivered by January 15, 1943 and the second one, designated N-9MA, was to be delivered by March 15th of that year. The purpose of the two additional aircraft was to have a backup should the first N-9M (now referred to as N-9M-1) be destroyed in an accident and to provide Materiel Division with an example to study.

First of four N-9M flying mockups to be built. First flight occurred on December 27, 1942. The diagonal line near the wing tip is the wing tip rudder. These control devices were often referred to as split flap drag rudders. As it was a time of war, and to show disdain toward the enemy, these devices were also referred to as "Jap Snappers;" teeth were painted on the inside surfaces. (Northrop/San Diego Aerospace Museum)

Ground testing of N-9M-1 started on December 20, 1942, with Northrop's chief experimental test pilot John Myers at the controls at Northrop Field. First flight occurred on the 27th with Myers flying the N-9M for 55 minutes. As Myers' services were required on other Northrop projects, follow-up flight testing was done by Max Constant, an experienced new hire at Northrop. The Menasco engines were the cause of constant problems and very little test data could be obtained. In five months, 44 flights produced only about 20 flight hours; only four or five of these flights were full term, the rest were terminated because of mechanical failures of the engines and other causes. On May 19, 1943, Constant took N-9M number 1 up for its 45th flight from Muroc. He was conducting aft center of gravity stability and control tests, including stalls, when the plane crashed, killing Constant. Investigations after the accident concluded that Constant got into a condition of control reversal which pushed the control column against his chest. He was not able to free himself in order to bail out.

It was initially feared that the plane had adverse stall and spin characteristics. As part of the investigation into this perceived problem, Change Order No. 8 to contract W535 ac-21920 dated August 7, 1943 called for a model of both the N-9M and XB-35 be constructed and sent to NACA's Langley Field, Virginia spin tunnel by September 1st of that year. The tests were to determine the spin and recovery characteristics of both the N-9M and XB-35, the correct size and location of the N-9M's spin chutes, and the tumbling characteristics of the XB-35. Subsequent accident investigation and wind tunnel tests (wind tunnel models at Langley and the second N-9M at NACA's Moffett Field, California, facility) indicated that the stall and spin characteristics were acceptable. The size of the spin chute was deemed too small and its location needed to be changed.

In meetings between Northrop and Wright Field Materiel Command representatives shortly after the crash of N-9M-1, Northrop was requested to produce a replacement aircraft (which would be designated N-9MB). He was given a verbal go-ahead and requested to provide a written estimate of the cost of the fourth N-9M. Northrop, for whatever reason, was slow in providing the estimate (almost $192,000). In his letter to Materiel Command he stated: "In case the amount involved is considered so excessive as to render inadvisable the construction of the fourth airplane, it is requested that the contractor be advised at the earliest possible date, in view of the fact that verbal approval of the construction of the fourth airplane has been received and work thereon already started." Northrop, who had quoted nearly $214,000 earlier for N-9Ms numbers 2 and 3, had spent over $404,000 to date (N-9M number 2 being completed at this time and the third craft was estimated to be 85 percent complete). Because of problems Northrop had with the Menasco engines in the first N-9M, which would continue in the second and third models, Materiel Command assisted Northrop in obtaining Franklin engines which had just become available for the fourth article.

The flight test program was on a hiatus for about a month when N-9M-2 took to the air for the first time on June 24, 1943. The flight was quite short, about five minutes, as the canopy came off during takeoff. Slight damage was sustained by the landing gear door, radio mast, and yaw meter. The craft was brought back to earth safely. Repair of N-9M number two put the test program back another month.

N-9M-2, with its used Menasco engines, seemed to suffer from the same problems as the number 1 aircraft. It wasn't until September 21, 1943 that the first reliable drag data was finally obtained. The results were not good. The data indicated that the B-35 drag at cruise speed would be between 7% and 12% greater than wind tunnel tests had indicated. Based on this data, Northrop provided Materiel Command with its first guaranteed performance figures. (Northrop had refused to provide guaranteed performance figures until drag data could be obtained from the N-9M flight test program.) Flying characteristics of the N-9M were deemed generally satisfactory for longitudinal and lateral stability, control at high speed, and in cruising ranges. There did seem to be some difficulty in obtaining satisfactory directional control, and severe reversal of elevator control forces at high lift coefficients was encountered.

Northrop test pilot John Myers flies the first N-9M (which would commonly be referred to as N-9M-1) over the Los Angeles area. Being part of a military project, the N-9Ms did not carry civilian registration. Because they were not considered an aircraft, but an engineering development tool, they also did not carry military serial numbers. (Northrop/Wolford Collection)

In January 1943 Jack Northrop got a ride in his N-9M. Both pilot Myers and his boss seem quite pleased. (Northrop)

Stability and control, and the development of associated systems and design features to be incorporated in the XB-35, were worked out on the N-9Ms. One of the members of Northrop's aerodynamics department was Irving L. Ashkenas. Mr. Ashkenas described this development process during a 1994 panel discussion of Northrop's flying wings:

Rudder control was always a problem. We tried two or three different things. One of the configurations was a flap, a conventional kind of flap with a scoop that came up on the opposite side – so that the flap went down and the scoop came up and the net effect was to increase the drag at the wing tip. That was a drag rudder.

These were [initially] all manual controls on these small airplanes [N-9Ms], so there was a limitation which we knew. We couldn't or didn't have the power to put a double split flap on, which is what we ended up with. We knew all along that would be the most logical thing to do, but working as we were at the time with purely manual controls – we hadn't quite developed the fully hydraulic system that we finally put on the XB-35. We tried various things that might work. I might add, incidentally, that nobody at the time was very anxious to trust an airplane, and the lives of the pilots, to a fully powered hydraulic system. They weren't considered reliable. Nobody knew how to design them. They often buzzed and buffeted and squirmed around. No one had ever built a fully powered hydraulic system. They were all boost systems of one kind or another, which magnified the pilot's force by a factor of, say 20, or there about. So, it was a rather tricky thing and neither Northrop nor the Air Corps at the time was willing to a priori to say 'we are going to have a fully powered hydraulic system.' Although that was obviously the thing to do to get rid of the tendency towards stick force reversal and the very high forces that you were bound to get on an airplane this size.

The double split flap has the advantage of being absolutely symmetrical. You minimize the rolling moments due to opening the rudder. On the other device [drag rudder] you have a flap for part of it and a scoop for the other half, and whether or not you got zero rolling moment out of deflection of that was a guess. Nobody knew. The

chances were that you weren't going to get zero rolling moments. You don't like to mix up controls in that way. So the double split flap arrangement we felt was a lot cleaner and more certain to work.

One of the ideas we had too in those days for improving the Flying Wing was to move the cg back into what would be normally an unstable aft cg and stabilize the airplane with a pitch autopilot. A very simple device. We actually did some flight tests on an [AT-6]. To prove the concept we flew at 10 percent unstable a number of times. The nice thing about making a flying wing unstable is that when you do instead of using 'up elevon' for the trip you have to use 'down elevon.' When you do that, you automatically get a high lift flap out of the elevon. You create a situation in which the airplane is balanced with a lot of positive camber, which is great, because then you get your maximum lift. You can reduce the wing area and thereby reduce the drag, and get the same landing speed that you would with a forward cg because of the increased lift due to carrying the elevon down. Some calculations that I made indicate you will pick up about 15 percent in range by doing that. By going from a forward cg to an aft cg on a tailless airplane.

That [control force reversal] was one of the things that we did experience. It was one of the things that was especially important about flying the N-9M. Because it clarified for us what the real control problem was, and the fact that when we got down to low speeds and were trying to bring the airplane closer to a stall that the stick forces would reverse and the pilot would have to push on the stick to keep the elevon from floating up. The pilots were very, very leery of that, of getting too far into the stall for that reason. We tried various ways. I started to say that one of the problems that we had in trying to get by with a fully powered system was that nobody would buy it. So we tried all kinds of aerodynamic ways of moving controls around, including flying tabs, floating tabs, and overhung balances, internal balances. The only thing that we came up with that we thought would work was the aero boost arrangement where you use the internal balance of the elevon as kind of a piston, [which was] subjected to the dynamic pressure of the air on one side and some suction on the other, and with that we moved the elevon around. The tests [were] con-

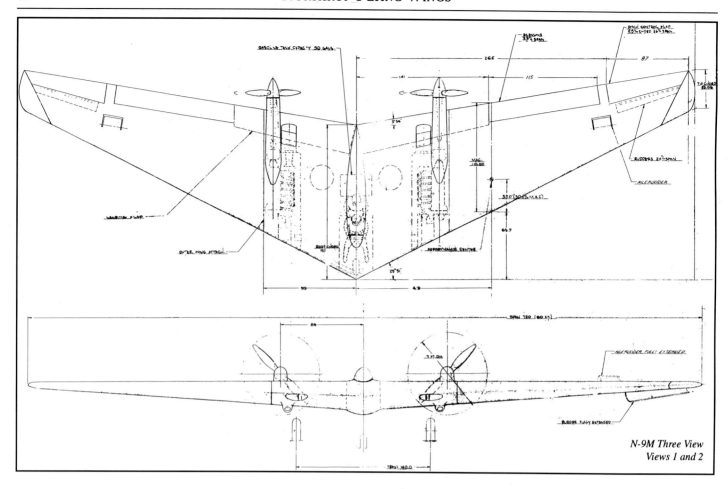

N-9M Three View
Views 1 and 2

ducted up at Ames [NACA laboratory] in the 40 by 80 [foot wind tunnel] on the N-9M[-2], where we had this system installed in the airplane. We could 'tweak' it in the wind tunnel to make the control surfaces go up and down. We were considered successful in view of the fact that it was our first attempt and we had leakage and excess friction. There were a lot of problems, but there were clearly ways to solve those problems if you wanted to pay the weight penalty. That was the thing that really killed all of our attempts to do things aerodynamically and put us back on the track with the fully powered system. Putting all those plates, seals, and the ducting and all that stuff, while it would have worked, would have made a mess of the airplane.

So we took the bull by the horns and developed that fully powered hydraulic system. And that wasn't easy either! We didn't have flutter per se. We had hunting and buzzing. To begin with we had a lot of problems in making the system really work. We would takeoff and buzz and shake and the pipes would rattle and everything would get tuned up. It was really pioneering work. I think the way they ended up strapping the valves to the cylinder so that the cylinder moved it closed the valve off automatically. The whole arrangement was really very rigid and free of backlash and play, which were important things to try to get out of a system like that. The idea of eventually allowing neutral leakage across the valve was an important contribution. Up to that point it was hard to make the flow characteristics linear with the valve displacement. It was hard to get a nice clean system. As soon as you allowed a little neutral leakage, it tended to linearize. Because you had flow to begin with, and just a little bit of movement of the

valve allowed the flow to increase and not only that, the neutral leakage kept the oil circulating throughout the entire system which kept it warm. Which is no small additional feature. So you didn't need heaters for the system, it stayed warm all by itself. Since it was a fully powered system and you wanted some forces fed to the pilot, we had to devise an artificial feel system that would make the airplane feel like a conventional system which we did by putting in a Q bellows on the stick. So as the speed increased, the stick got stiffer and stiffer just as it would on a conventional airplane. Because we had an artificial feel system, we could retrim the feel system so we didn't need trip tabs on the surface. We simply moved the zero for the stick force to a new position and that trimmed the airplane. If you want to look at the biggest legacy that the Flying Wing left, I think it was the fully powered hydraulic system.

By March 31, 1944, the second N-9M aircraft had completed 33 flights for a total flight time of 23 hours and 7 minutes. Data obtained was considered "constructive" to the B-35 program. It suffered its second accident on April 19th when it was forced to make a gear up landing at Roach Lake. Fortunately, the damage was slight and the pilot was not injured.

N-9MA, the third of the N-9M series, completed ground tests on April 20, 1944. First flight was accomplished on the 22nd of the following month. Instead of the wing tip clamshell rudder of the first two N-9Ms, the N-9MA had a pitch trimmer, with a split drag rudder incorporated, located along its trailing edge starting at the

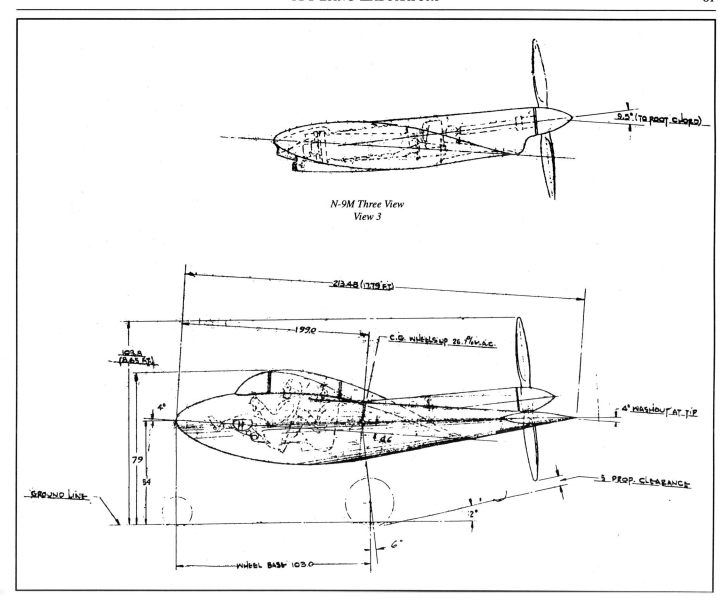

N-9M Three View
View 3

wing tip. This airplane contained practically all of the design features which were then scheduled to be used in the XB-35.

The replacement for the destroyed N-9M-1, the N-9MB, endured a protracted production period. This craft was to be quite similar to the N-9MA except the 260 hp Menasco engines were being replaced by Franklin's 300 hp XO-540-7 that were just becoming available. It was waiting for the delivery of these engines that was the major culprit in the delay. Additional systems beyond those included in the N-9MA that were contemplated for the B-35 were incorporated in the N-9MB. One of the features to be incorporated was an aerodynamic type boost control, which had initially been tried out in the N-9M-2. Additional advanced features included automatic wing tip slot doors and a fully powered, irreversible, hydraulic power control system.

Personnel of Bombardment Branch of the Engineering Division at Wright Field requested to fly N-9MA to determine whether it was suitable as a flying mockup on which to develop the flying wing bomber. On June 28, 1944, a series of flights were accom-

plished at Harper's Dry Lake near Barstow, California, with Col. Frank Cook at the controls. The post flight report concluded:

The flight characteristics of the N-9MA gave firm indications that the flying characteristics of the B-35 type airplane will be satisfactory. The flying scale model is small, light and very sensitive to its controls. The larger size and mass of the full scale airplane work in its favor in all respects so that the sensitiveness of the airplane to control applications, rough air, and landing gear retraction and extension should be damped out. The rudders have a flat spot at neutral and the elevators are too sensitive. Both of these deficiencies should be easily corrected.

The report included some interesting notes concerning the planes ground handling characteristics:

The airplane was taxied at slow and at very fast speeds. Its ground handling characteristics were excellent. Landings have been accom-

Max Constant was a new member to Northrop's flight test department when, on May 19, 1943, he apparently got the little craft in such an attitude that a condition of stick reversal occurred. Constant apparently could not regain control and was killed in the crash. (Northrop/Mike Petry, Planes of Fame Museum)

plished in emergencies with one main gear retracted and in forced landings due to engine trouble [where] the nose gear collapsed due to striking terrain irregularities. In all such emergency cases the airplane exhibited mild characteristics with no tendency to nose over when the nose strut collapsed nor to slow violently with one main gear retracted.

It was found that the plane showed good longitudinal stability and was found quite maneuverable and responsive in executing turns. Rudder control was found greatly improved over the earlier models due to its redesigned system. They also found that rough air performance, which was found to be unsatisfactory in the earlier versions, was quite satisfactory in the N-9MA; this too was attributed to the redesigned rudder system and to the powered elevons.

In the summer of 1944, discussions between Northrop and Wright Field were conducted concerning the use of the three N-9Ms. Materiel Command desired an extended flight test program beyond that which was planned by Northrop. Through a series of meetings and informal discussions, it was determined that 70 total additional test flights were required and Northrop was requested to provide a cost estimate. On August 1, 1944, Northrop estimated that it would cost about $1,523 per flight, or an additional $107,068.

Test pilot John Myers had taken over flying the N-1M in late June 1942, shortly after Jack Northrop had relieved Moye Stephens of his flying duties. It was natural that Myers would go on to the N-9M flight test program; he would be the principal pilot of N-9M-1 until the crash that killed Max Constant and would initially make a number of flights in N-9M-2 until his own accident in the XP-56 in October 1943.

Myers wanted the engineers to be personally acquainted with the project, and what better way than to give one a ride. Who could be a better candidate than the chief of aerodynamics, Dr. William R. Sears. In September 1974, Dr. Sears spoke of this experience.

Unknown to Jack, Johnny found that he could squeeze me in behind him sitting sideways. He wanted me to become personally acquainted with the good and bad features of the flying qualities of this little airplane. So, we made those flights together. As a matter of fact, I have to admit that I guess Jack found it out later – that I was with Johnny that day when we could only get two of the three wheels down. We flew back and forth over [Northrop Field] while Walt Cerny, Bob Catlin, and all wrote us notes on the runway about what we should do.

None of those things worked! So we went back and forth until one of the engines began to misbehave (had nothing to do with the landing gear of course). Johnny said, 'We're going to put this thing down, and we'll try not to hurt it any worse than we have to'. Well, those propellers were driven from the Menasco engines through hydraulic couplings that Jack himself designed, way ahead of the game of the hydraulic transmissions that we are all so familiar with now. (There was a young lady that they had hired that had to go around and turn the propellers of the airplanes that were not flown once a day, turn them over, to wipe the oil around in the cylinders. She religiously turned the propellers of the N-9M, which, of course, because of the hydraulic coupling, she wasn't turning the engines a bit, but she was happy.)

If the pilot had to bail out from this airplane, those propellers would have been windmilling and was considered to be hazardous. So Jack and Walt [Cerny] provided us with brakes, spring loaded propeller brakes, with two handles on the dash. If you would pull one, it would lock. After the engine was shut down or it quit running, you would have pulled it and it would have locked the [2-bladed] propeller [in the horizontal position] on one side or on both sides. I suppose the pilot would jettison the canopy and go out.

So Johnny said when we landed this thing with the two wheels, with one main gear still up, that we should pull the propeller brake, because then there was at least a chance that we wouldn't ruin both propellers, or the propeller on the lowest side. But it was too far for me to reach forward for those handles, and he figured he was going to be busy as he came over Crenshaw [Blvd]. So he says, 'Take your necktie' (we wore neckties in those days), 'and take my belt, and I'll tie one to each handle and when I say NOW, you pull those things.'

An N-9M makes a low pass at the field. Most pilots that flew the N-9Ms thought its performance was good though nothing exceptional. (Mike Petry, Planes of Fame Museum)

Thrust meter calibration for the second N-9M at the Northrop plant in Hawthorne, California. (Northrop/Wolford Collection)

We came down over Crenshaw Blvd. and he said, 'Now!' and I pulled on the belt and necktie. Neither propeller was touched. He held it on the one wheel until we got down to maybe 20 mph, when the aileron would pull it up, and the wing tip gently went down and we scraped a little paint off that wing tip. However, I want to tell you the necktie was ruined because of the sweat.

Jack Northrop did find out about N-9M-1's passenger carrying capability, and he too went for a spin through the wild blue with John Myers.

With the loss of Max Constant and John Myers, two of Northrop's other test pilots were brought into the N-9M program – Harry Crosby and Alex Papana. It is told that it was their flying that caused the unique paint schemes on the last two N-9M. Apparently their flying program went slightly beyond the scheduled events, including inverted flying and performing four loops in quick succession. The story goes that because it was difficult to tell the top from the bottom on the N-9Ms, the third aircraft (N-9MA) was painted blue on the top surface and yellow on the bottom. The fourth aircraft was painted in the reverse, yellow on the top and blue on the bottom. Thus you could tell if the craft was being flown right side up or upside down.

In the late summer and fall of 1944, N-9M-2 was sent to Moffett Field where it was installed in NACA's 40 ft. by 80 ft. wind tunnel. Earlier flight tests seemed to indicate that the anticipated drag on the B-35 would be greater than that indicated in previous tests with a model in NACA's 19 ft. wind tunnel. The results of the wind

tunnel tests with the N-9M revalidated the 19 feet wind tunnel results, and it was determined that the instrumentation used in the flight test was in error. N-9M-2 also tested out the aerodynamic boost control and a manual override control system at the Moffett wind tunnel. Once returned to flying status, these items would be test flown.

By the end of October, N-9MA had accomplished about 50 flights. The Aircraft Projects Section at Wright Field felt that the airplane had satisfied all test requirements and requested that it be put in such a storage status that it could be put back into flight readiness within 72 hours. All further flying of this airplane would "be limited to familiarization and educational flights." During its tests, it was found that this aircraft performed better that the earlier N-9Ms and that it recovered from spins satisfactorily. As with the two earlier N-9Ms, the aircraft was constantly having its control system modified and systems changed and added in its role as a platform to predict the performance and flying qualities of the B-35.

One of the pilots to checkout in the N-9MB was Capt. Glen W. Edwards. He concluded in his May 3, 1946 report:

An hour's flight is hardly a fair basis for drawing decisive conclusions. However, the airplane flew surprisingly well, was more stable and handled far better than most would expect. It would take a few hours practice to make good take-offs and get the proper coordination on turns. But the technique could be mastered without too much difficulty. It serves its purpose well as a flying model.

The second N-9M was constructed to the same basic instructions as the first. One lesson Northrop learned on the first N-9M was that the wing tip rudders were not necessary so they were wired closed on the second article. To distinguish this craft from the first, it became common practice to refer to this example as the N-9M-2. The flight test instrumentation probe attached to the nose of this craft was not installed for an extended period of time. (Northrop/Wolford Collection)

Ground and flight test crew pose with the second N-9M. From left to right: E. P. (Hetz) Hetzel, Bill Raikes, Ralph Freezeh, unknown, Tom Ruble, pilot John Myers, unknown, Hugo Pink, and Al Gardner. (Northrop/Wolford Collection)

Historical records are quite slim concerning the three remaining N-9Ms after 1944. They apparently continued as flying laboratories for the B-35 project as well as taking on the task of familiarizing AAF pilots with the handling characteristics of a flying wing. Some hint to their longevity is given when John Northrop presented the 35th Wright Memorial Lecture in London on May 29, 1947. In his lecture he stated, "Only recently have all desirable test programs been completed and the [N-9M] airplanes relegated to a semi-retired status from which they are withdrawn only for the benefit of curious pilots."

The last surviving member is the N-9MB. This aircraft has been restored by The Air Museum's Planes of Fame at Chino Airport, Chino, California. On January 8, 1994, the rebuilt beauty made its first taxi test. Then on November 8, 1994, this sleek little wing took to the air for the first time in over 40 years. A few days later, on the 11th, it flew again; this time for an audience (composed mostly of those who supported its restoration through contributions of money and labor).

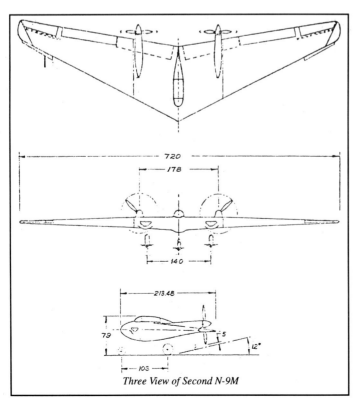

Three View of Second N-9M

Northrop test pilot Alex Papana is greeted by fellow pilot Harry Crosby, on the wing, and other well wishers after his first flight in the N-9M in March 1944. (Northrop/Western Museum of Flight)

Northrop's primary engineering flight test pilots are, from left to right: John Myers, Max Stanley, Harry Crosby, and Alex Papana. These pilots did the bulk of the test flying of the Northrop flying wing and tailless aircraft. (Northrop)

The second N-9M, as well as the next two examples, would receive many changes over its life as different configurations and operating systems were tried. Here leading edge slats have been added. An aeroboost intake has been added to the bottom of the wing as well as the corresponding exhaust on top (at about the 40 percent chord line). (Northrop)

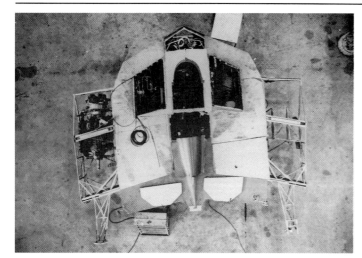

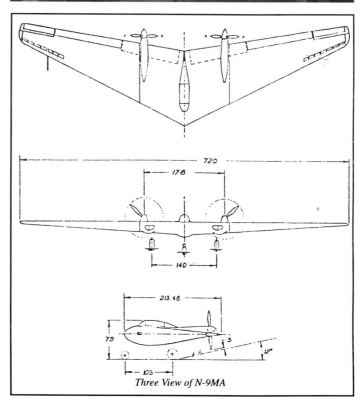

Three View of N-9MA

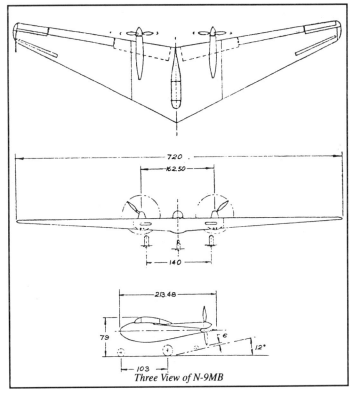

Three View of N-9MB

The Northrop ground crew at Muroc Army Air Base. In the foreground is the N-9MA, and the N-9MB is behind it. As the engineering effort wound down and the need to train Army Air Forces pilots for flying wing duty, the N-9Ms were pressed into service as trainers. (Northrop/Mike Petry, Planes of Fame Museum)

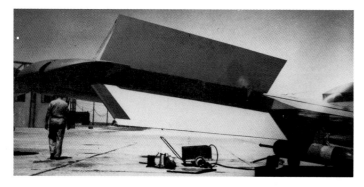

A closeup of the N-9MA's drag rudder in the open position. This control surface was itself mounted in another control surface, the pitch trimmer. Each of the surfaces could be operated independently or in conjunction with each other. To the right, mounted under the wing, is the spin chute canister (a closeup shown on the right). (Northrop/Mike Petry, Planes of Fame Museum and Northrop)

Flight operations at Muroc. Behind the N-9M are the second XB-35, now with single rotation four-bladed propellers, and the sole YB-35 to fly. (Northrop, Mike Petry, Planes of Fame Museum)

5Last of the N-9Ms was the Franklin powered N-9MB. With the change in engines, the engine air intakes were redesigned, setting this N-9M apart from the others. Its antenna mast was also unique. (Northrop/Wolford Collection)

Above: Norcrafters at Muroc. From left to right: Dick Hanna, Louis Welch, Bill Raikes, and Jake Superata. The Northrop crew at Muroc had their hands full keeping the N-9Ms and B-35s flying. (Northrop/Wolford Collection)

Right: Certificate issued by Northrop to pilots checked out in a flying wing. (Courtesy Mrs. Wm. B. Sellers)

Below: The only time the three remaining N-9M flew together, much less in formation, was on this day in February 1946. From left to right are the N-9MB, N-9MA, and N-9M-2. (Northrop/Wolford Collection)

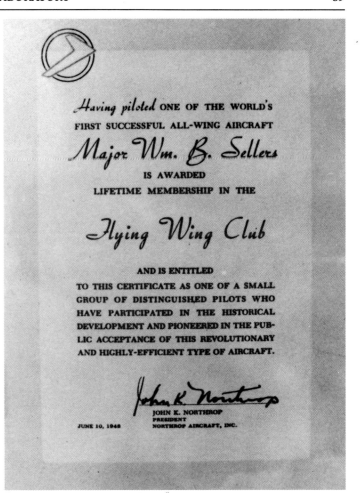

Having piloted ONE OF THE WORLD'S FIRST SUCCESSFUL ALL-WING AIRCRAFT *Major Wm. B. Sellers* IS AWARDED LIFETIME MEMBERSHIP IN THE

Flying Wing Club

AND IS ENTITLED TO THIS CERTIFICATE AS ONE OF A SMALL GROUP OF DISTINGUISHED PILOTS WHO HAVE PARTICIPATED IN THE HISTORICAL DEVELOPMENT AND PIONEERED IN THE PUBLIC ACCEPTANCE OF THIS REVOLUTIONARY AND HIGHLY-EFFICIENT TYPE OF AIRCRAFT.

JOHN K. NORTHROP
PRESIDENT
NORTHROP AIRCRAFT, INC.

JUNE 10, 1948

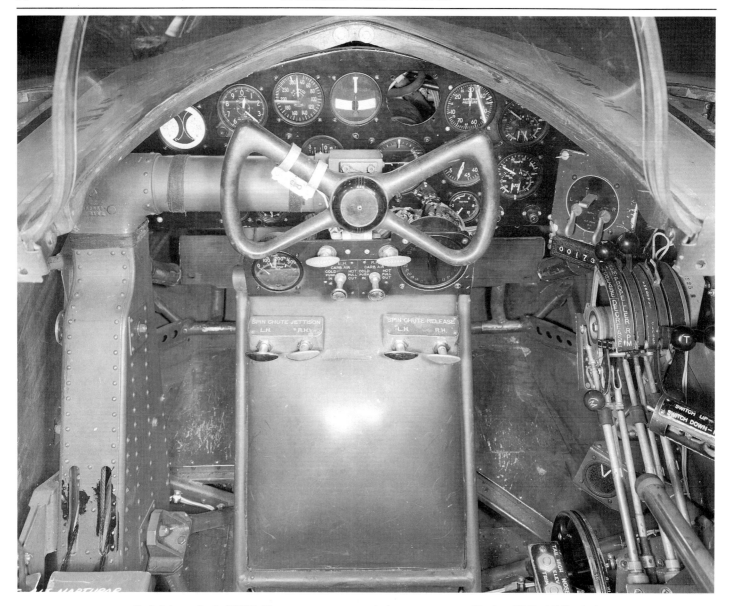

Cockpit layout for the N-9MB. There was no excess space in these snug quarters. (Northrop/Wolford Collection)

Opposite:
Capt. Glen Edwards, on the left, with the N-9MB. After his first flight in the craft he wrote a report with mixed reviews, though mostly positive. (Edwards AFB History Office)

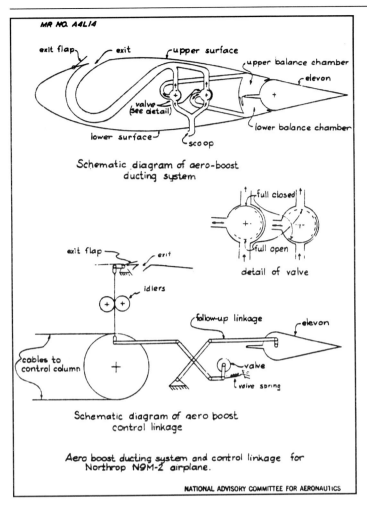

Schematic diagram of aero-boost
ducting system

detail of valve

Schematic diagram of aero boost
control linkage

Aero boost ducting system and control linkage for
Northrop N9M-2 airplane.

NATIONAL ADVISORY COMMITTEE FOR AERONAUTICS

N-9M-2 at Northrop Aeronautical Institute, then part of Northrop Aircraft, Inc., at Northrop Field. All three N-9Ms ended up at the school. The N-9M-2 was dismantled by the students and used as part of their studies. When the school became a separate entity and moved from the company's property, most of the school's aircraft were disposed of. The final resting place of only the N-9MB is known. It has been restored to flying condition by the Planes of Fame Museum in Chino, California. The present location of the N-9MA is unknown. (Northrop/ Mike Petry, Planes of Fame Museum)

Left:
Aeroboost System on Second N-9M

The MX-324 on display in October, 1945, at Wright Field, Ohio. Note the identification sign taped on the top entry hatch – "Jet Fighter Airplane." (Harold G. Martin photo, Kansas Aeronautical Historical Society Collection)

Chapter 6

PRONE PILOTS – NO PILOTS
XP-79 and the JB-1/10 Craft

By the fall of 1942 Jack Northrop must have felt that his dreams were coming true. He was finally able to form the company he had so longed for in 1939 and by the summer of 1940 he was showing the world that his wing could fly. Not more than a year later, this fact was punctuated by the US Army Air Corps contracting for a large bomber variant of his wing. What more could be asked for!

No doubt the close association that Jack Northrop had with Dr. von Karman had great influence on the next project. Northrop and his engineers put their thinking caps on (they probably never took them off) and came up with the idea of a fighter. But this time, unlike the XP-56, it would be a pure wing – no fuselage and no tail. To power it, they reached into the future. Heinkel had flown his rocket powered He 176 in Germany just as the present Northrop company was being formed in 1939, and Messerschmitt flew their Me 163 Komet for the first time in August 1941. Von Karman was quite involved in the design of rocket motors and was closely associated with Aerojet Engineering Corporation in Azusa, California, not far from Cal Tech in Pasadena, and most likely shared some of this knowledge with Northrop and his engineers. To enable the pilot of this new rocket propelled interceptor to take greater g-forces during violent maneuvers, it was designed for him to fly in the prone position (this idea came to Northrop at 2 a.m. one morning as he was trying to sleep). With the pilot in this position, it was possible to design the craft with a thinner airfoil.

In September 1942, Northrop presented to the Air Corps his proposal entitled "Jet-Driven Interceptor," which he designated as P-999. This unsolicited proposal was dated September 15, 1942 (the initials "JKN" were affixed after the date) and included Northrop drawing number 506400 which depicted a tailless flying wing craft. Apparently the proposal was a joint venture which included the Daniel Guggenheim School of Aeronautics at the California Institute of Technology (GALCIT) and the Aerojet Corporation. Undoubtedly Dr. von Karman assisted with this arrangement. The Army Air Forces was backing the development of various forms of jet-assisted takeoff devices and both GALCIT and Aerojet were participants. GALCIT laboratories were developing both liquid and solid rocket fuels while Aerojet was involved in the manufacture of such fuels. The engineers at Wright Field saw potential in the concept and negotiations began. Northrop had neither the manpower to design the plane nor the shop space to build it. The plant was at full capacity with the projects already on contract, so the majority of the design work and fabrication would be accomplished by Air Materiel Command and a subcontractor.

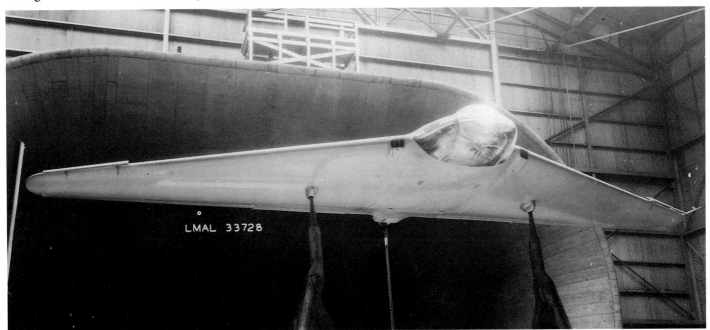

The first MX-334 was sent to the NACA full-scale tunnel at Langley, Virginia, before it entered the flight test program. (NASA Langley)

A number of leading edge slats and vertical fins were tried while the MX-334 was in the Langley full-scale tunnel. (NASA Langley)

Because of the radical design being proposed, the AAF Materiel Center at Wright Field felt that test data on the craft's flying qualities would be desirable so that the prototype XP-79 would not be completely an unknown quantity. To accomplish this, the Materiel Center decided that they would design and build a flying mockup, flight test it, and then incorporate into the prototype XP-79 any changes found desirable. But a closer investigation revealed that the expense in both time and money would probably be greater than if they allowed a contractor to participate. Northrop agreed to undertake the construction and flight testing of the mock-up. However, the engineering staff at Northrop was not of sufficient size to assume this added burden. Consequently, it was agreed that the Materiel Center would engineer the project and forward the necessary drawings to Northrop.

The terms of this contract were:

"...three (3) experimental glider models of a proposed interceptor fighter airplane, to be constructed largely of wood, in accordance with drawings which will be furnished from time to time by the Engineering Division, Materiel Center, Army Air Forces, Wright Field, Dayton, Ohio." The MX-324's were covered under Northrop specification NS-12, received the Air Corps classified project number MX-324. Because of the effort being endeavored, the project received a classification of SECRET. The engineering effort began on November 1, 1942.

Following close behind the MX-324 contract was one for three experimental versions of the rocket-propelled interceptor. Designated XP-79, these aircraft were to have the majority of the engineering and the fabrication accomplished by a subcontractor,

Northrop maintaining overall design responsibility. Northrop initiated the design in December 1942 under specification NS-14 (its classified project number was MX-365). For both projects, Aerojet was to design rocket motors, a small 200 lb. thrust motor for the flying mockup and a 2,000 lb. thrust variant for the Air Corps' new interceptor.

Authority for Purchase number 217608 dated January 12, 1943 called for three XP-79s, a static test article, and a wind tunnel model which was to be sent to NACA's Ames Laboratory. This resulted in contract W535 ac-36997 which was signed by the Secretary of War on May 21, 1943.

Thus the MX-324 was to serve as an engineering development tool (i.e. not considered an aircraft) for the XP-79 as the N-9M flying mockups were for the XB-35. No contractor or military serial numbers were assigned, and civilian registration was not required because they were to fly in military airspace (special permission had to be granted for the several times the N-9Ms were flown at Northrop Field).

Dr. William Sears, Northrop's aerodynamicist, recalled one of the first efforts on this project.

It [the MX-324] was a full size mockup of a fighter . . . At first it was flown as a glider with a prone pilot and later had an Aerojet rocket and made flights under its own power. This, of course, required that we develop a new type of controls for the pilot since he was lying prone.

It was necessary to have a support for the pilot's head so that when he made pullouts he could withstand something like 12 g's. In order to do that, he had to have support for his head – some kind of counterweight. One question that came up was 'How much does a human head weigh?'. At one time Walt [Cerny] and I had Jack on that leather covered sofa in his office, and we were measuring the weight of Jack's head with a string scale.

Security, though necessary, can make accomplishing engineering and flight testing quite difficult. Because of its classification, it was generally referred to as "Project 12." As the initial flights of the MX-324 was to be as a glider and the anticipated rocket-propelled flight slipped on a number of occasions due to developmental problems at Aerojet, it was agreed between Northrop and the military to lower the classification on the aircraft while it was being built and flown as a glider. A memorandum concerning this stated:

> Notification MX-334 applies to the gliders of the project and was classified confidential. This was done to facilitate handling of drawings, . . . (etc.). The classification of secret MX-324 was used when referring to the gliders with cruising jet power units installed and to all related installation drawings.

Some other aspects of the glider design, production and flight test program were even handled as unclassified.

The three gliders were constructed quite similar to the N-9Ms. The center section was of welded steel tubing while the outer wing panels were of wood interior members, all of which was covered with a plywood skin. Landing gear consisted of a pair of skids attached to the bottom of the craft. Initially the only control surfaces were elevons operated by the pilot's control bar. A vertical tail was not thought necessary. The craft was designed to be unusually strong in that an ultimate load factor of 18 g's positive and negative was designed in.

Much to Northrop's and Sear's displeasure, engineering calculations indicated that the craft would require a vertical stabilizer for its anticipated high speed flights. A plywood vertical (with no control surfaces) with wire bracing was designed with a promise to Sears that it would be reduced in size, if not completely eliminated, if subsequent flight tests proved it unnecessary.

The number 1 craft was completed in the late spring of 1943 and shipped to NACA's Langley, Virginia, facility for wind tunnel testing. It wouldn't enter the flight test program until late that November. Initial flight activities would fall to the second article.

In late August the number 2 craft had been taken to the Mojave Desert where on the 27th the first effort to get it into the air was attempted. At this time two wheels were attached to the fixed landing skids just behind the craft's center of gravity (cg). To get the glider into the air, it was attached to John Myers' Cadillac via a tow rope. As the car with glider dashed across the desert, the MX-334 experienced extreme porpoising and the attempt was aborted as it was uncontrollable. The test crew felt that the wheels were the major problem so they removed them. A second effort to get the glider into the air via vehicle tow was attempted, but it wasn't much more successful. The porpoising was reduced but not eliminated. With this result, they trucked the glider back to the Northrop plant in Hawthorne where a four-wheeled dolly was attached to the skids. This arrangement didn't work any better as the tow vehicle could only get to 35 mph, which was not enough speed to get the glider airborne. Using a truck as a tow vehicle, the MX-334, with Harry Crosby as pilot, finally took to the air on September 4, 1943.

A better way had to be devised to get the glider into the air. Northrop made arrangements with the Air Corps to get a P-38 modified for glider towing. Once again they went back to the desert. On October 1st, with test pilot John Myers in the MX-334's cockpit,

In this wind tunnel experiment, longer leading edge slats were installed. (NASA Langley)

Capt. Holbrook Schneider revved up his P-38 and sped across the desert at 70 mph to see how the pair of craft reacted to this arrangement. The ground run was successful. The MX-334 left the ground for momentary flights at regular intervals at about a foot altitude. The next day, October 2nd, the pair took the MX-334 for its first flight by aircraft tow and was by far of greater duration than the previous ground launched short duration flights. Myers' association with this project would be short lived as he was involved in the near fatal accident with the XP-56 about a week later. It is interesting to note that the official report of this flight states, "A vertical fin was mounted on this article for this flight." This would lead one to believe that the aborted attempts in August and the first flight in September were without the vertical.

Northrop test pilot Alex Papana joined Crosby for the remainder of the program. They would assist in discovering a number of needed changes along with a number of personal thrills. It must have been quite an experience to land that craft with your chin seem-

could do, he gently slid off the trailing edge of the craft. As he approached the desert in his parachute, the unmanned glider came quite close and landed not far from his landing site. If it wasn't for the vertical stabilizer hitting a rocky area as the glider touched down, it might have been salvageable. As it turned out, it was beyond repair. In about 10 months Crosby would be in a similar circumstance with the XP-79 in which the bailout ended tragically as plane and pilot met in mid-air.

Glider number 1 returned from Langley in late fall to join MX-334 number 2 in the test program. Harry Crosby and the P-38 tow ship took it up for its first flight on November 30th. Though it would make another flight in December, number 2 craft would perform a majority of the remaining test program. On this December 2nd flight, it would end up acting as a plow in the sand, though it would be repaired.

The landing skids were found not to be practical for either take-off or landing. A varieties of skids, wheels, and dollies would be

At this angle the craft's low stance to the ground is clearly visible. On each side of the canopy are tow cable attachment points. (Northrop/Wolford Collection)

ing to be just inches from the ground rushing up at you. On one occasion the craft touched down at a steeper angle than desired and the skids dug into the sand. As a result, part of the clear nose broke and the remaining structure acted as a shovel with sand partially filling the cockpit.

The third craft took to the air for the first time on November 9, 1943, with Harry Crosby at the controls. The following day Crosby was back in the cockpit, but what he was to experience would be a shadow of things to come. Unlike the number 2 glider, the number 3 craft had full-length leading edge flaps incorporated into its design. On this flight Crosby was towed by the P-38 to 13,000 feet where, as he was released from the tow cable for free flight, he found himself in the prop wash of the tow ship. The craft pitched up, stalled, flipped onto its back, and went into a spiral towards the earth. There was Crosby, hanging by his straps in the prone position, not able to reach the controls. He was able to release the bottom escape hatch, which was now on top, unstrap himself, and crawl out on top, which was really the bottom, of the flipped craft. He sat there for a few moments to gather his thoughts, as the craft was very gently descending. Deciding there was not much more that he

tried. In most of the dolly arrangements, the dolly would be dropped once the glider was airborne. Both articles 1 and 2 would suffer accidents from the use of this gear and ended up digging a hole in the desert with the craft's nose. This entire arrangement was deemed unsatisfactory and a set of fixed tricycle gear was designed. In this new arrangement, the nose gear was offset from the centerline because it would have extended the shock strut through the pilot's compartment. The pilot had no difficulty with this arrangement. To make them more aerodynamic, pants were attached to the gear.

In early 1944 MX-334 number 2 was damaged during ground runs at Muroc. While being repaired, the skid gear was replaced by the new tricycle gear. MX-334 number 3 was modified some months later as a result of Change Order No. 6 to the contract. It was at about this same time that glider 2 was modified to take the Aerojet XCAL-200 rocket motor. Under the security requirements of the program, this craft now reverted back to the original classified project number of MX-324.

Under the direction of Northrop project engineer Don E. Smith, Northrop technicians and Aerojet personnel installed the 200 lb. thrust rocket motor. The 427 pounds of weight added to the MX-

324 included the motor, four pressure tanks, two propellant tanks, and hydraulic and electric control equipment. This liquid rocket motor used monoethylaniline (aniline) for its fuel and red fuming nitric acid as the oxidizer. In the aircraft the tank containing the aniline was on one side of the pilot and the oxidizer on the other side. A heavy neoprene sheet was installed on each side to provide some measure of protection for the pilot should there be a leak from either tank or lines.

John Myers had an eye opening experience when he visited Aerojet's test facility near Azusa, California. There was to be test firing of the rocket motor that was to propel the MX-324. When all was ready, sirens went off, red lights flashed and every one around Myers scrambled for protective cover. This really gave John Myers something to think about. He was going to have the fuel on one side of him, the oxidizer on the other side, and the rocket motor behind him. There were no brick walls for him to hide behind in the tiny MX-324.

Northrop and Aerojet personnel went with the craft to Harper's Dry Lake where testing began. On June 22nd the installed rocket motor was fired for full duration. The following day Harry Crosby climbed into the craft to try out the new sling head rest that had been installed. As he taxied across the desert, he fired the rocket then turned it off and on again as this motor was capable of restarts in the air.

Not unexpectedly, adjustments and some rework were needed. This checkout and ground testing continued through June until July 4th when all was ready. On July 5th, with Northrop, Aerojet and Wright Field observers, Capt. Martin L. Smith climbed into his P-38 and Harry Crosby into the MX-324. As the 300 ft. tow line became taut, the pair moved out in unison. Gently gliding into the air, Smith brought the pair up to an altitude of about 8,000 feet and positioned them in view of the observers at which time Crosby disconnected and fired the rocket motor. America's first rocket powered aircraft had been successfully flown. The five minute burn of the rocket motor took the little craft to a maximum speed of about

There was no moveable control surface on the vertical fin. Its purpose was for directional stability. (Northrop/Wolford Collection)

There were other changes that took place as the test program progressed. The elevons were augmented with controls which served as both rudders and airbrakes, which were called "brudders." The vertical tail also went through a number of variations, though not eliminated. At least three configurations of vertical fins were flown.

In the months following John Myers' initial flight, the test team flew from Muroc and Harper's Dry Lake in California and Roach Dry Lake in Nevada, depending on the weather conditions and the amount of rain water in the "dry" lakes. At this time test pilot Alex Papana found out what a little mistake could do. At altitude, he reached for the tow line release. Instead of grabbing the correct release handle, he inadvertently pulled the handle which released the escape hatches. All of a sudden the upper and lower escape hatch covers went flying off. Their absence caused a dramatic increase in drag and the glider began buffeting severely. Using all his skills as a pilot, this three-time holder of the world aerobatics championship managed to bring the stricken craft in for a successful landing on the lake bed.

Modification of the MX-324 "Rocket Wing" was completed in June 1944. On about the 20th of that month, a contingent of

250 mph.

Crosby took the little rocket ship up for its second flight on July 11th. Once the rocket motor was fired, he made a spectacular dive to near-lake bed level and zoomed up nearly vertical as he raced back to about 6,000 feet. Not expecting these acrobatics, the observers were somewhat taken aback. Additional flights were accomplished with the Rocket Wing as 1944 waned.

Another feature of this test program was the early use of telemetry equipment.

The limited performance of the XCAL-200 and the developmental problems that Aerojet was having with the XCAL-2000 motor, as will be seen in the XP-79 development, probably shortened the life of the Rocket Wing as a flight test vehicle. The test program was concluded on August 1, 1944 and MX-334 number 1 and MX-334 number 2/MX-324 were sent to Air Technical Service Command at Wright Field for disposition. There is some indication that one or both were later sent to Freeman Field as part of the museum collection. One spent time at the AAF Museum at Wright Field where it was in an outdoors display until it, and a number of other aircraft, were scrapped around 1949.

Very aerodynamic pants were included with the fixed landing gear on this third MX-334. When the Aerojet XCAL-200 rocket engine was installed, this craft became the MX-324. (Northrop/Wolford Collection)

Project MX-365 – The XP-79

With the MX-324 effort signed and the follow-on XP-79 contract working its way through the War Department, Northrop completed specification number 14, which outlined the design requirements for the new pursuit ship. The tactical mission of the new pursuit interceptor was to intercept and destroy enemy aircraft by gun fire. To accomplish this, four .50 cal. model M2 fixed machine guns with 200 to 250 rounds of ammunition were incorporated in the design.

But this new pursuit was of a special design. By having the pilot in the prone position, it would enable him to withstand g-forces not ordinarily possible. The aircraft itself was to be designed to a maneuver load factor of plus or minus 12 g's.

Speed was also an essential element, and to accomplish this aspect rocket propulsion was to be used. Aerojet specification number A.S.-2 was called out and a main rocket motor and two 1,000 lb. droppable "jet units" (JATO) were to be installed in accordance with Aerojet drawing EO-256. With the 2,000 lb. thrust Aerojet rocket motor, to be designated XCAL-2000, the airplane was estimated to have a high speed of 538 mph at 40,000 feet. Cruising speed at the same altitude, with the rocket motor throttled back to 250 lbs. of thrust, was estimated at 390 mph. Endurance at 40,000 feet, at minimum cruise thrust (after takeoff, acceleration to climbing speed, and climb from sea level at maximum thrust) was 35.5 minutes. Time-to-climb to 40,000 feet was estimated at 6.1 minutes. This was all based on Aerojet's calculation for fuel consumption per 1,000 lbs. of thrust being 5.17 lbs. per second. Fuel provisions called for 8,400 lbs. of fuel at a ratio of 3.5:1 by weight of oxidizer to fuel.

The use of non-critical war materials was called for on this project and like the XP-56, Northrop chose magnesium. It was

lighter and stronger, but the construction process would always prove to be a challenge. The XP-79's skin thickness varied from approximately 3/4 inch at the leading edge to 3/16 inch at the trailing edge. Wing covering aft of the maximum thickness was to be 1/4 to 3/16 inch thick. With aniline as the rocket's fuel and red fuming nitric acid as the oxidizer, the results of battle damage were of great concern. This combination was a catastrophe waiting to happen. To protect the fuel tanks from ricocheting bullets (which were of greater concern, thus the use of heavy gauge constriction as opposed to penetration protection), armor plate was called for along the leading edge spar. The specification required:

> One-quarter inch steel armor plate shall be installed just inside the leading edge at 45 degrees to the chord plane. The armor plate shall be arranged to deflect any gunfire from the front parallel to the chord that could strike the airplane at an angle less than 70 degrees to the plane normal to the chord. Three-quarter inch skin shall be employed where each gunfire could strike between 70 and 76 degrees.

Like the MX-324, the XP-79 was to have skid-type landing gear. Four skids were called for – two on each side of the center section. They were to be retracted hydraulically. With this type of landing gear, it was proposed that takeoff would be accomplished by greased tracks, a wheeled dolly, or the use of a catapult.

A problem that would haunt Northrop in most of his flying wing projects impacted this project also. Being a relatively small company (when compared to Douglas, Lockheed, and North American at that time), shop space was limited. More accurately stated, it was always at a premium. Their initial production order of 24 N-3PBs was soon overshadowed by the 400 RAF Vengeance and USAAF A-31s they were to build and over 700 P-61 Black Widows. This did not leave much room for Northrop's wing and tail-

With the P-38 tow plane in the background and the MX-334 immediately behind them, the Northrop and Army Air Forces flight test team pose for this August 1944 photo. From left to right: Lt. Isely (Wright Field project office), unknown, Capt. Martin L. Smith (P-38 pilot), Harry Crosby (Northrop test pilot), Jack Northrop, Don Smith (Northrop project engineer), Maj. Duke Douglas (Air Corps Plant Representative), Tom Ruble, unknown, Jake Superata, Eddie Lesnick, and Al Nesshoffer. (Northrop/Wolford Collection)

less aircraft projects. Also, Northrop's size required a relatively small engineering staff. The military draft was constantly decreasing the staff's size and competent replacements were not found in most cases.

Northrop chose a new firm to subcontract the design and construction of the three XP-79s. Not far from the Northrop plant was a recently organized firm called Avion, Incorporated (no relationship to Northrop's earlier company of like name) just off Atlantic Avenue near Maywood, California. It had been formed by a number of ex-Vultee employees, and the XP-79 was their first and, unfortunately, only project.

In March 1943 the decision was made to modify the third XP-79 to be powered by two Westinghouse 19-B axial flow jet engines in stead of the Aerojet rocket motor. It was felt that these engines would provide greater range and endurance. These were US Navy engines and procurement had to be accomplished through that service. Arrangements for four examples was initiated in April. Authority for Purchase number 217623 dated April 27th authorized the modification work, this resulted in Change Order Number 1 to the contract. This jet-propelled version was designated the XP-79B.

A rather low thrust Westinghouse engine was initially chosen, and the aircraft's designation was changed to XP-79A, according to one source document (a second, and only other document relating to the XP-79A, stated it was to be rocket powered). This lasted only for a short time as Westinghouse had the more powerful 19-B version that would soon be available.

By May 1943 Northrop must have felt quite confident in both the XP-79 and XP-79B designs. In that month they submitted an unsolicited quotation for 13 service test variants of both types, designated YP-79 and YP-79B., for a total cost of $3,037,335. Air Materiel Command did not feel that development had progressed far enough and no action was taken.

By early July 1943, the skid idea was dropped and a retractable quadracycle was incorporated into the design. This decision would be proved a good one as the MX-324/334 flight test program would go on to show. A single centerline nose gear wasn't practical because of the pilot's position. But unlike the MX-324 where the fixed gear was offset by a few inches, the offset in the XP-79 would be 40 to 50 inches due to its retraction requirement. A single gear with this offset would not be very stable, thus the quadracycle arrangement.

The wing's leading edge canopy was redesigned in this July change and the overall dimensions grew somewhat. Wing span increased from 432 inches to 456 inches. Length went from 152 inches to 158.7 inches. With the change from skid gear to the quadracycle tired gear, the overall height (still no vertical) went from 41.5 inches to 57 inches.

The B Revision to Northrop Specification 14 covered the XP-79B and the installation of the two modified 19 inch Model B Westinghouse jet engines. The mission of the aircraft was still the destruction of enemy by gunfire (not by collision). The basic design was the same as in the basic NS-14 specification. The thick magnesium alloy skin and armor plate was for protection with the armor plate also serving as a deflector plate against enemy gunfire. Besides the engines, the only other major difference between the basic specification and Revision B was the quadracycle landing

With top and bottom access hatches open, pilot Harry Crosby is able to stand on the desert floor, giving a good perspective of the glider's size. (Northrop/Wolford Collection)

gear replacing the skid arrangement.

The change in type of powerplant did not seem to have a significant impact on performance. As stated in the revised specification, high speed at sea level was calculated to be 547 mph. At 25,000 feet it was anticipated to be 508 mph. Cruising speed at that altitude was 480 mph (with both engines running). Endurance at 25,000 feet at maximum thrust (after takeoff, acceleration to best climbing speed at sea level, etc.) was calculated to be 147 minutes. Maximum range (after takeoff, acceleration to best climbing speed at sea level, including climb at maximum thrust to 25,000 feet) cruising on one engine, except for the time two engines were required, for maximum efficiency at 1,200 degrees, operating temperature at 25,000 feet and glide to sea level was 993 miles. In other words: full bore to altitude, cruise, and glide down from altitude to land.

Through their detailed analysis of the design, Avion calculated that the stability/dynamics of the aircraft without a vertical fin, as the Northrop team envisioned it, were unacceptable. Through detailed studies of pitch, rolling motions, time histories and such, they estimated that by adding different designs of vertical fins this situation was improved but never resolved to be comparable to conventional aircraft. By the end of May 1944, Avion was still studying finless, single fin and two fin designs. With the two fin design, they calculated the airplane's maximum speed would be 499 mph.

Avion advised Air Materiel Command in July that the project schedule was being impacted due to Aerojets developmental problems with their rocket motors. The contractual first flight date of September 30th would slip to December 15, 1943. That September Avion would once again reschedule first flight to January 15, 1944 owing to the same problem. But Aerojet was not the only one having problems. From Avion reports arriving at Wright Field, AMC

Right: With the P-38 tow plane out of the picture, it looks as if the MX-334 is taking off on its own. Even with the rocket motor installed, the craft needs to be towed to altitude before igniting the rocket propellants. In this closeup of the MX-334 as it leaves the dry lake, one gets a good look of the pilot's position. It looks real uncomfortable. (Northrop)

felt that Avion was taking an "academic" approach and instructed then to stop all "unnecessary" work and concentrate on building the aircraft.

Avion sent the armament section mockup to Wright Field in November for testing. Firing tests at the Armament Laboratory proved satisfactory.

Delays in the rocket motor program continued. By the end of 1943 the earliest first flight date was predicted to be April 15th. By March orders were issued to give highest priority to the XP-79B. A mockup of the Westinghouse engine was shipped to Avion in mid April. Avion made the appropriate changes to the mockup to enable it to be installed in the XP-79B airframe and shipped the mockup back to Westinghouse. At this time the first flight of the XP-79B was estimated to be August 1st.

To prepare Northrop's test pilot to fly the little jet fighter, arrangements were made for him to make familiarization flights in the Bell YP-59A at Muroc AAB.

By spring of 1944, the design was not the only problem that Avion was wrestling with. They were a small company of 100 to 150 total personnel and manufacturing was greatly lagging. Welding heavy gauge magnesium was not an easy task, including the problem of the material buckling. Northrop, who had much more experience with the material and the development of Heliarc welding, had its share of similar problems in the construction of the two XP-56. Northrop also planned to make the twin tail booms on the P-61 out of magnesium, but they experienced extreme manufacturing difficulty with the two XP-61s that they reverted back to aluminum alloys for the remainder of the Black Widow program. Much time and wasted material was accumulating.

In June reports of excessive scrappage, undesirable shop practices and low shop morale at Avion were reaching Northrop and AMC. This, with Aerojet's admission that their rocket motor prob-

lems could not be solved in the foreseeable future, brought about the cancellation for the two XP-79 rocket planes in September 1944. The design and construction of the XP-79B would now be taken over by Northrop.

Indications are that Avion had only the outer wing panels in a near complete state. Scattered around their manufacturing area were the two panels, the wheels, and a number of parts and assemblies. The cockpit hadn't been worked out yet. What had been fabricated of the XP-79B was moved to the Northrop plant on December 1st.

Northrop had a good bit of "catch-up" to do. Engineers and production personnel had to be taken from other tasks to "fit in" the added work in their already full day. Manufacturing space had to be carved out of Northrop's limited plant facilities. Engine integration and test facilities had to be accounted for. Before they knew it, they were in a new year and the first engine had arrived. On January 13, 1945, engine tests were started. The second engine was received on February 26th.

Problems with landing gear actuators not functioning properly, doors not closing completely, as well as other interference problems provided assembly problems for Northrop. Some engine difficulties were also experienced once the Westinghouse engines arrived.

On May 26th a 689 inspection was held. The inspection was held with the point of view that no production would follow and only those changes affecting pilot safety would be required prior to first flight.

By June, with the two Westinghouse 19-B (J-30) engines installed and sporting the standard chrome yellow paint scheme of Northrop's test aircraft, it was trucked out to Muroc where taxi tests were begun. Low speed taxi tests started immediately. By July 11th these tests had been completed and high speed tests began on the 13th. Tire failures were encountered and delays followed because

of problems in obtaining replacements. To add to their problems, the brake system was found to be inadequate and had to be designed. The high speed taxi tests were extended into September.

Following taxi tests, test pilot Harry Crosby climbed into the XP-79B's cockpit on September 12, 1945 for the plane's first flight. Jack Northrop described this flight in his talk to the Royal Aeronautical Society in 1947:

> The takeoff for this flight was normal, and for 15 minutes the airplane was flown in a beautiful demonstration. The pilot indicated mounting confidence by executing more and more maneuvers of a type that would not be expected unless he were thoroughly satisfied with the behavior of the airplane. After about 15 minutes of flying, the airplane entered what appeared to be a normal slow roll from which it did not recover. As the rotation about the longitudinal axis continued the nose gradually dropped, and at the time of impact the airplane appeared to be in a steep vertical spin. The pilot endeavored to leave the ship, but the speed was so high that he was unable to clear it successfully. Unfortunately, there was insufficient evidence to fully determine the cause of the disaster. However, in view of his prone position, a powerful, electrically controlled trim tab had been installed in the lateral controls to relieve the pilot of excessive loads. It is believed that a deliberate slow roll may have been attempted (as the pilot had previously slow rolled and looped other flying wing aircraft developed by the company) and that during this maneuver something failed in the lateral controls in such a way that the pilot was overpowered by the electrical trim mechanism.

With the destruction of the sole XP-79B, the program was canceled. The cause of the accident was based only on conjecture because of two unrelated incidents. When the emergency equipment arrived on the scene of the crash site, the fire fighting personnel

Of the three XP-79s originally ordered, only one airframe was completed. Aerojet encountered developmental problems with their rocket motor and the one aircraft produced, designated XP-79B, was powered by a pair of Westinghouse 19-D jet engines. Here the nearly complete aircraft is waiting to have its magnesium skin painted. (Northrop/Edwards AFB History Office)

took standard procedures and applied water on the fire. In the case of a magnesium fire, this is not the thing to do. Water intensifies the fire. Thus, with the steady application of water, the complete destruction of the airplane was assured. The second, and unrelated incident, was the motion picture film. Personnel from the Northrop photo lab had their motion picture cameras going when the incident occurred and filmed every moment, including impact. In the past the Northrop photo people were allowed to use the Muroc AAB facilities to process their film themselves. On this occasion they were not allowed and Army personnel performed the processing. Unfortunately, it was not accomplished properly for the type of film used and the end product was nearly useless.

The reader of the foregoing story of the XP-79B might inquire why no mention was made of the aircraft's mission as a Flying Ram. It's simple; no official document suggests such a mission. The idea of it as a Flying Ram was an after-the-fact brainstorm of a Wright Field engineer. Fortunately, Willis D. (Bill) Vinson, who was an aerodynamicist on the XP-79, was at Wright Field at the time. As he relates the story:

> After Avion folded and I got drafted, I was assigned to Wright Field. I was in the Aircraft Division there where airplane proposals,

all kinds of new proposals, were coming through. While I was working there in the Aircraft Division, somebody in the air force, I have no idea who, but somebody in the air force who was somewhat familiar with the '79B design, came up with the idea. Said 'Well, look at the way this wing is designed. We could use this as a flying ram in combat and then deliberately fly it and try to cut off the wings of the enemy planes.' If you can imagine two planes getting that close together, it really is not practical. That was the idea. They said, 'This wing is so strong, you mess up the leading edge, but with that steel plate in there it should be able to simply cut off the wing of the enemy plane and it [the '79] will still be flyable. That was the idea of the Flying Ram. [It was felt that with the damaged leading edge,] it wouldn't be flying as good [due to disturbed air flow] but it would not make it crash at all.

There seems to be a couple of reasons why such a mission was not seriously contemplated. First, from an engineering perspective, the leading edge sheet that provided the airfoil contour would be totally decimated at the time of collision with another aircraft. The airflow over the wing would turn to a very undesirable condition and the control system would be totally useless because insufficient control authority would be left in which to maneuver the aircraft. Second, by late 1944 and 1945 the AAF had control of the skies in the theaters of war so why would they take on such a drastic tactic? Besides, the kamikaze mentality is not part of the American psyche. Then where did such statements as, ". . . the famed Northrop Flying Ram XP-79, a prone-piloted fighter with a heavy armored wing which was designed to be used as an aerial cleaver, shearing off wings of enemy airplanes and flying away safely" come from? Public relations most likely.

Jet Bomb

The designation "JB," for Jet Propelled Bomb, was the US answer to the German V-1 Buzz Bomb type weapon – a pilotless, jet propelled missile. Matter of fact, the second vehicle in this series of weapons, the JB-2, or Loon, was an American manufactured copy of the German V-1. First in this family of weapons was the Northrop JB-1.

Northrop came on contract for Project MX-543 on July 1, 1944, receiving an order for 13 JB-1s. Much of the work already accomplished with the MX-324/334 craft could be applied to this project also. As a matter of fact, they expedited the process by photo reducing the MX-324/334 tooling templates for use on the new project.

Construction of this little pilotless flying bomb consisted of aluminum alloy wings which were riveted and spot-welded while the wing tips were fabricated out of magnesium alloy. A magnesium alloy center section contained its powerplant with a bomb container on either side. The bomb containers were made out of formed and welded magnesium alloy plate. Two General Electric Type B1 (modified turbosuperchargers) turbojet engines were to power it. Each engine had a rated power of 200 lbs. of thrust. The explosive element of the JB-1 was one standard general purpose 2,000 lb. bomb, less fins, in each bomb container. Automatic con-

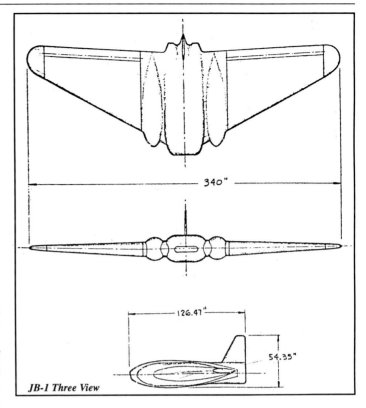

JB-1 Three View

trol equipment for the flying bomb was developed by the Hammond Instrument Co. of Chicago, Illinois. This equipment was mounted in the outer wing panels and consisted of a roll gyro and servo, a pitch gyro and servo, and an aneroid altitude control device. This all-electric equipment and the JB-2's pneumatic type were both scheduled to be flown in the JB-1 during its test program.

The pair of vertical stabilizers did not please Northrop, but wind tunnel data and engineering calculations indicated that they were needed. Jack Northrop felt that if the program had continued he would have been able to have one smaller vertical stabilizer. (Northrop/Edwards AFB History Office)

The requirements for the design called for a speed of 400 mph, a 200 mile range, and a 6,000 foot service ceiling. It would be ground launched and guidance would be pre-programmed. It was meant to strike against area targets such as did the JB-2/V-1.

For flight test purposes, the first vehicle was built as a glider. In place of the jet engines, a cockpit for a pilot was carved out and the engine air intake faired over. Attachment points were installed at the forward end of each bomb container where tow cables could be connected so the glider could be towed to altitude and released.

On August 27, 1943, Harry Crosby flew the JB-1 glider for the first time out at Rogers Dry Lake in the Mojave Desert. The cameras were rolling. To the surprise of many as he came down to land, he went by the pre-set camera position and just kept floating along the desert floor at a couple of feet in the air. They hadn't counted on the ground effect phenomena under that wing. It just kept floating along until, with a jarring thud, it "plopped" to the ground. No shocks, though the pneumatic tires helped to cushion the blow.

Not only was this little glider testing the airworthiness of the design, but that of the automatic control equipment developed by the Hammond Instrument Co. As the flight test program progressed, the construction of the second article, this time a powered pilotless bomb, was coming along. As December approached, all seemed to be ready for a first launch.

Northrop's Dr. William Sears and project engineer Don Smith arrived at Eglin Field, Florida, in early December. There great difficulty was experienced in assembling and removing the wing panel covers because of the large number of self threading screws incorporated in its design. When fueled, they found one serious and several minor fuel leaks in the integral tanks – the former caused a day's delay in launch.

At Eglin's Range 64, the JB-1 was placed on a modified JB-2 launching sled on a 500 track. To get it airborne were two Monsanto rockets which propelled the sled, with bomb, along the track. Before the sled rockets were fired, the jet engines were started. Though no details were given, the flight test report stated that, "The 50%

Opposite:
From this angle details of the cockpit can be seen. The pilot's headrest along with the control handlebars on either side are somewhat visible. (Northrop/Edwards AFB History Office)

power reduction of these units from the original requirements necessitated the flying of this bomb in a light-weight condition." Starting the engines was accomplished by turning the turbines with compressed air and at the same time applying a spark through the spark plugs by way of a high voltage transformer. There was great difficulty in starting these engines and once again the flight test was postponed.

On December 7th all seemed to be well. The missile was mounted on its launching sled, which ran along a level track, and was adjusted to a nine degree nose high attitude. The elevons were placed in a nine degree up from the streamlined position per the calculation of Northrop engineering. The engines were fired up and launch was achieved.

At about 10-feet distance from the launch sled, the missile nosed up about 45 degrees, climbed rapidly for a short distance, and then went into a stall. During its five second flight, it covered about 400 yards from takeoff. Post-flight investigation showed that the elevon setting needed to be recalculated. But, even if the elevon setting had been correct, the flight probably would not have been a success as the right engine had failed.

It was recommended that the GE turbojets be dropped from the program as unsuitable powerplants for the JB-1 because they had failed at turbine speeds only half of the thrust required. It was also recommended that the correct elevon settings be determined. Northrop was requested to improve the accessibility to control equipment and powerplants, and a thorough check under pressure of all integral fuel tanks for leaks be accomplished on the next airframes prior to delivery.

The first priority was to find an appropriate powerplant for the flying bomb. Whether it was a Northrop decision or an AAF recommendation, the JB-2's Ford Motor Company-built PJ-31-1 pulse jet engine was selected. On February 19, 1945, Northrop's flying bomb was redesignated the JB-10. A second JB-1 pilotless vehicle had been completed at the time of the abortive launch in December. This craft would now be modified into the first pulse jet-powered JB-10. The remaining 10 vehicles from the original JB-1 order would also be completed as JB-10s.

To house the pulse jet engine, the center section of the flying wing required major redesign. This included the design and instal-

Above: With the pilot flying the aircraft in the prone position, it was impossible to place the nose gear on the center line of the nose area. The retractable quadracycle gear, though unusual, was the answer. (Northrop/Edwards AFB History Office)

Below: Final adjustments are made to the XP-79B shortly before trucking it to the Muroc area. (Northrop)

lation of a cast magnesium shroud. The shroud was a circular section surrounding the engine in such a way that a flow of cooling air was permitted between the shroud and the engine.

Two cast magnesium warhead sections, one on either side of the center section, were bolted to the outboard stations of that section. They were shaped to the contour of the airfoil and extended from the wings leading edge back approximately two-thirds of its chord. Each warhead section weighed 1,815 pounds (1,604.5 pounds of that being Tritonal explosive). Trailing sections made of aluminum sheet metal were attached to the rear of the warheads and constituted the remainder of the wing contour.

As in the JB-1, the JB-10's wing leading edge swept back at 27 degrees while the trailing edge was relatively straight. The fixed vertical fin was used for directional stability while elevons along the wing's trailing edge provided directional control. Both Hammond Instrument Company's electric servo control system and the JB-2's pneumatic system were considered for the JB-10.

Ten of the 11 JB-10s produced would be test flown from Range 64 at Eglin Field, Florida, between April 13 and December 19, 1945. They were launched from a 500 foot level launching ramp using a rocket propelled sled to accelerate the aircraft to flying speed. A fully loaded JB-10 required a sled speed of 225 mph to get it airborne. To accomplish this, five 11,000 lb. thrust, 1.8 second duration rockets were used.

The first flight occurred on April 6, 1945. Not much is known of this flight, except that it was not successful. Of the 10 total flights accomplished, only two were considered partial successes. On April 13th the flight had to be terminated prematurely because of a combination of control and fuel system malfunctions. On this flight the craft had flown 26 miles. The second partially successful flight, on October 1st, was terminated when the JB-10 went into a divergent pitch oscillation after a flight of approximately 20 miles. The primary causes for the other eight test flight failures included structural failure of the launching sled, control gearing or follow-up ra-

Don't believe all that you think you see. Here the XP-79B has been skillfully integrated with some southern California urban scenery. (Northrop)

tios of improper value, improper longitudinal trim settings, premature launchings which did not permit full usage of the accelerating run, powerplant failure, and failure of control equipment uncaging mechanism. Two of the failures were directly caused by a malfunctioning of the control equipment which caused the craft to roll over and crash immediately after launching. Two others were apparently successful launches which nosed down at takeoff and crashed. For these, it was thought that improper trim was the cause of the failures.

The project was closed out as 1945 came to an end. With the termination of the project in early January 1946, the Army Air Forces planned to scrap the JB-1 glider and to send the one remaining JB-10 to Seymour Field in Indiana for inclusion in the display of historical aircraft then being assembled. By some quirk of fate, the JB-1 glider remains today in a small southern California museum while the whereabouts of the sole remaining JB-10 is unknown.

The test crew work on the XP-79B on the hot Mojave Desert dry lake bed. It had arrived at its desert test base in June 1945 with taxi tests commencing soon thereafter. On September 12, 1945 the little jet took to the air. Pilot Harry Crosby must have felt very comfortable with how the plane was behaving, as he started putting it through its paces. Then something went drastically wrong. Crosby lost control, bailed out, and was killed when hit by the craft before it crashed. (Northrop)

One of three JB-1s produced, out of an order for 13, was this glider variant. Its purpose was twofold. First, it was to demonstrate the flying qualities of the basic design. Second, it was to test the telemetry equipment that was to be installed in the pilotless weapons. (Northrop/Wolford Collection)

This craft was most often referred to by those working on the project by its project number, Project 16. The designation JB-1A pops up in literature, but it seems to be an unofficial designation as it does not appear in official Army Air Forces documents. At various times Northrop personnel and publications use the JB-1A designation in reference to the glider, the powered weapon, and early on to what became the JB-10. (Northrop/G. H. Balzer Historical Archives)

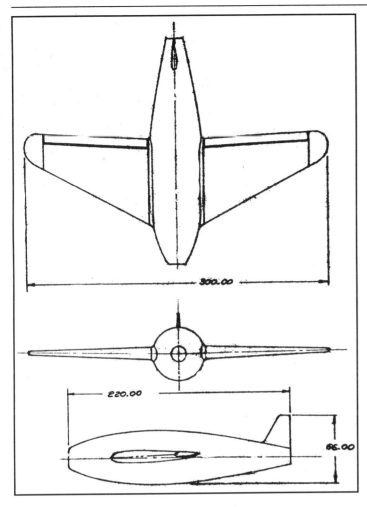

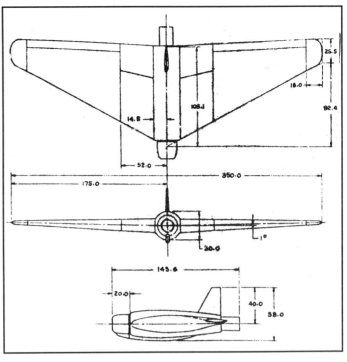

Above: JB-10 Three View

Left: Proposed JB-1B Three View

Below: The JB-1 glider with an enclosed cockpit and new windscreen. From dates on photos it appears that this modification took place in September 1944. (Northrop/G. H. Balzer Historical Archives)

Above: The size of the JB-1 glider is brought into perspective with the man in the cockpit and the other two at the vertical stabilizer. On his first flight, pilot Harry Crosby had some trouble getting the glider to touch down due to the ground effect caused by the aircraft's design. (Northrop/Robert Gerhart)

Left: This threesome was an act in a Northrop employees variety show. (Northrop)

The powerplant installation of the JB-1 pilotless flying wing. The engines were modified General Electric turbo superchargers. (Northrop/G. H. Balzer Historical Archives)

One of two JB-1 pilotless craft produced is being hoisted at the Northrop factory. The cylindrical-shaped areas on either side of the center section were each meant to carry a 2,000 lb. bomb. (Northrop/G. H. Balzer Historical Archives)

The one and only JB-1 to be launched is in position on its sled at a test range in Eglin Field, Florida. The flight controls had to be manually set prior to flight. Apparently there was a miscalculation and the craft nosed into the ground shortly after takeoff. Analysis of the flight showed, though not responsible for the actual failure of the flight, the General Electric engines were not adequate to power the craft. Redesign would bring about the JB-10. (Northrop/G. H. Balzer Historical Archives)

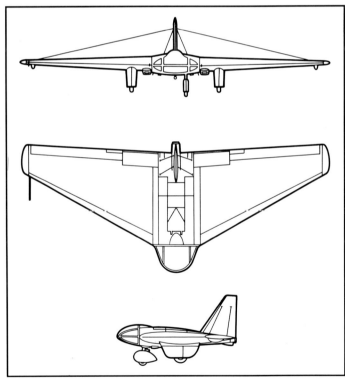

MX-324/334 Three View

Center left: A model airplane club? No, this really is serious stuff. Probably part of the JB-1/JB-10 redesign effort. (Northrop)

Left: A scale model of the JB-10 on a small test track. (Northrop)

Eleven JB-10s were produced from the one complete and 10 partial JB-1s manufactured. The JB-10 was powered with a Ford Motor Company version of the German V-1's Fiesler pulse jet engine. (Northrop/G. H. Balzer Historical Archives)

A JB-10 sits on its launcher at one of Eglin Field's test ranges just prior to it's first flight on April 6, 1945. Ten of the 11 JB-10 produced were launched from the Eglin range. After only a few partial successes, the Army Air Forces discontinued testing and planned to put the one remaining JB-10 on display. (Northrop/G. H. Balzer Historical Archives)

Wind Tunnel testing continued for a while in an effort to design an improved version. (Northrop/Wolford Collection)

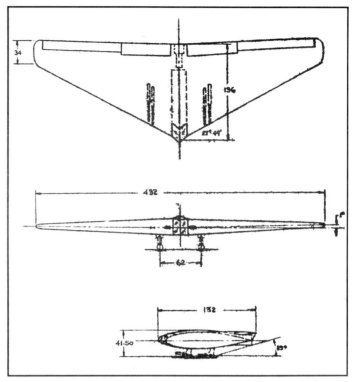

Early Three View of XP-79 with Skid Gear

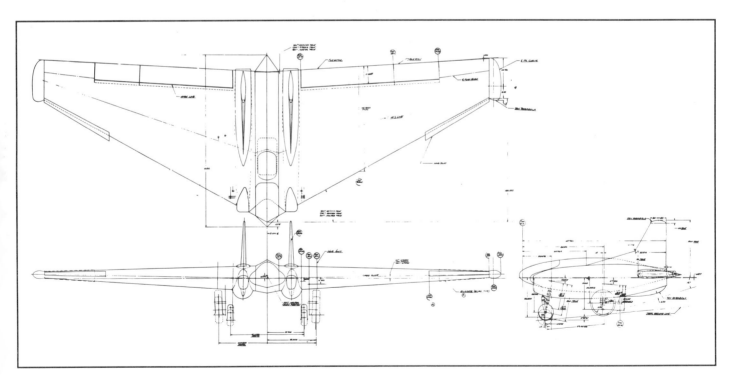

Near-Final Configuration of XP-79B

Chapter 7

A DREAM ALMOST REALIZED
B-35 Design and Flight Test

When the October 1941 contract was awarded, the approximately 1,200 employees at Northrop were already quite busy, and the company's original 9,000 sq. ft. of floor space had grown to 216,280 sq. ft. On the brink of a world war, Northrop's dream was about to come true. The time seemed right. But the company's size (Jack Northrop always wanted a small company to devote to research and development) would become a liability. In both personnel, especially engineering, and manufacturing floor space he would soon reach his limits. Manufacturing was filled with orders for V-72 Vengeance dive bombers for the British and soon would be building its A-31 counterpart for the Air Corps. Between September 1940 and November 1943, 400 of these aircraft would be produced. Major subcontract work was being accomplished for Consolidated and Boeing as well as for the XP-56. Engineering had been busy on the XP-56 since early 1940, was supporting the N-1M project, and the Air Corps had ordered two XP-61 night fighters in late January 1941 (an order for 13 service test YP-61 followed six months later). Besides the crunch on technical talent and floor space, the banks were worried that the company was over-extending itself.

With delivery dates two years off, Northrop had a lot of work to do. The XB-35 was grossly larger than anything Jack Northrop had ever contemplated undertaking and most of the flying wing theory had not been proved yet. The N-9M effort, which was to go far beyond the N-1M experience to date, was to prove much of this theory. One N-9M flying mockup was called for as part of the October 1941 contract. The engineering talent that could be spared from the XP-56 and XP-61 projects were put to work on the N-9M and XB-35 designs.

When the Air Corps and Northrop were discussing the flying wing bomber contract in September and October, the Air Corps desired to contract for two experimental examples; Northrop felt that his facilities were not adequate for the fabrication of two of these aircraft simultaneously. Apparently Jack Northrop and his staff re-evaluated the situation, for in late October he informed the Materiel Division that they could take on the task of constructing a second article. It was at this same time that discussions were being conducted between these same two parties concerning a second XP-56 also. As the Air Corps was concerned about the impact a second XP-56 would have on the XB-35 effort, Northrop replied:

It is estimated that little difference in engineering is involved, whether one or two [XP-56] airplanes are constructed. It would be impossible to undertake the second airplane if it involved appreciable additional engineering time, as the Engineering Department is definitely overloaded at present and is the critical spot in our organization with regard to the completion of the XP-56 and Project MX-140 [XB-35].

The Air Corps apparently felt that the XP-56 program would have a marked influence on the XB-35 project. As part of Materiel Division's support for the procurement of a second XP-56 and the renegotiation of that contract from a fixed price type to a cost plus fixed fee contract (at the behest of the company's bank), the Division stated:

A second airplane provides insurance against the loss of the first airplane. This is doubly important in this case because the XB-35 project follows so closely behind the XP-56 project. The loss of the one and only XP-56 could have a disastrous affect upon the bomber project. If a second XP-56 airplane were available upon which to work out the corrective measures deemed necessary as a result of the loss of the first airplane, this adverse effect could perhaps be entirely alleviated.

So on November 26th the Materiel Division informed Northrop that Article 42, the option for a second XB-35, was being exercised. In their letter, the Division requested a satisfactory delivery date for the second article, though the delivery of this airplane could not interfere with the XP-56 or XP-61 schedules. Northrop's reply was that they could deliver the second XB-35 approximately five months after the first aircraft.

As the shortage of engineers was just noted above, in Northrop's December 1, 1941, reply on the second XB-35, they stated:

The governing factor in this instance is the estimated length of time necessary for the assembly of the airplane from its component parts. In this case parts for two airplanes will be run through the shop departments at the same time. However, we do not have shop space available for the final assembly of these airplanes and must therefore build additional space in which to undertake this work. It is now contemplated to put up a temporary building approximately 75 X 200 feet, which will be of sufficient size to house one assembled airplane, but not two at the same time. As soon as one airplane has been completed, assembly of the second can be started at once, and delivery will be made as soon thereafter as assembly is complete. In view of

Opposite: YB-35, serial number 42-102366, made its first flight on May 15, 1948. By this time, nearly two years after the maiden flight of the first XB-35, and with both YB-49s already flying, the piston engined B-35 series were of limited value and production for them was no longer a consideration. (Northrop/Smithsonian Institution)

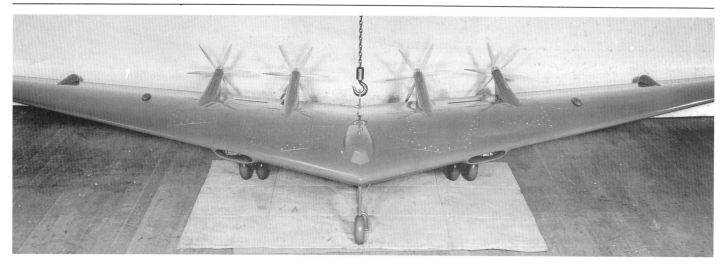

This 16-foot model of the XB-35 is one of many wind tunnel models produced. The models were tested at NACA facilities on both coasts of the United States as well as at universities and Northrop's own wind tunnel. (Northrop/G. H. Balzer Historical Archives)

the fact that we have been informed Government aid is not available to construct the necessary assembly floor space, we desire to reduce the expenditure for this building to a minimum.

In early December a rough mockup of the crew's quarters in the XB-35 was nearing completion, and Northrop felt it would be worthwhile for representatives from Materiel Division to visit his plant and review the progress to date. He felt that at this stage it would be useful to inspect the mockup for purposes of determining whether the pilot's vision and general roominess of the crew's quarters were satisfactory. Overall mockup completion, Northrop felt, was still several months off.

What would be the first of many delays in the B-35 program came in mid-December 1941. America had been at war for but a few days. The production of war materials of all sorts needed to go into high gear. Production, not development of new war machines, was of top priority at the moment. To expedite production deliveries of V-72/A-31 dive bombers and subcontracted components for Consolidated and Boeing, Northrop was informed by the Air Corps' Western District Supervisor to halt performance on the XB-35 contract and that the duration of the delay could not be determined at that time.

Progress was slow as 1942 moved along. Northrop's engineering department seemed never to be able to have the numbers or talent required for Jack's Wing. Air Corps changes and normal engineering difficulties were requiring additional engineering time on the Black Widow night fighter. The drafting of personnel was exasperating the situation.

As the XB-35 design effort approached its one year mark, Northrop had only 30 to 35 engineers working on the design. The XB-35 mockup was completed in the summer of 1942 and a mockup inspection was called to begin on July 6th; this was 47 days ahead of that required by contract – the Flying Wing bomber was starting off on a positive note. The Air Corps felt that British representatives should not be present for the inspection because of the experimental nature of the project. The inspection took place between the 6th and 17th. The inspection team found the mockup generally satisfactory. Many of the details which normally would have been worked out on a conventional airplane had not been solved and

could not be truly represented. This situation would necessitate many changes in the mockup later on, creating delays. The powerplant installation was found unsatisfactory and a complete redesign was required. All this would require another mockup inspection at a later date. Not only was the mockup, which consisted of a full-scale crew nacelle and a portion of the left wing, discussed, but future program plans. Two additional N-9Ms and thirteen YB-35 service test aircraft were also part of the agenda.

Northrop-Martin Partnership

Northrop would have to expand its facilities to take on the job of producing 13 more large Wings. The engineering shortage would be exacerbated with the engineering required for the service test variants of the Wing. In September Northrop sent representatives to the Glenn L. Martin Company in Baltimore, Maryland, to discuss some of the design engineering of their B-33 which they thought might be applicable to the Wing, particularly the fuel system. The representatives also went to Seattle, Washington, where they visited Boeing to obtain data on the B-29, the bomb rack design in particular.

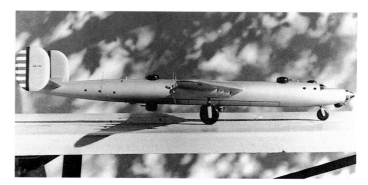

A model of the competing XB-36. The development of both aircraft would be much longer, and costlier, than initially envisioned. Both would come close to cancellation on a number of occasions. (Consolidated Aircraft Corp./San Diego Aerospace Museum)

Scale model of the XB-35 flying wing undergoing free-spinning test in the Langley 20-foot free-spinning tunnel. (NASA Langley/Smithsonian Institution)

To expedite matters, Brig. Gen. Lawrence S. Kuter, Deputy Chief of the Air Staff, wrote General Echols at Materiel Command in late September 1942 that the highest priority should be given the research and development activities relating to the XB-35 and XB-36 projects, and in particular to Northrop's engineering personnel problem. Two days later Echols replied that the highest priority possible had been given the XB-35 by both Materiel Command and the NACA in connection with wind tunnel work. In an attempt to ease the shortage of engineers that Northrop was experiencing, Brig. Gen. Charles E. Branshaw of the Western Procurement District was attempting to borrow engineers from other west coast aircraft manufacturers to assist Northrop. So far, the manufacturers told Branshaw that the only way they could free up any engineers was for the Air Corps to cancel a project. Materiel Command recommended that Douglas lend engineers currently on the A-26 to Northrop and that North American Aviation lend engineers from the P-78 Merlin Mustang project. The Air Staff contemplated this

problem and in early November the Director of Military Requirements and Plans concurred with Materiel Command's recommendation of a higher priority for the intercontinental bomber projects but disagreed with the removal of engineers from the A-26 and P-78 projects. As an alternative, they reviewed the B-29, B-32, and B-33 projects and considered their "real value." Their decision was to discontinue the Martin B-33 project and use that engineering force to expedite the B-35 and B-36 projects. For Martin, this was the loss of two XB-33s and 400 production aircraft.

On November 7th the stop work order was sent out to The Glenn L. Martin Co. in Baltimore, Maryland. General Echols soon talked with Mr. Martin personally to explain the situation. Mr. K. Ebel, Martin's chief engineer, and a number of other engineers (including the chief of structures) and the factory manager with manufacturing representatives arrived at the Northrop plant on November 16th.

As 1942 came to a close, the feeling at Northrop must have been close to an all time high. On December 17th the contract for the 13 YB-35s was approved and ten days later N-9M-1 made its first flight. In Materiel Command's technical instructions CTI-735, Addendum No. 14, dated December 11th, 100 production B-35 bombers were called out for both Northrop and Martin. But time was passing. The first N-9M was about three months behind schedule when it took to the air, and half of the 24 months had passed since the XB-35 was contracted for in which Northrop promised to have the first XB-35 flying. There was much to be accomplished. As a matter of fact, with Northrop's new engineering and assembly facilities, which would be ready in January 1943, they still lacked adequate manufacturing space for the 100 aircraft production buy. In a December 28, 1942, Materiel Command message, it was stated that Northrop had informed them that "their (Northrop's) facilities as now existing, they will be unable to fabricate more than the XB and YB type airplanes already on contract, and asked that they be relieved of the load of fabricating these additional 100." Martin vice president Harry T. Rowland, informed Materiel Command at this time that Martin could take over this work if the Air Corps so desired. It was so recommended.

Col. J.W. Sessums, Jr., the Assistant Chief of Staff (AC/S(P)) in Washington, D.C., wrote Materiel Command's headquarters in Washington, in which he stated that the original contemplated quantity for the B-35 production program was 400, 200 going to each Northrop and Martin. This quantity was halved when it was decided to place interim orders in the Fiscal Year 1943 budget. He went on to state that he felt the 100 aircraft under the present Northrop contract should be canceled outright and that a quantity of 50 should go to Martin under the Fiscal Year 1944 budget.

An interesting meeting took place at Langley Field, Virginia, in which Martin representatives, Air Corps liaison officers and NACA representatives discussed the B-35 project; there was no Northrop representation. Vernon Outman and Paul E. Hovgard represented Martin. During this conference, the Martin representatives stated that at the present time Martin was a subcontractor to Northrop. Present plans called for Northrop to construct the first XB-35 and Martin would construct the second and all 13 YB-35s as well as producing a majority of the engineering. This was due to Martin having a much larger engineering organization and more shop space. Martin also questioned the airfoil section Northrop had chosen for their big bomber along with other design details.

The thousands of miles separating Northrop and Martin, and each company's own agendas, did not bode well for the B-35 project. Part of the difficulty in developing this plane was in the structure under which it was carried out. When Martin became part of the program, both they and Northrop were to work on the experimental, service test, and production airplane designs at the same time. Considerable indecision and confused communication abounded as to where the most emphasis should be placed. There was also a question as to which company was responsible for accomplishing which tasks. A January 1944 Wright Field report details the situation as of mid-July 1943:

> As a result of telephone conversation between Mr. Martin and General Carroll, in which Mr. Martin expressed doubts as to the feasibility of the B-35 design, Materiel Command personnel visited the Martin Company on this date [July 12, 1943] to inspect progress and the reported difficulties with design. Most of these problems concerned the power plant installation as regards clearance, excessive temperatures, difficult duct design, maintenance features and increased weight empty. It was the feeling of the Materiel Command representatives that, while some of the concern of the Martin Company was justified, most of the items were arguments being used to substantiate the lack

of enthusiasm of the Martin management for the project and to further their efforts at having the project dropped so far as the Martin Company was concerned. At the Preston Street office where the Martin and Northrop engineering was being carried on, the project was being pursued with vigor and the problems considered serious by the Martin management were not worrying the people actually doing the engineering. However, it was requested that studies be made showing new arrangements of power plant installations which would relieve the so-called difficulties.

As the contractual delivery date of November 22, 1943 approached, the project seemed to have more than its share of troubles. Besides its problems with Martin, Northrop was experiencing difficulties of its own in 1943. The limited flight test program to date with the N-9M indicated problems with stall characteristics, rudder effectiveness, and elevator force reversal. The B-35 designers were struggling with the electrical and hydraulic control systems. Accidents in May and October resulted in the loss of the first N-9M and XP-56 aircraft, which set the program back. Martin was striving to overcome bomb bay and engine accessory temperature problems, duct design and maintenance difficulties, and overweight of the structural design. For its part, Pratt & Whitney was having its own

XB-35 mockup at the Northrop plant in August 1942. (Northrop/G. H. Balzer Historical Archives)

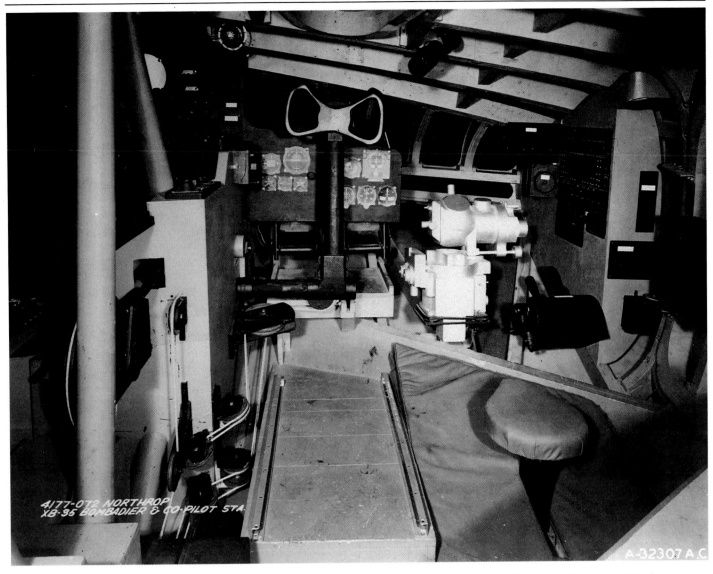

Copilot's and bombardier's station in the XB-35 mockup. The pilot sits to the left and at a higher elevation. (Northrop/Smithsonian Institution)

problems with the development of the R-4360 engine. In the XB-35 program, the airplane and engine was a coordinated effort which required additional data not normally obtained during test stand running. Pratt & Whitney's engine test stand was a major component in their part of the program. Engine changes which included relocation of engine cooling fan and redesign of propeller gear box to incorporate drive for alternators impacted both engine and stand development. Their developmental problems caused the schedule to protract and would also impact the delivery of this model engine for the two aircraft scheduled to use it – the B-35 and Hughes F-11 photo reconnaissance airplane. All had to admit that the delivery date had to be changed. Best estimates were that about an additional year and a half was required to complete the design and to fabricate the first XB-35, so April 15, 1945 was now the delivery date.

As 1943 came to a close, the XB-35's design was about 29% complete (this was a month after its original contractual delivery date). Engineering difficulties, engine development problems, lack

of government furnished equipment, and possibly an unworkable relationship with Martin added to the lack of progress on the B-35 program. On December 10th, General Chidlaw at Materiel Division Headquarters in Washington, phoned Brig. Gen. Orval R. Cook at Wright Field in which General Chidlaw indicated that he felt that range and speed were the two most serious problems at that time with the B-35. They decided not to make any changes on the B-35 production program at the time but would hold that option open pending further information.

Partnership Unraveling

Engineering personnel in January 1944 stood at 354 in Hawthorne and 357 in Baltimore. At this same time negotiations were proceeding with the Otis Elevator Company of New York City to contract for an additional 350 to 400 engineering draftsmen to assist the Baltimore contingent. Martin had used this same group

Rear gunner's station in the XB-35 mockup. Visible in this photo is the gunner's periscope sighting equipment and two bunks for crew rest during long missions. (Northrop/Smithsonian Institution)

of Otis engineers in the design of Martin's Mars flying boat. Materiel Command was now pushing Martin to start construction of the production aircraft as they felt that Martin should be able to do this from essentially the same engineering as Northrop was using to build the experimental and service test airplanes.

Even with the infusion of the Otis Elevator personnel, Martin was now projecting that the first production B-35s would not be available until early 1947. This did not sit well with the AAF as Brig. Gen. Mervin E. Gross, Chief of the Requirements Division stated in a memorandum to the Chief of the Air Staff on March 22, 1944:

> The Glenn L. Martin Company has executed no production engineering on the B-35 to date. 350 Martin engineers are now wholly engaged in executing experimental engineering to enable the Northrop Company to produce the first XB-35. Martin expects to begin about 15 April 1944 to put additional engineers, secured from the Otis Elevator Company, on the experimental and production engineering, bringing it up to an additional 400 or a total of 750 engineers. Martin has made no commitments for material and has done nothing productively and feels that their Company would not be justified in doing

more, pending the solution of the aero-dynamic difficulties by Northrop.

Northrop's greatest troubles at present include aero-dynamic difficulties with elevator and rudder control surfaces, hydraulic boost control and a new electrical system. These difficulties are inherent in the design of the airplane and are recognized as such by Martin and Northrop, except that Martin believes his company has already developed a hydraulic boost control which is satisfactory.

The Glenn L. Martin Company is very much concerned over the employment of its production force on an airplane which, to date, has not been completely experimentally proven and on which certain aero-dynamic problems have not been solved. It has executed its part of the experimental contract approximately on schedule, but probably contemplates the employment of more engineers in converting the experimental drawings into production drawings than actually required. This concern on the part of Martin appears justified.

The airplane at present, though some 8,000 pounds overweight, does represent an advance in airplane design of sufficient value to continue in spite of the 18 month delay.

Materiel Command is now fully aware of all pertinent circumstances and has taken, although perhaps somewhat late, appropriate action to bring the two Companies together and has set a definite date of May 1, 1944 as a deadline on making a decision as to the future of the project.

On May 3, General Gross would write:

> The time would appear propitious to decide whether we want the B-35 or not. If the decision is that we do not, then the "Y" models might also be eliminated and only the "X" models built or even only partially built. Due to new proposals which have recently been coming in, the value of the B-35 appears to be vastly reduced. Under the circumstances, it is recommended that the B-35 and YB-35 both be eliminated, unless comparison of the XB-35 with more recently submitted proposals would indicate production justified.

From all this the Air Staff would conclude that the B-35 project was being unduly delayed under the existing arrangement and that further delays would be expected. The delay in the project was understood to be occasioned largely by the loss of engineers to the draft and that as things were going the production model probably would not be available until after the war. The Air Staff felt that the project was suffering from these factors, plus Martin's reluctance to continue the project through production, and recommended cancellation of the production contract. It was also recommended that Martin continue assisting on the experimental and service test airplane engineering. On May 18th Headquarters, Materiel Command issued a Technical Instruction canceling the production contract which was followed by a Notice of Termination on the 26th.

Critical Period

The year wore on and the design of the XB-35 continued at a slow rate. Northrop was ever battling the understaffed problem in their engineering department. In gross numbers, the engineers at Martin and Otis Elevator swelled the ranks of engineering and drafting personnel, but much seemed to be lacking in making the design effort cohesive.

Northrop's engineers found that the stability and control system required for the flying wing bomber was one of their toughest challenges. A number of aerodynamic systems were tried on the N-9M flying mockups. All attempts led them to a conclusion that they felt from the beginning would be required. Irv Ashkenas of the aerodynamics department commented on this effort during a symposium in early 1994:

> So we took the bull by the horns and developed that fully powered hydraulic system. And that wasn't easy either! We didn't have flutter per se. We had hunting and buzzing. To begin with we had a lot of problems in making the system really work. We would takeoff and buzz and shake and the pipes would rattle and everything would get tuned up. It was really pioneering work. I think the way they ended up

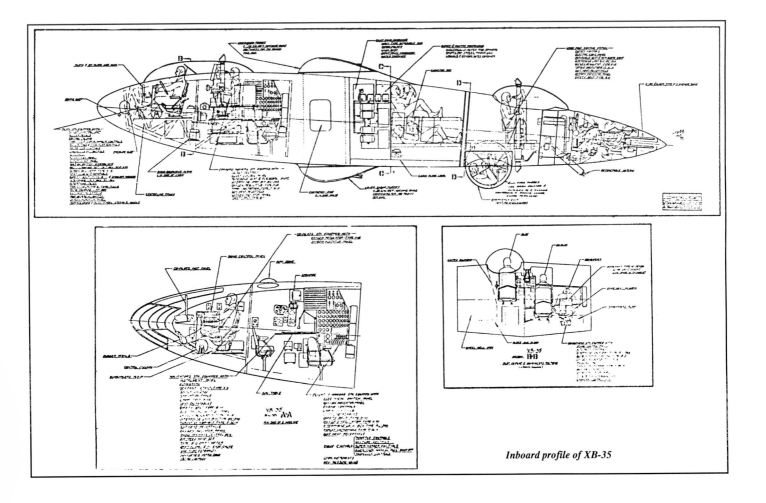

Inboard profile of XB-35

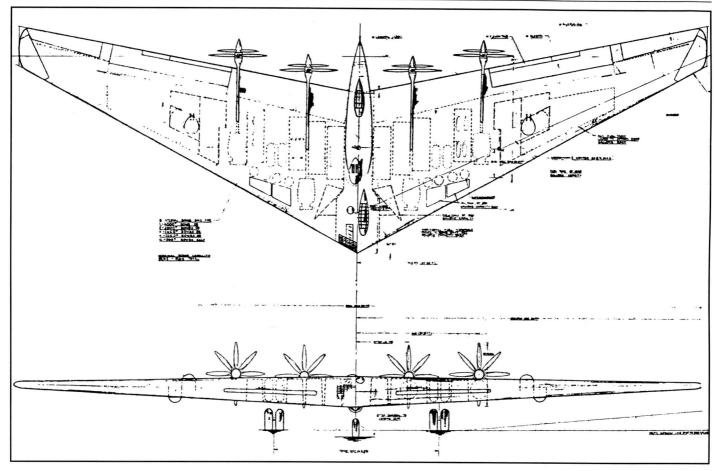

Above and below: Early Three View of XB-35

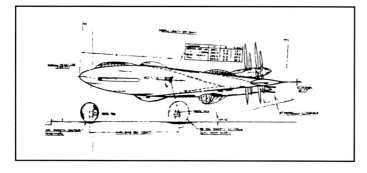

strapping the valves to the cylinder so that the cylinder moved closed the valve off automatically. The whole arrangement was really very rigid and free of backlash and play which were important things to try to get out of a system like that. The idea of eventually allowing neutral leakage across the valve was an important contribution. Up to that point it was hard to make the flow characteristics linear with the valve displacement. It was hard to get a nice clean system. As soon as you allowed a little neutral leakage, it tended to linearize. Because you had flow to begin with and just a little bit of movement of the valve allowed the flow to increase and not only that, the neutral leakage kept the oil circulating throughout the entire system which kept it warm. Which is no small additional feature. So you didn't need heaters for the system, it stayed warm all by itself. Since it was a fully powered system and you wanted some forces fed to the pilot, we had

to devise an artificial feel system that would make the airplane feel like a conventional system which we did by putting in a Q bellows on the stick. So as the speed increased, the stick got stiffer and stiffer just as it would on a conventional airplane. Because we had an artificial feel system, we could retrim the feel system so we didn't need trim tabs on the surface. We simply moved the zero for the stick force to a new position and that trimmed the airplane. If you want to look at the biggest legacy that the Flying Wing left, I think it was the fully powered hydraulic system.

By mid-1944 flight test data from the little N-9M flying mockups was coming in which indicated that the B-35's flight characteristics would be satisfactory. Though the N-9Ms were found to be quite sensitive to flight control movements, the Materiel Command personnel felt that the larger size and mass of the bomber would work in its favor. They felt that, based on the results to date, the B-35 project should continue. At this same point, they also felt that another mockup inspection should take place in the near future. In particular, the mockup should be complete with either actual or wooden models of all equipment in the crew positions and to the location of radio and radar equipment.

Support for the B-35 was ebbing fast as November 1944 opened due to the lack of progress being made on the project. In a telephone conversation with Col. Donald Putt at Wright Field, General Echols remarked, "It's gotten to the point here everybody's so discouraged that every time you say B-35 they just all look the other way." To overcome the situation somewhat and to get a number of flying wing bombers into the air sooner, it was decided to construct the first six YB-35s to the XB specifications (at this time the first XB-35 was about 75% complete and the second airplane was about 72% complete). By doing this, it was projected that the first XB-35 would be in the air by August 1945, the second in December, then the others at two month intervals after that. By this action, General Echols felt that it "assures us of getting something!" Under this scheme, the engineering effort would go towards the XB design only. Some improvements might be incorporated, such as weight reduction in the fourth airplane and the aeroboost in the fifth, though no change would be incorporated that would hold up the construction of any of them. The use of jet engines in the B-35 was suggested to Northrop that past August and the inclusion of the jets might take priority over other YB-35 efforts. As a result of the above, the first six YB-35s maintained that designation, the last seven were redesignated YB-35A, and the production aircraft were designated B-35Bs.

In early March 1945 it was decided to reduce the YB design effort and emphasize the jet powered B-35 variant. Four major improvements or additions were to be added to the YB-35 over the XB-35 variants. These improvements included the thermal de-icing on the center section of the wing; structural change to allow 1,000, 2,000, and 4,000 pound bombs in the inboard bomb bay; removal of structural armor plate with accompanying weight reduction; and provision for carrying bomb bay fuel tanks. At this time the AAF felt that speed, and the jet engine, was the future. Lt. Col. H. E. Warden of Wright Field stated at this time:

It is certainly not believed that the expected performance from the R-4360 installation will even approximately meet the new required performances. On the other hand, the predicted performance with jet installation is extremely attractive.

Northrop was not the only one experiencing troubles on this project. Pratt & Whitney informed the AAF that delivery of the R-

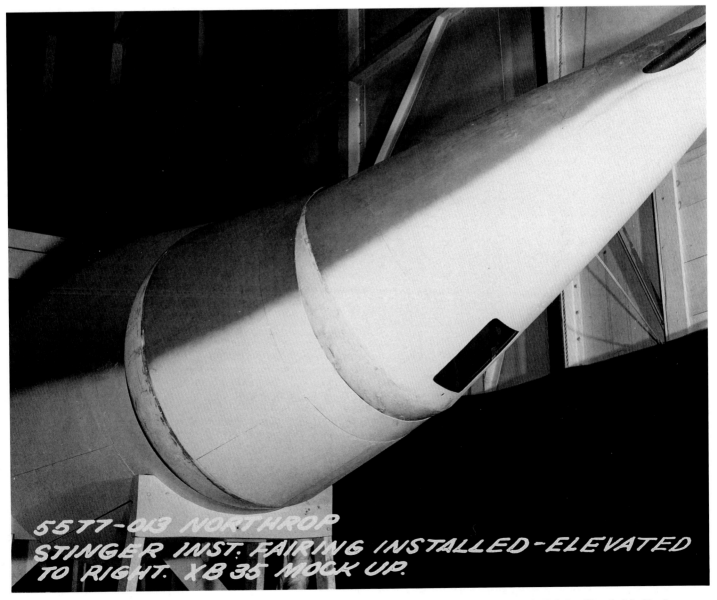

Tail gun, or "stinger," installation on the XB-35 mockup. Here it is in the elevated to the right position. (Northrop/G. H. Balzer Historical Archives)

This photo, taken in July 1942, shows the XB-36 mockup. Both Northrop and Consolidated found going from the mockup stage to designing a flyable aircraft to be quite a chore. (Consolidated Aircraft Corp./San Diego Aerospace Museum)

Arrangements had been made for express delivery of these engines to Northrop as short a time as ten (10) days ago. Apparently no trouble has occurred on the engine, and it is therefore hard to understand an engine manufacturer not knowing until three (3) weeks before delivery date that delivery will require an additional two (2) months.

There was still considerable work to be accomplished as April drew to a close. The Otis Elevator contract would end on October 31st. Though some Martin effort would continue to the end of 1945, a majority of their effort would also cease at the end of October. Emphasis was on getting the XB-35 into the air and the engineering modification effort associated with the jet powered version of the XB-35, now designated the YB-49. Some assistance would be realized at Northrop with the reduction of the P-61 Black Widow effort which would allow those technical personnel to be transferred onto the big wing.

4360 engines scheduled for May would be delayed for a least two months. The dual rotation gear box thrust bearing was the major problem. Col. Victor R. Haugen, the chief of Aircraft Projects Section at Wright Field, reported to Brig. Gen. Lawrence C. Craigie:

Configuration of the 15 flying wing bombers in late May called for the first XB-35 to be of non-military configuration. The next two were to have the original fire control and armament systems

Lt. Gen. William S. Knudsen (center) of the War Production Board on one of his visits to Northrop Aircraft, Inc. Flanking General Knudsen are Jack Northrop to his left and La Motte T. Cohu, Chairman of the Board and General Manager of NAI, on his right. (Northrop)

The XB-35 engine test stand under construction at the Northrop plant in Hawthorne, California. (Northrop/G. H. Balzer Historical Archives)

installed. Airplanes 4 and 5 were to be modified to the YB-49 configuration. Numbers 6 and 7 were to have the leading edge thermal de-icers installed. The status of airplanes 8 through 15 remained questionable, being contingent on flight test results of the YB-49s. It was recognized at this time that because of the protracted development time, the XB-35 would now "fall far short of present military requirements."

As 1945 came to a close, the project office at Wright Field felt that the 689 Inspection should be scheduled for January 21, 1946. The airplane would still be incomplete at that time, but all safety of flight items would be in place, thus enabling the inspection team to make all necessary recommended safety changes. Wright Field felt these changes could be incorporated in conjunction with the remainder of the airplane construction still to be accomplished.

Delivery of the Pratt & Whitney engines were still unsure in early 1946 and the Aircraft Projects Section at Wright Field let their concern be known.

In May Northrop requested permission to dismantle the B-35 mockup in order to obtain required storage space. Wright Field agreed with the exception that the crew nacelle portion be maintained. That same month the first XB-35 was rolled out and ground engine guns were started. On June 13th Northrop test pilot Max Stanley performed the first taxi tests. About a week later Air Technical Service Command outlined the parameters of the XB-35's

first flight. Operating speed range of the propellers would be 1,800 to 2,200 engine RPM, landing flaps would not be used at any time. Maximum speed would be 200 MPH, maximum flying time would be 60 minutes, and maximum manifold pressure was to be 46 inches.

Into The Air

On June 25th the XB-35 made its maiden flight going from Northrop Field in Hawthorne to Muroc in just 44 minutes and flying at a maximum altitude of 10,000 feet. The Northrop flight test

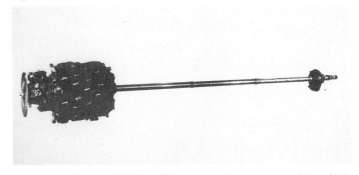

The Pratt & Whitney R-4360 Wasp Major engine with the extension shaft and XB-35 mounts installed. (Western Museum of Flight)

crew consisted of Max R. Stanley as pilot, Fred C. Bretcher as co-pilot, and Orva H. Douglas was the flight engineer. Takeoff from Northrop Field's 5,000 foot runway didn't weigh too heavy on test pilot Max Stanley's mind, as he "had the solemn promise of Jack [Northrop] and Bill [Sears, chief aerodynamicist] that was plenty long enough and there was no need to worry." But as a precaution, Stanley did not make his takeoff into the prevailing winds towards the west but waited for the winds to calm and took off to the east, the direction in which he would have to head to get to Muroc. Stanley has recounted this event:

As I look back on the first flight of the B-35, there is one event that seems to stand out more clearly than anything else. It was an event that led to really the only concern that I had during the entire first take off and first flight. The B-35 was towed into take off position at the end of the runway, and then backed up to within about 3 inches of the fence. Then the engines started and we went through the preflight checklist and the engine runup. While all this was going on, my attention was pretty well all within the cockpit. And when Orva Douglas, the flight engineer, said everything was okay back there and we were ready to go, I looked out on the runway for the first time. And there right in front of me, right in front of this big airplane, was

the biggest jackrabbit I ever saw. As I released the brakes on the airplane and began to roll, to accelerate, the jackrabbit took off down the runway ahead of us. Well, it wasn't long before I noticed that we weren't gaining on him. I thought, 'Holy Toledo!' If we can't catch a damn jackrabbit, we'll never going to get this thing into the air! Fortunately about that time the jackrabbit veered off into the weeds alongside the runway and the take off was accomplished and the flight to Muroc was completed in a fairly uneventful way.

At the conclusion of this historic flight, Lt. Gen. Ira C. Eaker, Deputy Commander of the AAF wired General Carl Spaatz, Commanding General of the AAF, that a "35 minute initial flight successfully completed today flying from factory to Muroc Lake. Reached altitude 10,000 feet. No trouble."

About a week later, on July 3rd, a second flight was achieved in which a maximum speed of 250 mph was reached. During this flight the number one propeller governor operated erratically and the number three governor "hunted" with a variation of about plus or minus 100 rpm. The gear box temperatures were high, but considered satisfactory. The first XB-35 would fly only once again in September 1946, before it was grounded because of the severe, and persistent, propeller governor and gear box problems. By March

Here the Northrop proposed XB-35 tail gun installation has been installed in a B-29 for flight testing. (Northrop/G. H. Balzer Historical Archives)

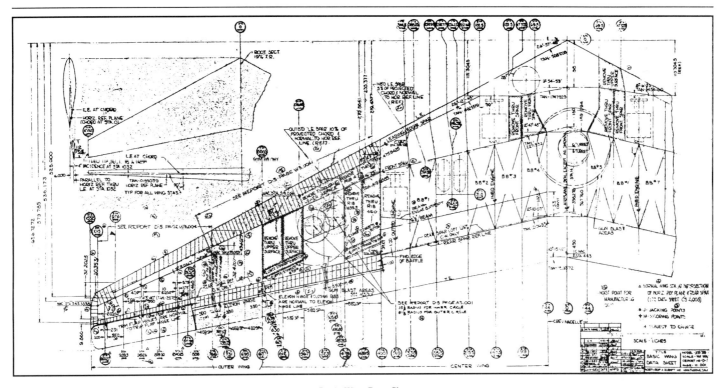

Basic Wing Data Sheet
General Structure, Crew Nacelle

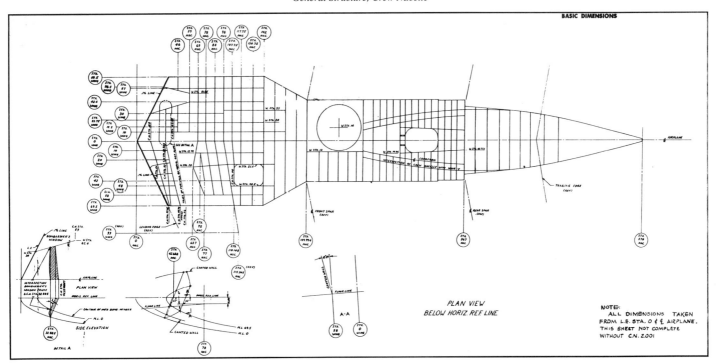

1947, some progress had been made in solving these problems and the XB-35 was back on flight status. But they were not solved. The number one experimental flying wing bomber was only able to get into the air nine times that year. The second XB-35 joined the flight test program when Northrop's flight test crew of Stanley, Bretcher, and Douglas took off from Northrop Field on June 26th. This aircraft, as well as the sole YB-35 to fly, was equipped with operational turrets. Having the same government furnished propellers

and gear boxes, it too was soon having similar problems, making only three more flights in 1947.

As part of the XB-35 flight test program, Max Stanley had to fly a series of stall tests. This veteran test pilot told of his exploits in a symposium in January 1994:

> I ran a series of stall tests with a forward cg. When each time I would stall it, we would move the cg back just a little bit. Finally got

In this March 1945 photo the XB-35 is starting to take shape in final assembly jig number one. (Northrop)

to the point where the behavior of the airplane was erratic. It felt like nobody was in control of this thing. I said, 'I will not continue on with this stall test, including the cg change, unless you provide some way for me to get out of this airplane.' It was very difficult to get into the seat and get out of the seat, even when you were under control. To get out of the seat when the airplane was out of control was an impossibility. Somebody came up with the idea that 'Maybe we can get rid of the canopy.' The canopy on this airplane was fastened to the airframe itself with fiberglass tape around. Somebody had the idea 'We'll imbed a resistance wire in this tape and give it a shot of electricity, it will get real hot and blow off.' We ran a test on this thing. We took a canopy and suspended it between two saw horses, filled it with lead shot to simulate the airload, and on a signal somebody applied the electricity. We waited and waited and waited and finally it began to smoke a little bit. I don't know, it must have been at least five minutes before the thing finally gave way. It turned out to be not a very good idea.

The B-35, as a piston-engined bomber, was no longer in contention as an operational airplane. The B-36, which had its own troubles and was near cancellation a number of times, was faring somewhat better. The XB-36 first flew on August 8, 1946; almost a month and a half after the first XB-35. But, production aircraft would start equipping Strategic Air Command's 7th Bomb Wing at Carswell AFB, Texas, in June 1948 while Northrop was still trying

to get service test aircraft into flying status. That same month a B-36A dropped 72,000 pounds of bombs in a test to demonstrate the aircraft's vast capacity (the B-35 was designed for a maximum bomb load of 40,000 pounds). Combat radius, in nautical miles, was 3,370 for the B-36A while the XB-35 was estimated at 1,300. The greater bomb load and combat radius out weighed the maximum speed at optimum altitude that the XB-35 was estimated to have over the B-36A (381 knots for the XB-35 and 300 knots for the B-36A).

The YB-35 service test program was having even greater difficulties than the experimental aircraft. When Martin finally dropped out of the B-35 design effort, Northrop found itself with very little achieved in the design of the YB-35. With World War II over, downsizing of the military, and drastic cuts in defense budgets, the Army Air Forces, still seeing value in continuing the flying wing bomber project, opted to build six of the first eight YB-35s (YB-35 number two and three were already slated to become YB-49s) to XB-35 specifications. This was to get more wings into flying status sooner. The remaining YB-35s would be to YB specifications, with additional changes added over time, and were redesignated YB-35As.

Northrop would have the YB-35 airframes ready but delivery of government furnished equipment such as propellers, gear boxes, and armament would cause excessive delay. The problems the XB-35s were experiencing with this equipment added to the difficulties. Only one YB-35 would get off the ground. The rest would be

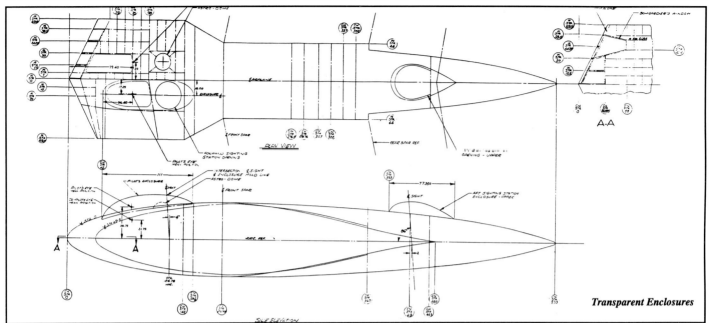

Transparent Enclosures

in storage a good bit of the time awaiting the government furnished equipment or in many phases of modification as their mission was changed. All would be in some state of modification to accommodate jet engines when the entire program was canceled.

In late 1947 the counter-rotating propeller and gear box problems seemed insurmountable. A solution did not seem to be in sight and the most expeditious action seemed to be a change. The dual-rotating propellers and associated gear boxes were to be replaced with a single-rotation four-blade propeller with new gear box. With this change, the two outboard R-4360-17 Wasp Major engines became -45s and the inboard R-4360-21s were redesignated -47s. In February 1948 XB-35 number one made its first flight with its new propeller system. In an attempt to squelch growing skepticism over the project, General Spaatz, who picked up the baton of flying wing bomber support from General Arnold, stated in early January 1948 that failure to obtain flight data in the XB-35 flight test was not considered to be the fault of Northrop because the problems lie with equipment provided by the government.

The change in propellers did not help the project. In the few flights that the two XB-35s and the one YB-35 (which first flew on May 15, 1948) would make in 1948, they found that the new propellers produced excitations which caused cracking in the propeller housings and control surface ribs. A marked decrease in the wing's performance was also noted by the pilots. Other problems were experienced. The auxiliary power unit, or APU, which was government furnished, experienced numerous failures. Design problems were also experienced. Several flights were terminated because of landing gear door failures. Engine cooling fans were also a problem area and the associated ducting needed major redesign.

As the jet-powered YB-49 was seen as the only possible hope in keeping the program alive, and millions of dollars of over runs had occurred in a tight budget economy, the two XB-35s were put in storage in the fall of 1948. That winter it was thought that they might be used for other purposes, but this was soon dropped. XB-35 number one was ferried from Muroc back to the Hawthorne plant where it was accepted by the Air Force on November 22,

Here the night shift has taken over from the day shift in trying to get the aircraft built and into the air. The Second World War was just about over and time was running out for the XB-35 project. (Northrop)

1948. The second experimental airplane followed suit on January 7, 1949. This apparently ended their career as Air Force records show that the first XB-35 accumulated a total of 24 hours in 19 flights while the second had 12 hours in only eight flights.

All contracts on the big Flying Wing programs were over budget and, in 1949, the Air Force was having it's own budget troubles. Congress had slashed budgets and President Truman was pushing a reduction in fighter and bomber wings. In order to keep some of the Flying Wing program going, Air Materiel Command recommended in a February 17th correspondence that the two XB-35s, the one flying YB-35, and one of the YB-35 at Northrop be stripped of all useful items and be scrapped. The remaining funds, it was estimated, would support the EB-35B, YRB-49A, the YB-49 flight test program, and the jet conversion of the remaining YB-35s. Northrop provided an estimate of $52,000 to accomplish the scrapping and on March 7th Headquarters USAF authorized AMC to accomplish this action. On July 20th the sole flying YB-35 was scrapped and in August the two XB-35 and a YB-35 were scrapped.

Typical outer wing construction is visible in this photo submitted as part of regular progress reports by Northrop. (Northrop/Smithsonian Institution)

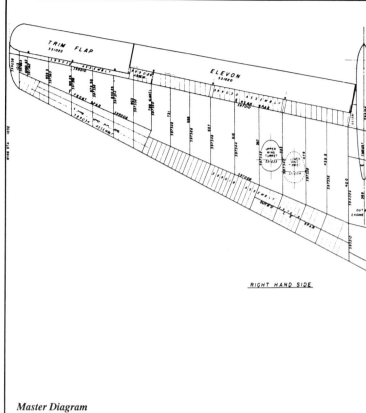

Master Diagram

Though Jack Northrop's passion was the flying wing, he did have other interests. Sitting on his desk is a lightweight anchor which he designed and was produced under the Northrophill name (Blanche Hill was his partner in this venture). (Northrop/Western Museum of Flight)

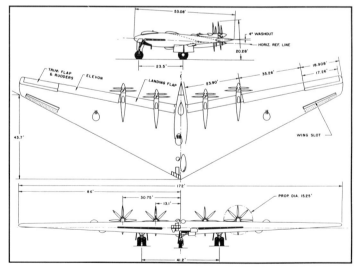

Three View of XB-35 No. 2

Opposite: First YB-35, and only example to fly, is taking form in this photo from a April 1946 progress report photo. (Northrop)

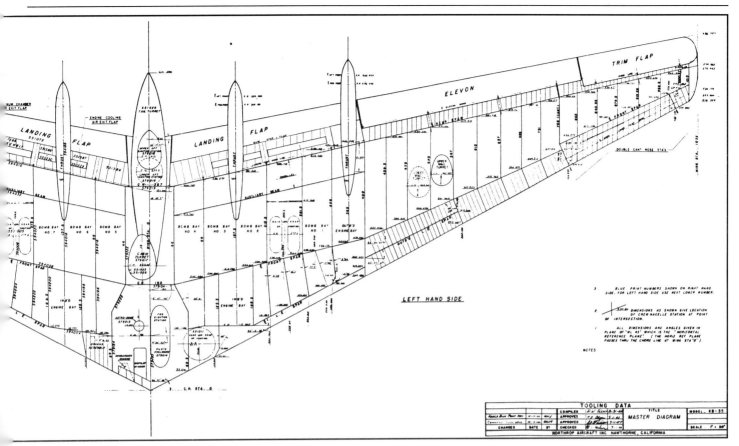

LEFT HAND SIDE

First XB-35, Northrop construction number 1484, is shown here nearing completion. Note the structural shapes which are to simulate the turrets which, like all tactical equipment, were not included in the first article. (Northrop)

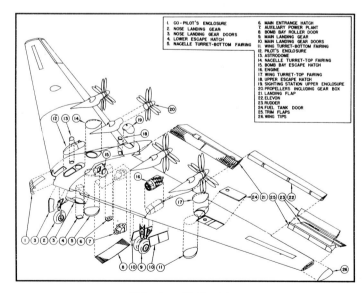

1. CO-PILOT'S ENCLOSURE	6. MAIN ENTRANCE HATCH
2. NOSE LANDING GEAR	7. AUXILIARY POWER PLANT
3. NOSE LANDING GEAR DOORS	8. BOMB BAY ROLLER DOOR
4. LOWER ESCAPE HATCH	9. MAIN LANDING GEAR
5. NACELLE TURRET-BOTTOM FAIRING	10. MAIN LANDING GEAR DOORS
	11. WING TURRET-BOTTOM FAIRING
	12. PILOT'S ENCLOSURE
	13. ASTRODOME
	14. NACELLE TURRET-TOP FAIRING
	15. BOMB BAY ESCAPE HATCH
	16. ENGINE
	17. WING TURRET-TOP FAIRING
	18. UPPER ESCAPE HATCH
	19. SIGHTING STATION UPPER ENCLOSURE
	20. PROPELLERS INCLUDING GEAR BOX
	21. LANDING FLAP
	22. ELEVON
	23. RUDDER
	24. FUEL TANK DOOR
	25. TRIM FLAPS
	26. WING TIPS

Major Assembly Breakdown

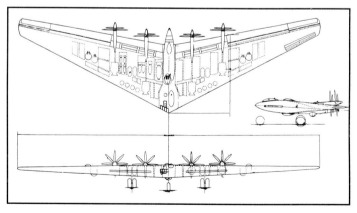

XB-35 Interior Layout

This photo, like the preceding one, was taken April 1946. Here the first XB-35 has just been rolled out from the production building and is still on the dollies used to move these giant flying wings through production. In the background are two Northrop P-61 Black Widows. The one to the left, painted olive drab and grey with yellow cowls is a P-61A used for Northrop flight testing. The other, in the center of the photo, is the first P-61C. (Northrop)

The first XB-35 being prepared to commence engine run and taxi tests. Note that a six-bladed counter-rotating propeller has replaced the standard eight-bladed configuration on the left outboard engine. This configuration was only used in ground tests. (Northrop)

A. M. Schwartz, Northrop's chief of structures, stands on the pilot's seat to get a good view from within the pilot's canopy. From this angle it can be clearly seen how the pilot's position is offset to the left of the aircraft's center line and the copilot and bombardier are to the right of the center line. (Northrop/Smithsonian Institution)

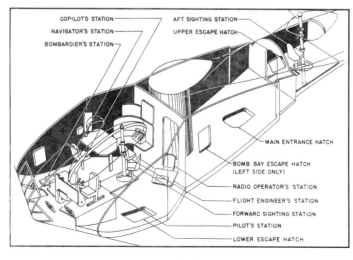

COPILOT'S STATION
NAVIGATOR'S STATION
BOMBARDIER'S STATION
AFT SIGHTING STATION
UPPER ESCAPE HATCH
MAIN ENTRANCE HATCH
BOMB BAY ESCAPE HATCH (LEFT SIDE ONLY)
RADIO OPERATOR'S STATION
FLIGHT ENGINEER'S STATION
FORWARD SIGHTING STATION
PILOT'S STATION
LOWER ESCAPE HATCH

Crew Stations

Jack Northrop speaks to an audience of Northrop workers, families, and others at the May 1946 Family Day open house. Mr. Northrop strived to make Northrop Aircraft, Inc. "A good place to work."

The main attraction at the 1946 Family Day was XB-35 number one. By this time the aircraft had been painted overall with silver paint. (Northrop)

Shown in this perspective is the flat construction of the bombardier's station glass. (Northrop/Stu Luce)

From this rear view the two different propeller installations then being tested and the upper cooling air exit flaps are clearly visible. (Northrop)

*The flight controls along the trailing edge of the XB-35, from outboard in, were split-flap rudders attached to pitch trimmers, landing flaps, and then the elevons.
(Northrop)*

To Jack Northrop, it must have seemed that his dream was finally coming true as the giant flying wing bomber took to the air from Northrop Field on June 25, 1946. (Northrop)

Taxi tests began on May 22, 1946. According to an Associated Press news release test pilot Max Stanley stated that the plane, moving under its own power for the first time, handled "very successfully." Some sources indicate that taxi tests started in April, which is when engine runs began. (San Diego Aerospace Museum and Northrop)

On their way to Muroc Army Air Field in California's Mojave Desert. XB-35 number one, AAF serial number 42-13603, took only 44 minutes to reach its destination on this historic flight. Crewing the big plane were Max Stanley, pilot; Fred Bretcher, copilot; and Orva Douglas, flight engineer. (Northrop)

The welcoming. From left to right are Max Stanley, Fred C. Bretcher, Col. Signa Gilkey (Muroc's commanding officer) and Orva Douglas. Stanley immediately phoned Jack Northrop to report a very successful flight. (Northrop/Western Museum of Flight)

Jack Northrop welcomes test pilot Max Stanley after XB-35 number one's second flight on July 3, 1946. Stanley reached a speed of 250 mph on this flight. Trouble with the governors occurred on this flight, which would plague the B-35 program throughout its life. (Northrop)

About two weeks later, on August 8th, the competing XB-36 also took to the air for its maiden flight. (Consolidated Vultee Aircraft Corp./San Diego Aerospace Museum)

General Kenney, Strategic Air Command's first commander, on the left and General Arnold, in the center, were strong supporters for the B-35 program, but they realized that more of the big wings had to get into the air if the program had any chance to get into production. (Western Museum of Flight)

The Northrop ground crew pose with the second XB-35 around the time of its first flight (June 26, 1947). (Northrop/G. H. Balzer Historical Archives)

A nice front five of the second XB-35 (AAF serial number 42-38323). The installation of wing and tail turrets distinguished this plane from the first XB-35. (Northrop/G. H. Balzer Historical Archives)

XB-35 takes to the air from Muroc Army Air Field. Flight testing with these aircraft would be quite limited due to persistent, and seemingly unsolvable, engine gear box and propeller governor problems. (Northrop)

In this rear view of the second XB-35 the gun ports in the wing and tail turrets are visible. (Northrop/G. H. Balzer Historical Archives)

Preparing for a test flight. Only the pilot rode in the high seat (which moved up and down) in the bubble. The copilot and bombardier stations were at lower levels (sometimes referred to as "the sump"). (Northrop)

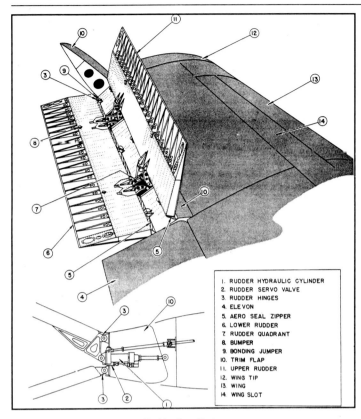

1.	RUDDER HYDRAULIC CYLINDER
2.	RUDDER SERVO VALVE
3.	RUDDER HINGES
4.	ELEVON
5.	AERO SEAL ZIPPER
6.	LOWER RUDDER
7.	RUDDER QUADRANT
8.	BUMPER
9.	BONDING JUMPER
10.	TRIM FLAP
11.	UPPER RUDDER
12.	WING TIP
13.	WING
14.	WING SLOT

Rudder Installation

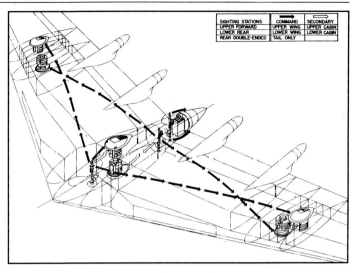

Turret and Sight Installation

REF	NAME	REF	NAME	REF	NAME
1	NOSE SIGHT BOX	11	UPPER CONTROL BOX	21	TAIL COMPUTER
2	PANEL ASSEMBLY	12	ENGINEER'S JUNCTION PANEL	22	LOWER COMPUTER
3	SINGLE PARALLAX COMPUTER	13	TERMINAL BLOCK ASSEMBLY	23	UPPER AND LOWER LEFT O.W. SERVO AMPLIFIERS
4	NOSE JUNCTION BOX	14	SWITCH	24	CAPACITOR BOX
5	TRIPLE PARALLAX COMPUTER	15	PRESSURIZED PLUG "A-B"	25	TAIL AMPLIDYNE JUNCTION BOX
6	UPPER JUNCTION BOX	16	PRESSURIZED PLUG "Q"	26	PRESSURE PLUG "G"
7	PANEL ASSEMBLY	17	PRESSURIZED PLUG "A-A"	27	LOWER CENTER TURRET SERVO AMPLIFIER
8	NOSE CONTROL BOX	18	CENTER AMPLIDYNE JUNCTION BOX	28	TRIPLE PARALLAX COMPUTER
9	COMPUTER VOLTAGE REGULATOR	19	UPPER AND LOWER CENTER TURRET AMPLIDYNES	29	TAIL SERVO AMPLIFIER
10	ALTITUDE AND AIRSPEED HANDSET	20	UPPER CENTER TURRET SERVO AMPLIFIER	30	UPPER AND LOWER RIGHT O.W. SERVO AMPLIFIER
				31	LOWER JUNCTION BOX "B"
				32	TAIL JUNCTION BOX
				33	LOWER JUNCTION BOX "A"
				34	TAIL MOUNT AMPLIDYNE
				35	PANEL ASSEMBLY
				36	LOWER CONTROL BOX
				37	D.C. LIMITER PANEL
				38	TAIL CONTROL BOX
				39	SWITCH
				40	PANEL
				41	TAIL BOOSTER CONTROL BOX
				42	PRESSURIZED PLUG "N"
				43	AMPLIDYNES
				44	AMPLIDYNE JUNCTION BOX
				45	PANEL ASSEMBLY

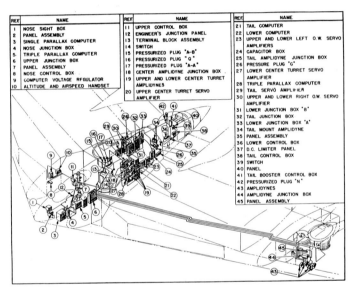

Armament Equipment Wiring Diagram

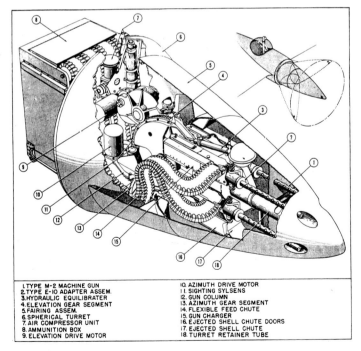

1. TYPE M-2 MACHINE GUN	10. AZIMUTH DRIVE MOTOR
2. TYPE E-10 ADAPTER ASSEM.	11. SIGHTING SYLSENS
3. HYDRAULIC EQUILIBRATER	12. GUN COLUMN
4. ELEVATION GEAR SEGMENT	13. AZIMUTH GEAR SEGMENT
5. FAIRING ASSEM.	14. FLEXIBLE FEED CHUTE
6. SPHERICAL TURRET	15. GUN CHARGER
7. AIR COMPRESSOR UNIT	16. EJECTED SHELL CHUTE DOORS
8. AMMUNITION BOX	17. EJECTED SHELL CHUTE
9. ELEVATION DRIVE MOTOR	18. TURRET RETAINER TUBE

Tail Turret

In flight the large flying wing bomber was quite beautiful. (Northrop)

A family portrait. XB-35 number one with one of the N-9Ms to its left await their turn as one of the YB-49s climbs to altitude overhead. (Edwards AFB History Office)

The sole YB-35 is accompanied by a P-61 chase plane during one of its test flights. Northrop chief photographer Roy Wolford got many good shots from this plane. (Northrop/Smithsonian Institution)

A B-17G and the YB-35 fly in formation on about May 1948. (Northrop/San Diego Aerospace Museum)

Above: Twin .50 cal. machine guns in the raised position in the top turret of the right wing. (Northrop/G. H. Balzer Historical Archives)

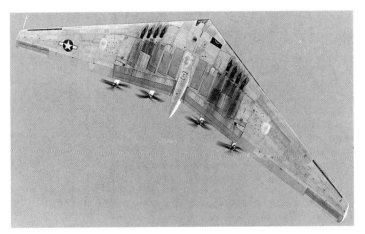

Above and right: Bottom view of the first XB-35 and the YB-35. Besides having armament, the YB-35 was the only one of the three flying B-35 aircraft to carry "buzz" numbers. (Northrop, YB-35 via San Diego Aerospace Museum)

Above and below: XB-35 on the Muroc ramp. Col. Signa Gilkey, Muroc's commanding officer (in the center), visiting the flying wing operations. (Northrop)

The three propeller-driven B-35s spent their last months back at the Northrop plant. Initially they were to be converted to jet and/or turboprop but finally they, and one of the non-flyable YB-35s, were ordered to be stripped for useable parts and then to be scrapped in order to save money. The project was already grossly overrun and the savings realized from scrapping these four airplanes would enable other aspects of the flying wing bomber/reconnaissance program to continue. (Northrop/San Diego Aerospace Museum)

Because of the constant problems with the counter-rotating propeller system, the two XB-35s were modified to carry the single-rotation, four-bladed propeller as the YB-35. Here the first XB-35 is parked along side the two YB-49s at Muroc. (Northrop)

Opposite: Will missiles doom the bomber? That was not one of the B-35's problems. By the time this magazine came out all three flying B-35s were scheduled for jet or turboprop conversion programs. (Northrop)

THE TRUE STORY OF PEARL HARBOR page 15

FLYING

JANUARY 1949 · 25 CENTS

WILL MISSILES DOOM BOMBERS?
page 20

★

JOBS IN AVIATION
page 26

★

JET-PROPELLED LIGHTPLANE
page 24

Eight Jets Roar in First YB-49 Take-off

MAX STANLEY, PILOT

NORTHROP'S GIANT FLYING WING YB-49 EIGHT-JET bomber roared out of Northrop Field on its first test flight, October 21 at 9:46 a. m. Thirty-four minutes later the big airplane settled to a normal landing at Muroc Army Air Field 85 miles away where it is now undergoing a series of extensive flight tests. The plane was airborne after a takeoff run of 3500 feet. Built to the efficient Flying Wing design the YB-49 has a wingspread of 172 feet and a gross weight of 100 tons. Its eight J-35-A5 engines have a combined thrust output equal to 32,000 horsepower.

Chapter 8

A DREAM DASHED
YB-49 Development and Flight Test

In the fall of 1944 the Flying Wing program was years behind in its development and cost overruns were skyrocketing. Northrop's partnership with Martin was a failure, and the design effort was in a shambles. The AAF and Northrop knew that they had to get the big wing into the air soon and in numbers. By this time it was also realized that the 1941 design had been passed up by technological advances over the intervening years, particularly with the turbojet engine becoming a practical mode of propulsion.

Northrop and the AAF discussed two routes the program might take. First, to get more airplanes into the air it was decided to build the first six YB-35s to XB-35 specifications. The other was to investigate the feasibility of replacing the reciprocating engines with jets (apparently the AAF had initiated conversations with Northrop concerning using jet engines in the summer of 1944). It was felt that the piston-engine planes would be good for proof of concept purposes and that any idea of producing them was now out of the question. Because the YB-35 design effort was so woefully behind, it was decided that all emphasis would be on producing the new total of eight XB-35s and incorporating jet power plants in two of the YB-35 airframes. Maj. Gen. Oliver P. Echols of Air Technical Service Command would remark at this time, "That assures us of getting something!"

A telephone conversation between Col. Donald L. Putt at Wright Field and General Echols on November 9, 1944 gives some insight into the situation with the jet-powered wing:

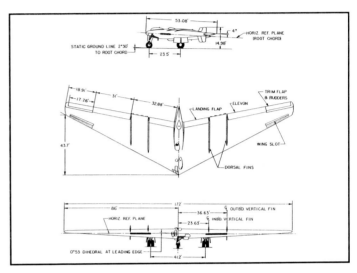

YB-49 Three View

Echols: Have you talked to them about the jet business?

Putt: Yes, we've talked to Jack [Northrop] about that and we're going to give him all the engine data, and he's going to make a little study as to the possibility of actually getting the things into the airplane. I thought perhaps they had already done that in view of his discussion with you.

Echols: You see, his proposal is to leave out two bomb bays. Well, I hate to see the ship come out with less bomb carrying capacity than the B-29, you see. I think that if we could . . . [have] three bomb bays, that would give us 24,000 [lbs. bomb load]. To cut down to 16,000 [lbs.], that's lower than the 29.

Then he thought, (he didn't know) with the TG-180 [jet engines] he might be able to stack them. Getting rid of turbos and one thing and another, he could get the four in. The thing that intrigues me about this is this business of having eight and cutting out four and you begin to get three.

That looks like it's really the first fellow that's come in with a solution to this thing that's been worrying us so much.

I think there is a gem of an idea there that may pay off.

What do you think about his [Northrop's] speed when he begins to get up in some of those figures?

Putt: Well, the preliminary report of the aircraft lab based on the data that he had submitted back here in August, they seemed to think that the performance was reasonable.

The race for the first post war long range heavy bomber had gone to the B-36 out of default—the XB-35's counter-rotating, eight-bladed propellers with their governors and gear boxes provided unsolvable problems. More time, and money, could not be allocated as the jet-powered bomber was already on its way into the Air Force's inventory. (Convair/San Diego Aerospace Museum)

Echols: Well, he had some 475 mph and something. That's all guns and everything on it.

Putt: Yes, that's right, and there may be some possibility if he got a little of that off it can even do better.

Echols: Well, what I thought was that if I told him I didn't want to do it now, but as we go along, then take a look at maybe taking off some of the guns. They may try to get 500 miles an hour.

The point was brought up on account of the [wing] thickness.

Putt: Yes, it is a little thick, but we're pouring quite a bit of power in there. The thing that worries me probably more than what the drag is going to do is how compressibility will affect the control.

Echols: Well, Don, will you go ahead with that and sort of keep me informed from time to time?

Putt: Yes, sir, we're giving Jack all the installation data of both the engines and the latest fuel consumptions and what not. He's going to make some preliminary lay outs just to see if it's feasible to fit it in.

Dr. William R. Sears, Northrop's chief aerodynamicist for most of the 1940s, would remark in 1980 concerning the conversion effort to jet power:

The simplifications afforded by these [jet] engines in comparison with the complications [of the R-4360s] . . . were almost unbelievable, and it is, naturally, the 49's that one remembers with pride . . . They were, or course, modified XB-35 airframes; nothing about them had been optimized for the turbojet power-plants or the transonic flight regime that they afforded. The structure bore the compromises inflicted by the buried air-cooled engines, propeller shafts and gear boxes, etc. . . . Four small vertical fins, with low-aspect-ratio extensions forward, were added to replace the side-force and directional-stability contributions of the propellers and shaft housings of the XB-35 and to inhibit spanwise boundary-layer flow.

Within months Northrop's design team was working on what was now designated the YB-49. The second and third YB-35 airframes had been selected for the powerplant modification and initial design data was being passed to Air Technical Service Command. In late May 1945 the Command issued an evaluation of the project. Their conclusions were that the TG-180 powered wing should be restricted in its maximum performance because of limi-

Jack Northrop's flying wing bomber only had one chance in the mid-1940s and that was as a jet propelled airplane. But because of the performance, including the high rate of fuel burned by these new powerplants, the jet version of the B-35, now designated the YB-49, would be in the medium range bomber classification. Here the second YB-35, on the right, has nearly completed its metamorphosis into the first YB-49. On the left is the third YB-35 soon to become the second YB-49. (Northrop)

Originally designed to have a tail gun turret as its sole armament, this was soon replaced with a fibreglas tailcone. (Northrop)

ing gears for the alternator drive on the TG-180 jet engine was causing some headaches, and Northrop was having difficulty in finding space within the design for their installation as well as that of a hydraulic pump on each engine.

As 1946 progressed, so did the jet modification effort on the big wing. Air Materiel Command felt that the projected performance figures for the YB-49 were looking good. By May it was projected that the first YB-49 would be delivered in September 1947. The Command felt that at the time of delivery it would be the only jet bomber available and would be valuable for use as a "research" airplane.

Engineering progressed at a quicker pace than anticipated and in August, 1946, Northrop requested that the delivery of the TG-180-A7 engines being built by Chevrolet (they were a General Electric design), as well as reversing gear necessary for the TG-180 unit and associated constant speed drive, be accelerated. The answer came nearly two months later, delivery uncertain! The problem was that General Motors was in the process of changing production of the engines from their Chevrolet division to their Allison unit.

As the B-35 project trudged along, yet another conference was held in October 1946 to discuss the configuration and disposition of the 13 service test YB-35 airframes. One of the recommendations to come out was for a preliminary study to estimate the work and cost that would be associated with modifying the last five YB-35 airframes into YB-49 configuration.

In November the question arose concerning the B-35/B-49 aircraft's bomb carrying capability. The Assistant Chief of Air Staff for Requirements and Materiel replied that the bomb bay limita-

tations of structural integrity and a limiting Mach number of .65 caused by an extensive separation flow and elevon ineffectiveness.

To compensate for these restrictions a number of recommendations were suggested. Because the structural members had not been tested in combination compounded by the constantly changing loading requirements which affected the previous stress analyses, they felt that one of the airplanes should be static tested. To eliminate the speed restrictions in the near future, they felt that one of the YB-49s should maintain two of the R-4360 engines and have only four TG-180s installed. The thick wing of the YB-35, going from 19% at the root to 18% at the tip, needed to be thinner in order to resolve the separation flow and elevon ineffectiveness problems by increasing the critical Mach number.

Change order number 11 to YB-35 contract W545 ac-3390, dated June 1, 1945, officially authorized conversion of YB-35 numbers two and three to the YB-49 configuration. The YB-49s differed from the XB/YB-35s in a number of ways. All armament were deleted except for the four .50 cal. machine gun turret in the tail. The bomb bays had been reduced from eight to six; this was necessary to provide adequate space for the eight turbojet engines and additional fuel for the fuel guzzling engines. As noted earlier, four vertical fins, projecting above and below the wing (no moveable control surfaces) and wing fences were added. The leading edge of the wing was highly modified to accommodate the air intakes for the jet engines.

Engineering on the jet-powered flying wing bomber continued through 1945, being about 20% complete by year's end. But, as with the B-35 program, required government furnished equipment was once again an obstacle to be overcome. Design of the revers-

The size of the YB-49's elevon is put into perspective with this worker standing next to it. It measures 34 feet six inches long. (Northrop/San Diego Aerospace Museum)

Above and opposite: First Flight of YB-49 number one occurred on October 21, 1947. Once again test pilot Max Stanley was at the controls while Fred C. Bretcher was copilot and O. H. Douglas was the flight engineer. (Northrop)

tions of the flying wing bombers had been addressed at a Bomb Conference held in January 1945. It was felt that the service test (YB-35s and YB-49s) aircraft were being procured to evaluate the flying wing configuration. It was stated that further procurement of the B-49 jet-powered bomber would "be predicated on its ability to carry the atom bomb." Apparently at this time there was some thought that 11 YB-49s might be proposed under fiscal year 1948 funding and that these aircraft would be atomic bomb capable.

The Procurement Division's Bomber Branch at Wright Field issued a revised first flight schedule for the YB-35s and YB-49s in April 1947. They stated that all the aircraft would have completed their first flight by June 1948 if all government furnished equipment were received on time. In actuality, the lack of the government equipment would delay the first flight of the sole YB-35 to fly as well as the two YB-49s. At this same time period, the tail turret was eliminated from the two YB-49s then being produced, and Northrop was directed to make tail cones instead. In May the government informed Northrop that the automatic pilots were being deleted from the YB-35s and YB-49s because none would be available in the foreseeable future. (Northrop was to maintain provisions in the airframes for this government equipment.)

Northrop felt that the YB-49 was "originally conceived as a purely experimental jet-powered version of the XB-35" in which the existing XB-35 structure was revised only to the extent required for the installation of the TG-180 engines and additional fuel capacity. There had been no attempt to increase the structural strength of the basic XB-35 airframe, and Northrop felt that certain flight

restrictions should be imposed on the YB-49. Air Materiel Command disagreed though Northrop broached the subject on a number of occasions. One might wonder what impact this decision had on the destruction of both YB-49s at later dates.

Once again engine delays were impacting first flight. The TG-180-A7, now designated J-35-A-5, were to be reworked to a J-35-A-15 configuration, which produced 3,750 pounds of static thrust. Availability of other government furnished equipment such as the constant speed drive and auxiliary power plant also continued to impede progress.

The 689 inspection for the first YB-49 was conducted on September 18, 1947. The inspection was concerned with features different from the YB-35 such as powerplant and associated components, engine instruments and controls, electrical system, and structural changes. The plane was complete except for government engine starters which had not been received yet. The inspection team found the plane to be in "excellent condition and complete in accordance with the detail specification." At this time the second YB-49 was about 95% complete. J35-A-15 engine modifications were still going on.

Flight Test Begins

On September 29th the sleek YB-49 was rolled out and ground testing of engines and other systems commenced. Northrop's flight test crew of Max Stanley, Fred Bretcher, and O. H. Douglas performed the first taxi test on October 20th. The following day this

same crew flew the YB-49 for the first time. The 34 minute flight from Northrop Field to Muroc was uneventful. The crew found the performances of the YB-49 and the XB-35 to be as different as night and day. The lack of noise and vibration was quite noticeable. Performancewise it was all that they had hoped for in the Flying Wing.

As the XB-35 spent most of its time on the ground, the YB-49 was flying. General flying characteristics were quite good. Northrop's concern that the jet powered flying wing which received minimal design analysis associated with the changeover from piston to jet engines might suffer from this, proved true. On the second flight the rear nose wheel door blew off at 280 indicated air speed. When the pilot attempted to put the gear down for landing, the nose wheel remained in the up and locked position. Fortunately he was able to release the gear using the emergency system, and the hour and a half flight ended without further incident. It would be common practice throughout the YB-49 test program for the pilot to pull up sharply, or reduce power drastically, immediately after takeoff to keep the airspeed down in order to reduce the danger of damaging the landing gear doors which had not been modified for the higher speed of the jet-propelled bomber.

On December 11th the seventh flight was scheduled to determine rate of climb, check operation of the emergency elevon electrical system, and to perform speed vs. power runs. At 300 mph the time to climb from an altitude of 6,000 feet to 13,000 was 3 minutes 19.5 seconds. During "gentle maneuvers," the emergency elevon system exhibited an undesirable interconnection of control movement between stick and wheel. It was reported that control by the electrical system was awkward, but it was believed to be ad-

equate for normal flight and landing conditions if excess stick forces and interconnection of control movement were corrected.

Air Force Major Robert L. Cardenas became the Air Forces' chief test pilot on the YB-49 project in December 1947. This was actually his second stint with Northrop. He had been selected quite some time earlier to participate in the Phase I Flight Test program of the XB-35. Phase I was usually flown by the contractor but arrangements were made for Cardenas to fly with Northrop's Max Stanley. Arriving at Muroc from Wright Field in August 1946, Major Cardenas made a number of flights in the N-9MA and N-9MB between August 14th and 20th. But within a month he was assigned to head up the group attempting to break the sound barrier in Bell's X-1. This was accomplished on October 14, 1947 and by December of that year he was back on the flying wing program. Max Stanley checked Cardenas out in the YB-49 during three flights that month.

The second YB-49 joined the flight test program on January 13, 1948. This time Major Cardenas and an all Air Force crew flew the plane from Hawthrone to Muroc. Like the first YB-49's initial flight, this one was flawless also. This was good news for the program. General Spaatz' comment that month that the failure to get flight data on the XB-35s to date was not considered Northrop Aircraft's fault – that is, it was not an inherent flaw in the wing design but caused by design and delivery problems with government furnished equipment – served to buoy the spirits of Northrop even more. This was a good month for both the flying wing program and Jack Northrop. With the performance of the YB-49 to date being so promising, Jack Northrop must have felt that the world would soon see what he always knew, the flying wing was not only practical, but superior to "conventional" aircraft design. In this same

Here Northrop chief photographer Roy Wolford, in the P-61's gunners seat, prepares to photograph the YB-49 on its first flight. Unfortunately, an engine fire forced Wolford and pilot L. A. "Slim" Perrett to bail out. (Northrop)

month Jack Northrop got his first ride in the YB-49. All seemed to be going well.

Air Force crews were quite active in the YB-49 flight test program. During a talk in early 1994 at the Planes of Fame museum near Chino, California, retired Air Force Brig. Gen. Cardenas described the early test program:

> We started the tests for performance first. We were doing okay, had my own tests. The stall series, had first stall, power off at 40,000 feet, attitude kept increasing, you pilots know what a stall warning is, you begin to get a little nibble, well I got no nibble, I got nothing. Just the attitude kept increasing. Suddenly it dawned on me that I was down to 80-90 knots and the rate of descent was going down, and I had no control. I tried the controls and they didn't work. I knew I couldn't go over the top so I tried to go over the side – didn't matter, the clam shells didn't do anything. So about the time I was trying to decide what the hell happened, it flipped over backwards. I knew how to get out of a spin, I knew how to get out of many things, but I had never been taught how to get out of that. But the designers for that '49, I don't know who ever designed the interior cockpit, but at that moment I could have kissed him because they put the throttles up here [motioning up in the air about his head]. Now normally the throttles are down here; well they had the throttles up here. When it went over backwards the centrifugal force put my hands up in the air, and I was able to reach one throttle and get 100% power and get out of it and recovered at about 1,000 feet off the ground. I immediately called my boss, Boyd, and told him the stall series were completed. I wrote a report. The airplane did not give you a stall warning. At slow speeds you would encounter a rather odd aerodynamic and at high speeds you might encounter inertial coupling that would be more severe. So I said it should be placarded against intentional stalls. You didn't really need to stall this airplane.

> Because one of the toughest jobs in the airplane was landing it, not because it was hard but just power off, you didn't need the flaps because the ground effect of that huge wing, more than twice as big as the little one, kept you afloat like a surfer. It was like surfing down to the ground. But then they put the clam shells out on the wing tips, and this was an odd airplane. You could shut both of the rudders at the same time; this was normal. I used to win a lot of money from the troops on the ground on spot landings. Because I could come in floating on that air surface and when I wanted to touch down, I would just hit both rudders at the same time and plot it down where I wanted it.

By mid-March the first YB-49 had accomplished 27 flights. The pilots found it flew more like a fighter, out turning its P-80 chase plane on numerous occasions. Because of the clean design of the all-wing bomber, the pilots found that it accelerated very rapidly and decelerated very slowly. Problems with the auxiliary power plants (also true for the B-35 program) and low reliability of the J-35 engines would be constant problems throughout the program.

In March the second YB-49 performed the first bombing tests. The crew was all Northrop except for the bombardier from Air Materiel Command. He brought along his Norden bomb sight, which he wouldn't let Max Stanley or the rest of the crew take a look at – secrecy, and all that. The first mission was flown on the 12th. Because of poor weather over the bombing range, only practice runs were made without dropping any bombs. Three days later they were in the air again. Only dry runs were flown again. Problems with the number two bomb bay door not completely opening and the number seven door failing to function properly prevented dropping ordnance on this flight. With repairs accomplished, they went aloft again on the 18th. A report by the Air Force Inspector In Charge at Muroc Sub-Office described this flight as "satisfactorily accomplished" and "was considered highly satisfactory by the crew." A final bombing mission was flown on March 22nd. Not much is known of it except for a brief statement in an Air Force report: "Seven satisfactory runs." Apparently the airplane was then grounded for an engine change in preparation for a "special project" and the beginning of Phase II testing by Air Force crews.

Jack Northrop was always conscious of the right publicity at the right time. In the early 1940s he was concerned with news leaks on the N-1M and inquired with the Air Corps on a regular basis concerning the proper release of information. The same held true with the XB-35 in the mid-1940s. Reality, in the case of the XB/YB-35's poor showing in flight test, was sometimes lost in the potential that Northrop saw in the wing design. In March of 1948 he suggested to the Air Force that a program be set up to break the current world records using the XB-35 and YB-49. Because of the reduction in performance and increased ground and flight vibration that the three flying B-35s were experiencing with the single-rotation four-bladed propellers and the newness of the YB-49 in the flight test program, the Air Force recommended that additional testing was required prior to any such undertaking.

Northrop attempted to show, if on paper only, that this flying wing design was superior. In January 1948 he stated that the B-35 would equal the range of the B-36, fly at higher speeds, and require only two-thirds weight and two-thirds the power of the B-36. He proclaimed that the B-35 offered "greater performance per dollar of first cost" and that at equal ranges, speeds, and bomb loads, the flying wing would require only half the fuel necessary for the B-36. The use of the flying wing bomber would double the striking force for a given expenditure.

One of the high points in the YB-49 flight test program occurred on April 26, 1948. The Northrop flight test crew of Max Stanley, Fred Bretcher, Orva Douglas and Don Swift, along with Air Force Captain Jay D. Wethe, flew two "round robin" circuits of Muroc-Bakersfield-Fresno-Oakland-Fresno-Bakersfield-Muroc-Riverside-Blythe-Phoenix-Blythe-Riverside-Muroc followed by a Muroc to Oakland to Muroc flight. This flight pattern was intended to reduce wind effect. A similar flight was attempted three days earlier but was terminated because of a cabin pressure valve. The flight took an elapsed time of 9.5 hours (a record length of time for jet powered aircraft); 6.5 of those hours were flown at 40,000 feet. The aircraft carried a simulated bomb load of 6,000 pounds. Both an auxiliary power unit failure and an engine failure were experienced; the YB-49 flew two hours with one engine out. Ground mileage was estimated to be 3,007 at an average ground speed of 330 knots.

Though the plane set records for jets for both endurance and time at altitude, there were a couple of limiting factors from the start. The gross takeoff weight for the mission was limited to 192,000 pounds, rather that the design gross of 213,500, because the aircraft had not been static tested. And a maximum altitude of 40,000 feet was imposed because of the auxiliary power unit, which was the main source of electrical alternating current.

With the success of this long range mission, a mission with a 10,000 pound simulated bomb load was set for May 12th. General Hoyt S. Vandenberg, Air Force Chief of Staff, sent his congratulations to Jack Northrop on his work on the B-49 and the results of the long range flight.

In mid-May the Phase I flight test program concluded. YB-49 number one (42-102367) had flown 33 times and accumulated 47 hours and 44 minutes and the second aircraft (42-102368) had accomplished 20 flights, accounting for 44 hours and 54 minutes. Phase II would be flown by the Air Force. These test flights would concentrate on stability and control of the aircraft. At this same time the Air Force's job of chief pilot on the YB-49 changed hands.

Major Cardenas had received permission to finish his aeronautical engineering studies at the University of Southern California and had nominated his friend Capt. Glen Edwards to take his

In flight the YB-49 was not only quite eye appealing, but most pilots found it handled more like a much smaller plane than as the large bomber that it was. (Northrop)

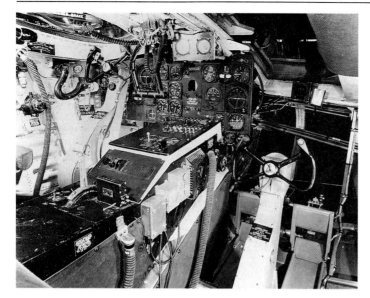

A comparison of the pilot and copilot stations in the YB-49 (on the left) and the XB-35 (on the right). The copilot, his station is on the right in each photo, could neither takeoff nor land the aircraft and did not have engine controls at his station. The pilot had one throttle for each (left and right) set of four engines in the YB-49. In the XB/YB-35 he had individual throttles for each of the four engines. (Northrop)

place. Edwards seemed to be the perfect pilot for the job, having a graduate degree in stability and control from Princeton University. The first flight under Phase II took place on May 20th (the 34th flight for YB-49 number one) and was also Capt. Edwards' familiarization and checkout flight.

During the first two weeks of Phase II, testing the program went along without incident. A total of 11 flights, accounting for 27 hours and 43 minutes of flight time, was logged by the two aircraft. At least two of these flights were familiarization flights for Air Force aircrew, the rest were "performance" flights. The Air Force crews reported findings which had earlier been documented by Northrop, in some cases as warnings. Some of these findings included, ". . . that the airplane had not been reconfigured to handle jet engines. Landing gear extension and retraction were too slow, the electrical system was inadequate, bomb bays had to be pressurized to keep auxiliary power units running," etc. Other items included the fact that the canopy was bolted down and no escape mechanism was provided. The control system also caused severe vibrations, thus making the plane difficult to handle. Fuel cells leaked, which they felt was due to lack of baffling. They also felt that the aircraft sank in a nose-high position instead of "stalling properly." Overall, Air Materiel Command realized that these items were due to the YB-49 being just a test bed for jet engines and not a "designed" jet bomber. Overall performance to date was encouraging.

Tragic Event

With the success of the program to date, Air Materiel Command was pushing for purchases of bomber versions, though the emphasis was on a photo reconnaissance adaptation. The present flying examples needed a number of items incorporated before that model could be considered a tactical aircraft. Included were de-icing equipment, climatization, autopilot, refueling system, armament, radar, and camera. A number of items already part of the

aircraft needed extensive redesign. These included the constant speed drive, trim flap actuator, engine bays, bomb bay doors, landing gear, and engines.

Disaster struck on June 5th when the second YB-49 went airborne on its 25th flight. The purpose of the flight was to make speed runs at altitude, measurements of engine tailpipe temperature, shutdowns and air restarts on two engines, and a stall test. On board were Maj. Daniel H. Forbes, Jr. as pilot, Capt. Glen W. Edwards in the right seat as copilot, Lt. Edward Swindell at the flight engineer's station, and two government civilians flying as observers, C. Leser and C. LaFountain. At their last report all was going well, then 20 minutes later the plane plunged to earth. In horror, fellow test pilot Major Russ Schleeh witnessed the wing tumbling through the air as it plummeted. All were killed. In honor to the pilots, Topeka (Kansas) AFB was renamed Forbes AFB in June 1949 and Muroc AFB became Edwards AFB on January 25, 1950.

There had apparently been a catastrophic structural failure, both outer wing panels were located some three miles from the main crash site. The subsequent accident investigation was unable to determine the cause of the structural failure. Speculation was that it was probably in a dive; the crew, not used to the rapid acceleration of a clean all-wing design, over stressed the large plane when attempting to recover from the dive at a low altitude with a very abrupt attempted pull up.

As a result of the accident, Northrop reviewed the stress analysis of the wing section which failed and was asked to build and test a wing panel. Northrop engineer Stu Krieger shed some light on this matter during an early 1994 panel discussion on the Northrop flying wings.

> The flying wing had a different type of spin property than any conventional airplane. It was something that worried a lot of people – pilots particularly. They looked at the flying wing and said, 'Where's the tail?' and 'How do we operate this thing if we get into a spin?' Also, another thing that came up frequently is 'Well, wouldn't this

thing, if it got into a steep climb or dive, tend to actually tumble rather than spin?'

Well, those were things we got worried about in the testing program and in the wind tunnel testing program. We made some balsa type models. There was a vertical wind tunnel at Langley Field in those days where you could actually spin airplane models. They would stay there and just spin; they're balanced by the upward movement of the air. So they're spinning exactly like they would in a true maneuver. We made these models to test the controls and to test the recovery from a spin, or what caused the spin in a flying wing type of airplane. (I happened to be the one that ran a lot of those tests back at Langley.)

What we discovered, strangely enough, was that in a wing if you get in a spin and you want to get out, the normal reaction of a pilot is to kick the rudder the opposite way. Well it turns out that when you kick the rudder on a flying wing it actually tends to unstall the wing that is rising and helps stall the one that's going down, so it actually forces you into a spin. So we quickly learned from the tests that you don't use the rudder to get out of a spin in a flying wing. But you do use the aileron, and the aileron will recover very quickly and very positively and easily. We ran those tests with little radio controlled controls on it, actual models of the controls, and it worked beautifully. Put the model in [the wind tunnel] and get it spinning. Reverse the ailerons and the airplane would snap out of the spin, and we would have to recover it with a net because it would tend to dive into the tunnel. But we also found that if you wanted to get into a spin, all you had to do was kick the rudder, which you would normally do by instinct if you were a pilot on a conventional airplane [to get out of a spin].

We didn't want them to spin the airplane in the first place, but if they happened to get into a spin, or a wing starts falling off, we said 'Just turn the aileron against it, don't touch the rudder.' Well, we never got direct contact with the Air Force test pilots on this subject. I remember that I tried to impart that knowledge somehow through chan-

Flight engineer's station. The three major panels on the top are the direct current (DC) control panel, alternating current (AC) control panel, and the upper electrical control panel. In the center and lower left is the main instrument panel. On the center right is the lower electrical control panel (fuel control). To the lower right is the throttle quadrant with controls for each individual engine. (Northrop)

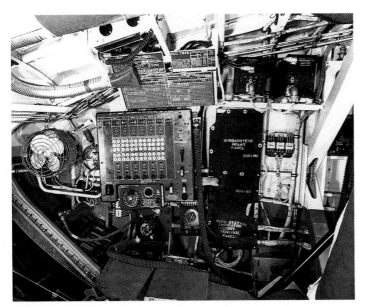

Bombardier's station on the YB-49. To the left of the photo is the aircraft's leading edge and the window through which the bombsight is aimed. On the bombardier's control panel, just left of center, bomb bays one and eight have been blocked out. The space originally used in these bays in the B-35 models was required for engine and fuel tank space in the YB-49s. (Northrop)

nels to them but, as Max will tell you a little later possibly, Forbes and Edwards were very uncommunicative with Northrop pilots. They wanted to test the airplane themselves. They didn't want to hear anything about our experience because I think that the rule was 'We want to see how this airplane reacts from the Air Force view since we are under Air Force directions. We don't want to hear all your stories.'

One of our pilots, some months later, [Chuck] Tucker, made some stall tests in which he got into a spin on the YB-49. He claimed to me that he had never touched the rudder, that he had followed our instructions. But when we looked at the flight box, indeed he had kicked the rudder as soon as the thing started to fall off on one wing. In order to correct it he held it there for something like three seconds which is a long time. That actually accelerated it into the spin. He then got out of it and recovered nicely and was able to pull it out. It's obvious to me that the Air Force people had the same problem, but they were flying at a much lower altitude. They did recover from their spin, but they pulled the wings off trying to get out of the dive. That's what I think happened.

The net result of the accident, I'm convinced, is that Forbes had the same exact experience that Tucker had later. Namely, he started falling off on the wing very sharply, and he was stalling. (He was doing more of a true stall test, probably a lot more than we would have done. There is really no point in stalling an airplane that huge,

Northrop News

Issued Every Two Weeks at Northrop Field, Hawthorne, California   Wednesday, January 28, 1948

Suggestion Awards Tops At Northrop

By CECIL CALLAWAY
(Northrop Suggestion Plan Representative)

Awards paid Northrop Suggestion Plan winners top the industry!

A recently completed survey shows that Norcrafters who won suggestion award prizes received on the average more than winners in 39 other factories.

On V-J day (August 15, 1945) the War Production Drive Plan in effect at Northrop was discontinued, and no suggestion plan was in operation for several months. Wishing to share with the employees the savings resulting from their constructive ideas, the Management, after reviewing the various plans being used in other organizations, installed the present Suggestion Award Plan in June, 1946.

January 1, 1948, completed the first year and one-half of the Plan's operation. The response and participation has been very gratifying—in that time over one thousand suggestions have been submitted.

Of this number, 18% of the

NORTHROP YB-49 FLYING WINGS ARE WORLD'S LONGEST RANGING JETS

SECOND Flying Wing YB-49 leaves Northrop Field.

The U. S. Air Force has disclosed that its unconventional new Northrop Flying Wing YB-49 bombers are the world's longest-ranging jet aircraft, and are each capable of packing over 15 tons of bombs.

The giant eight-jet bombers are designed for top speeds in the 500-mile-an-hour class, with a range several hundred miles farther than that of any other jet airplane known to aviation authorities.

The YB-49 tests, it was indicated, have gone far toward proving the design in which Northrop Aircraft, Inc., has pioneered. Northrop designers have maintained that the cl~ all-wing design, which every part of the airpl~ working surface, will res~ greater speed, longer rang~ greater load-carrying ~ than is possible with con~ al designs.

With Air Force a~ N~ pilots aboard, two cf the F~ Wing YB-49's have been mak~ ing regular flights over the California desert near Muroc, in a~

NORTHROP CRACKS SONIC

On January 13, 1948 the second YB-49 took to the air for the first time. Air Force Major Robert Cardenas and his flight crew accomplished this flight. Minor damage was sustained by the main gear doors on this flight. (Northrop)

especially if the cg is back. I think the Air Force wanted to really wring the airplane out, which I guess they do with all the airplanes. It was more of a daring type test than we would have run.) I think what happened is he [Forbes] started spinning and kicked the rudder and forced it into a steeper spin and finally did recover.

I made calculations from the ground back up, which I was convinced was the actual flight path of the accident, because the airplane landed flat and not on one wing. If it were spinning, when it hit the ground, one wing would have hit first. But instead it pancaked flat, which indicated he had gotten out of the spin and went into a dive and then tried to pull out but overstressed the airplane.

We went through all the calculations to see what the altitude loss and two turns and a turn and a half would be, and how much room was left. My calculations, as I remember, said that if he had used only two g's or two and a half g's in this pullout, that he would have still made it. But I think they immediately put on four or five g's and snapped the wings off. What happens then, of course, is that your aerodynamic center of the flying wing goes extremely far forward, your cg still stays pretty far back and you have a violently unstable airplane. I think what happened then is that the center section tumbled, because we actually made tumbling tests of the flying wing, because of the worry about tumbling, rotating . . . instead of spinning. We did

do some tumbling tests in a wind tunnel and proved indeed that a wing will tumble, just like a leaf, a falling leaf. Anyhow, when the outer panels snapped off, I also calculated that the thing went into a negative tumble, rotation and speed was so fast that it put at least 10 to 15 negative g's on the pilots' heads. I think six or seven negative g's will kill a person, and I think they apparently were killed instantly.

The remaining YB-49 had been grounded at the Northrop factory while the investigation of the crash of its sister ship was being conducted. At the same time, extensive testing and the installation of strain gages in the area failure occurred on the second YB-49. It was to be flown by Northrop test pilots in an Interim Phase I flight test program in which extensive control and stall tests were to be conducted.

The fatal accident had put a shadow over the program. Air Materiel Command had proposed to Air Force Headquarters that B-49s be procured as a medium bomber. On June 25th the Requirements Division in Washington, D. C., stated they disagreed with AMC and suggested that the FB-49 reconnaissance aircraft should be thoroughly service tested before any decision be made for the bomber variant. The question was asked as to the status of the one remaining YB-49 as a bomber. The answer was that it had no bomb

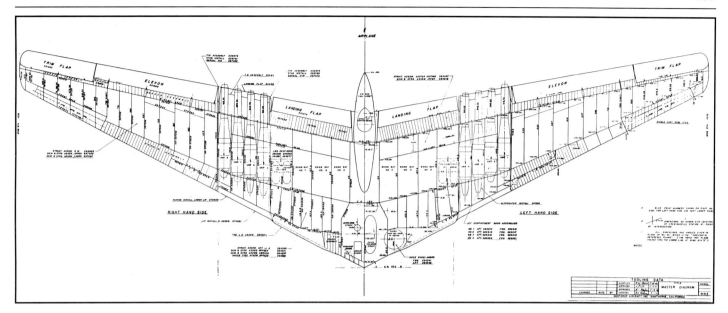

Master Diagram

racks, shackles, or autopilot. Its bomb bay design could not accommodate large bombs. It was also stated that "the general design of this airplane is suitable for the installation of the K-1 Optical - Radar Bombing System. The anticipated high altitude and high speed operation of this aircraft precludes the use of the Norden M-9B Bombsight." A recommendation was made that the B-49 comply with Specification 34040 to insure its suitability for bombardment use.

The loss of YB-49 number two had put a crimp in the Air Force's bombing test plans. The plane had been scheduled to be used along with a North American Aviation B-45 Tornado in high speed bombing tests that were scheduled to be carried out by Air Materiel Command in the near future. The purpose of the tests was to determine bomb bay turbulence, stability of the bombs, and the resulting ballistics of those bombs when dropped from very high speed and at high altitude.

Phase I Contractor Flight Testing Re-Instituted

On July 21st with strain gages and other added test instrumentation in place, Interim Phase I flight testing commenced when the sole YB-49 took to flight for the first time since the issuance of the grounding order following the June accident. During this 52 minute

"shakedown" flight a minor problem occurred: the left hand rudder stayed partially open. Two more flights were accomplished that month and then it was grounded once again. This time for engine changes. Within a month the plane was in the air again. On September 18, 1948, the crew consisted of Max Stanley as pilot, Charles Tucker flying copilot, O. H. Douglas in the flight engineer's seat, Frank Schroeder flying as assistant flight engineer, Don Swift the flight test engineer, Roy Wolford the photographer, and Col. Gates from Wright Field went along as an observer. On this flight they flew inland to California's capital at Sacramento, then southwest to the San Francisco area and finally south along the coast back to the southern California area.

During the above mentioned flight and others like it, a phenomena was observed, but not much was made of it for about 30 years. It was noticed that the YB-49 was nearly undetectable to the air defense radar at Half Moon Bay just south of San Francisco due to the reduced radar signature produced by its shape. Northrop test pilot Max Stanley recalls:

> We made a series of flights over the coastal defense radar at Half Moon Bay. There was one time we played a game with them. We made a call on the telephone and told them 'We'll be over your station tomorrow' but wouldn't tell them what time of day or what altitude or what direction to see if they could pick us up with their radar.

As much as the XB/YB-35s did not fly, the YB-49s did. Their major equipment problems were in the auxiliary power units (APUs) and their J-35 engines. (Edward AFB History Office)

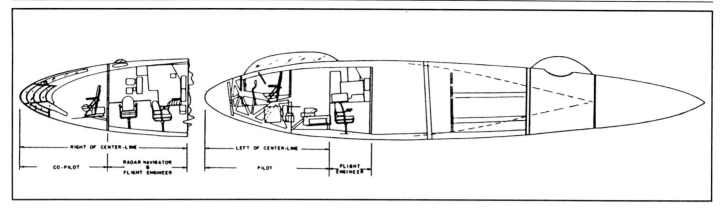

YB-49 Inboard Profile

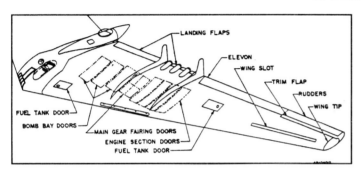

YB-49 Interior Layout

Without exception they were unable to pick us up until we were directly over head. I think this was the first indication that this airplane had something special about it; low observeability.

Northrop chief photographer also participated on these flights.

One flight that I was on – we were making these tests for the coastal defense people. We went out over Half Moon Bay and went out to sea. We were at about 44,000 feet and went out about 100 miles and flew a big figure eight that was probably 100 miles long. We were on radio silence and the coastal defence, when they made a detection, were supposed to give us the position. I think Max was flying that day. We flew for quite a long time. We had contrails – all you had to do was walk out the door and you could have found where we were! Finally we broke radio silence and asked them for a position. And even after that it took them about five or six minutes before somebody came up with some indication that we were even in the area.

Stall Tests

The YB-49 stall tests are quite a story in themselves. Charles Tucker was the test pilot who performed the test. In October 1993 he told his story to a meeting of Northrop aircraft enthusiasts:

We were pretty sure that the Edwards airplane that crashed had started their stall at 20,000 feet and in a clean position (which means no flaps, no wheels, or anything like that). We, the aerodynamicists and Northrop engineers, decided that it would be better if we left the wheels down during the stall maneuvers because that wouldn't have

any serious aerodynamic effects on the airplane but would help to slow us down if we got into something nasty. I also suggested that we maybe put down 15 degrees of flap which would also help slow the airplane down, and they agreed that that was okay. We also decided that we would have a minimum crew.

Besides the pilot, the engineer was critical to manage the various fuel tanks and maintain proper cg. So Frank Schroeder flew in the flight engineer's seat with Tucker on the spin test. Because of the danger of the flight test, and no compelling need in this flight scenario, a copilot was not included.

So we started these tests at 30,000 feet instead of 20,000. We climbed up to our 30,000 altitude and put the gear down, put down 15 degrees of flap, and proceeded to stall the airplane. We started with a forward cg, about 24%. At 24% the airplane was very reluctant to stall. It took all the poop I had to try to get the nose up. It would drop off and we would come out of this semi-stall position and I would apply power, retract the gear, and climb right up to 30,000 feet altitude. We kept repeating this thing with me progressively moving the center of gravity back in slow increments. I finally got back to about 27%, and the airplane would go into this stall maneuver quicker, earlier – it didn't take so much backforce. And the nose would come up 15, maybe 20, degrees, I'd pull the stick back and the airplane would drop off on its right wing. We got the thing to recover at about 140 mph and gently pull back on the wheel and recover.

I got the cg back to 29 plus, almost 30 degrees, I got the nose going up. I pushed forward on the wheel and the nose kept going up until I thought I was going to stand on my tail. Very gradually the wing dropped, seemed like forever until the nose came around. When I got down to 140 mph and started my recovery, the airplane snap rolled and did two and a half turns [observers in chase aircraft state it was one and two-thirds] of an almost vertical spin. I guess it scared the wits out of everybody on the ground, and of course it startled me. I gave it the old flying school recovery. I gave it full up rudder and forward stick, and boom, it popped right out. When it did, I found myself flying straight down and the desert coming up at me awful fast. Well, thank God I had the gear down and started at the altitude that I did. I then started my gentle recovery. The plane was stressed at only two g's, and I pulled about two and a half g's, but it stayed together. I made my pullout at about 8,000 feet.

After I made my pullout, one of the engineers on the ground radioed up and said, 'Do you want to do another one?' I just kind of croaked and said, 'No, that did it. I'm all through.' They agreed that that was enough.

Northrop photographer Roy Wolford was in a P-61 Black Widow chase airplane. Roy recalls:

> We were flying escort on Tucker when he was doing the stalls. On that test there was Gil Nettleton [flying the P-61] and I. We sat at about a three-quarter rear from the '49. Tucker pulled the airplane up and he kept riding, and the nose kept coming up and he rode along – we were having trouble slowing down enough to stay in a proper position for me to photograph. Finally, the airplane started to fall to the right. We had a plan that if he did stall the airplane and it fell off, we were going to do sort of a diving spiral so that I would try to keep in touch with the airplane for as long as possible. We actually saw him fall off, and he made about one and two-thirds turns. He stopped the rotation and we were now looking down over the top of him. It looked as though, you couldn't tell really, whether he was absolutely vertical or even a little past vertical, and he started his recovery. He got to a position, we had to break off, he went underneath us and we picked him up as he went out on the other side.

This wasn't the first time Roy flew in the escort plane during these type of tests.

> Max [Stanley] was flying stall tests on the B-35s and we flew a number of escort flights on those. On the B-35, my recollection was Max would bring it up and it would stall and it would be rather gentle. It would fall off, and he would just push the nose over a little bit and the recovery was a very smooth, really uneventful stall and recovery.

Max Stanley confirms:

> That's very true. I should point out that with all the stalls I made we had a forward cg. When Tucker ran his stalls, the cg was in an aft location, and that made a vast difference to the stall characteristics and behavior post stall.

On the same day that Major Cardenas took the second YB-49 on its first flight, Jack Northrop got his first flight on the first YB-49. Test pilot Max Stanley is on the far left and Jack Northrop is the fourth over. (Northrop/Western Museum of Flight)

Concerned over the minimal changes and design analyses undertaken in the changeover from propeller-driven to jet-powered, Northrop once again wrote the Air Force in August 1948. In this communique ground load conditions were discussed and that when modifying the YB-35 into the YB-49 that the effort had been limited to only that work required for the engine changeover and that the landing gear design had not been changed. Northrop also reiterated its conviction that certain restrictions should be imposed because structural deficiencies brought about by gross weight changes and weight distribution had occurred.

Critical Tests

By October 23, 1948, the Interim Phase I test program had accumulated 38 hours and 45 minutes of flight time in 16 flights. The Air Force was anxious to test the YB-49 as a bombing platform and once again Major Cardenas was given the assignment. To replace Major Dan Forbes, Capt. Wilber W. "Pete" Seller was to be copilot.

The capability of the YB-49 to drop bombs needed to be proved. For stability purposes an autopilot was required but the government was not able to provide one. Still, the Air Force felt the tests could not be put off. AMC felt that the March bombing tests were

With the elimination of the propellers and propeller shaft housing, the fixed vertical fins were required for directional stability; though later is was determined that they needed to be somewhat larger. The fences along the top of the wing acted as physical barriers to prevent spanwise boundary layer flow. (Northrop/ San Diego Aerospace Museum)

Pleasing the home team. The YB-49 with a P-80 chase plane make a low pass at Northrop Field for one of Northrop's Family Day open houses. (Northrop/Stu Luce)

insufficient because "a very limited number of bombs were dropped" and that "these bombs were not dropped at maximum speed and no actual quantitative data is available." For comparative purposes a B-29 was to be flown on identical missions. Because of the YB-49s lack of an autopilot, the B-29 bombing runs were to be made manually. Cardenas was pilot while Capt. R. A. Fulton of the 3208th Strato-Bomb Squadron, Aberdeen Bombing Mission at Muroc AFB acted as copilot and Major Warren C. Williams of AMC's Armament Laboratory was the bombardier. The tests were accomplished between October 19th through the 29th at the Aberdeen bombing mission precision range at Muroc AFB.

Though the Norden bomb sight had been recommended not to be used earlier, it was once again used. This sight needed a very stable platform. Though the YB-49 was not "unstable," that is, dangerous to fly, it did have yawing characteristics that as a bombing platform made it unstable. It was reported that Major Williams got air sick while peering through the Norden bomb sight as the landscape continually translated back and forth.

Slowly the pilot could get the plane down to zero yaw, but this took a long time. During this test period the YB-49 was not able to make a bomb run under four minutes. For the B-29, no bomb run exceeded 45 seconds. Accuracy, for the YB-49, measured in circular average error and range error, was about twice those of the B-29, at all speeds and altitudes. Other problems were also encountered. Bomb bay doors could not be opened or closed in flight on a number of occasions. Air Force flight test personnel felt that further testing was required to prove the aerodynamic soundness of the YB-49 (aerodynamically they felt the major problem to be in flap flutter). Until these deficiencies were corrected, they reported, the YB-49 would not make a sufficiently stable platform for either the bombing or reconnaissance missions.

To muddy the waters somewhat, the terms that then-Major Cardenas used in reporting the airplane's flying characteristics were misinterpreted and picked up by many writers/historians. Now retired-General Cardenas has made a great effort to correct this error, including a talk in early 1994:

> I never said the airplane was unstable. What I said was, and I said this to a Lt. Col. whose name I have forgotten. [He thought this person was technically qualified to understand his terms.] So I told him that it had displayed marginal stability about all three axes. Therefore, in any turns, climbing or diving, you had phugoid oscillations. That's what I said. Well, he printed out in his . . . document that I had said the airplane was unstable.

On September 18, 1948 the YB-49 flew a special test flight from Muroc, up inland California to the capital, Sacramento, then back down the state and to the coast and San Francisco, down along the coast for a ways and then back to the Mojave Desert and Muroc Air Force Base. Pictured here, from right to left, are the members of that flight: Don Swift (tech rep engineer), Frank Schroeder (assistant flight engineer), Max Stanley (pilot), Stan Erbeck (assistant project engineer), O. H. Douglas (flight engineer), Chuck Tucker (copilot), Colonel Gates (Wright-Patterson AFB observer), and Roy Wolford (photographer). (Northrop/Edwards AFB History Office)

In May 1948 the responsibility for overseeing the YB-49 on the Air Force side passed from Major Robert Cardenas to Captain Glen Edwards. Pictured, from left to right, are: unknown, Major Cardenas, Captain Edwards, and Major Daniel Forbes. (Edwards AFB History Office)

Mr. Northrop knew better because in November of '48 they had a general officers panel convene at Patterson Field, Materiel Command, and the board had me present to the general officers the history of all the flights, including Glen Edwards' report of the few flights he made. He was killed on the 5th of June. So in November I did that, Mr. Northrop was present at the briefing. When it was over he got up and said he had great faith in Major Cardenas' abilities as a test pilot, and he looked around and said, 'It looks like I have a lot of work to do.' I tell you, he was a cool cat, because some guy sprung up from the audience and said, 'Sir, you don't have a lot of work to do, you've got an impossible task.' He didn't look at him, just kept looking at the four stars up there, and he said, 'General, I'm surprised to see you have people in your employ who think the impossible is impossible.' That ended the briefing.

Final Chapter

Close on the heels of the bombing test, General Cabell, Director of Intelligence, called a conference on November 12th. In attendance were representatives of the Air Staff, Strategic Air Command, Air Materiel Command, and Air Proving Ground. The poor results of the bombing test and the inherent instability of the wing was one of the main topics. A conclusion from this conference was that early availability of the B-49 as a bomber was doubtful since its design apparently rendered it unstable as a bombing platform. Most of the B-49's problems could be overcome but aircraft such as the B-47 and B-52 would be available before the B-49 was tactically capable. Besides, these aircraft already had most of the B-49's problems designed out, were faster (a major requirement of the time and for some years to come) and had greater range. The B-49's future was becoming quite uncertain.

In January 1949, Air Materiel Command proposed flying the YB-49 to Andrews Field in Maryland as part of an air show scheduled to take place there. As part of a demonstration and goodwill tour for the YB-49, it would make several stops at air bases on its return flight to the west coast. On February 9th a crew including Major Cardenas and Max Stanley took off from Muroc for Andrews. In four hours and five minutes they were over the field, a total of four hours and twenty-five minutes from takeoff at Muroc until they were parked at Andrews. Their average speed of 511 mph compared with the transcontinental record set on January 26, 1946, when Col. William H. Council, flying a Lockheed P-80A Shooting Star jet fighter, made a similar flight (2,435 mile trip) at an average speed of 580 mph. Unfortunately the feel of victory didn't last long. For unbeknownst to them the day before, Major Russell E. Schleeh

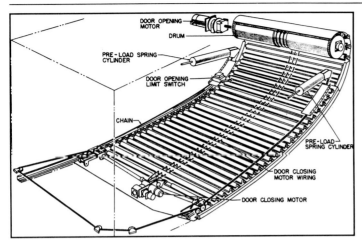

Bomb Bay Door Operating Mechanism

had flown the Boeing XB-47 from Moses Lake AFB in Washington state to Andrews at an average speed of 607 mph.

When the YB-49 arrived at Andrews, "Everybody was real interested in this weird looking thing," according to General Cardenas, so the tower had him make a couple of passes over the field. While at the Andrews air show, President Harry S. Truman climbed aboard the giant flying wing bomber to get a look for himself. After climbing down the airplane's entry ladder, both Max Stanley and Major Cardenas reported hearing the President saying to the Chief of the Air Force words like: "General, this looks pretty damn good to me. I think we ought to buy some." But General Cardenas adds:

And then he walked away a few feet, came back and said, 'General, why don't you have this young Major fly it down Pennsylvania Avenue. I want people to see what I'm going to buy.' Mentally I was saying to myself, 'No way that's going to happen. But, you know, what the heck, even if he's a Democrat, sounds like pretty common sense.' Well, I was wrong, because my boss came up and said, 'Now, Bob, be God damn careful. You got to do that.' So I did; I flew down Pennsylvania Avenue. I throttled back. I got down to about roof top level making sure I didn't hit anything. So when I got to the end there was the Capitol dome ahead of me. So I had to pull up to go over the Capitol dome.

There was a photo taken of the big wing as it went over the dome. It is a story of its own and General Cardenas has recently retold it:

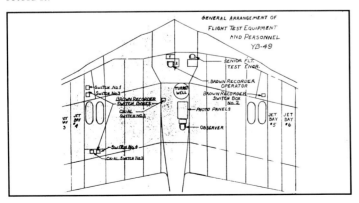

General Arrangement of YB-49 Flight Test Equipment and Personnel

There was a civilian standing on the steps of the Capitol and just as I went up over the dome he snapped a picture. I didn't know it. But about two, three months later or so I got a letter, no return address but stamped Washington, and in it was a 35 mm slide and a little note saying that he had taken this picture but afterwards he understood this was a 'top secret space plane' and he was sending it to me; he didn't want to be caught with it.

The original plan for the YB-49 to stop at a number of bases was changed in the end to just Wright-Patterson AFB in Ohio. The flight from Wright-Patterson towards California turned out to be quite an experience for the Flying Wing crew. General Cardenas tells us of this experience:

On the way home we stopped at Wright[-Patterson AFB] to show the people [the YB-49 there] . . . because they had a deep interest in the airplane. Then we took off from Wright[-Patterson] and headed

In the air most pilots heaped praises on the flying qualities of the YB-49. It was a different story for the bombardier. Oscillation problems needed to be solved before it could become an acceptable bombing platform. Here Northrop personnel and Air Force aircrew members differ All Northrop people the author has had contact with swear that these problems were solved and it was a perfectly acceptable bombing platform. On the Air Force side is exactly the opposite response, to a man. No logical explanation can be found for these absolutely opposite opinions. (Northrop/San Diego Aerospace Museum)

back to Muroc. I got out over the Rockies and the guy in the Stinger started ringing out 'fire on 6, fire on 4, fire on 3.' And every time Sgt. Cunningham would cut the throttle.

So I asked my copilot Pete [Seller], I said, 'Pete, give me a bearing to the nearest airport that we can land this thing.' He said, 'Well, I've been looking and the only thing you got here, (because we were down to six engines out of the eight) is Winslow, Arizona, and the runway is long enough but you got to remember it's about 7,000 feet high. So you got that problem.' I said, 'No problem, I think we can make it.' Coming in he said, 'Oh, yeah, I forgot to tell you, but the runway at Winslow is just 50 feet [wide].' The tread on the gear was 41.2 feet. But we got it down all right. No problem, we landed on the first three feet. That's when I thanked God for those little clam shells out there. Stopped about five feet from the other end of the runway.

They had to get one of those great big Caterpillar tractors from the forests up there to come down and tow me backwards down the field. Northrop came in and changed all eight engines. They thought the cause was oil starvation. In the entire plane each engine was in its own individual engine bay. And in the bay there was an oil tank. They were J-35 engines. They used to pump overboard one gallon of oil every hour of operation. It would have been mathematically improbable to have all eight engines lose roughly 20 gallons of oil, because we had only flown four to five hours.

When I got back they put new engines in and everything. I flew it for the last time in late '49. High altitude, high attitude to see if we were getting oil siphoning at attitude and altitude. We didn't. To this day it remains a mystery to me what happened to all that oil. I have to presume that it just was not filled at Wright Field.

There was somewhat of a humorous side to this incident also. There wasn't a regular fire department there. It seems that whenever an accident occurred at the Winslow airport, the local mortuary would send out its hearse. Well, that's just what happened when the big Wing landed. Except some reporter saw the hearse going out, apparently knew that the Wing had declared an emergency, put out the word that the Wing had crashed. Word reached Base Operations back at Muroc with lightning speed (where Cardenas' wife worked). There were some anxious moments in Operations, but it was soon straightened out.

From this incident has arisen speculation of sinister actions on the part of M/Sgt William Cunningham, one of the flight engineers on the YB-49 flight test program. On Capt. Edwards' fatal flight of June 5, 1948, he was to have been the flight engineer but had turned himself into the hospital. In like manner, when Major Cardenas was prepared to leave Wright-Patterson AFB in February 1949 on his return flight from Andrews AFB to the west coast he found that once again Cunningham had turned himself into the hospital (though he sent Capt. Seller to get him, which is what occurred); this flight culminated in the emergency landing at Winslow, Arizona.

From those who flew with Sgt. Cunningham come an explanation of these "facts." Apparently, according to those that knew him, he seemed to be somewhat sickly, putting himself in the hospital on a regular bases (though he didn't seem afraid to fly on the YB-49). There might have been additional incentive for him to wrangle a way to stay longer at Wright-Patterson during the Wing's stopover there – his wife was living in that area and he, stationed at Muroc, hadn't seen her for quite some time.

His "mystery" death has also been seen as an indication of his hand to destroy the Wings. The fact is that he was involved in the 1950 accident that destroyed the remaining YB-49, suffering from serious head injuries. He experienced periods of blacking out afterwards. It was on a rainy Sunday afternoon, quite some time after the 1950 accident, that he was killed while riding a motorcycle. It is felt that the motorcycle accident was probably caused by one of his blacking out spells.

Soon the Minneapolis-Honeywell E-7 would be available for the YB-49 and bombing tests commenced. Getting this for the B-49 seemed to be a major obstacle. The manufacturer's schedule and squabbling between government agencies were not helping the flying wing program (the XB/YB-35s were having the same difficulties). Air Materiel Command at the same time was developing a precision autopilot for high performance aircraft which would be tried later.

By early April 1949, the first YB-49 had completed 85 flights. An E-7 autopilot (affectionately known as Little Herbert) was finally installed and a bomb drop program scheduled in which ten 500 lb. bombs would be dropped from 10,000, 20,000, and 30,000 foot altitudes. These tests were carried out late April through June. Unfortunately, the official documents relating to the test results have either been lost or cubby-holed away. The remembrance of the participants (Major Russ Schleeh and Northrop test pilots Max Stanley and Charlie Tucker) are diametrically opposed. During the 11 bombing missions that Major Schleeh flew, he found the results to be "very poor." When dropped, the bombs tended to show pitching and oscillation motions. Schleeh felt that this was due to turbulence in the bomb bay and that this contributed to the bombing inaccuracies. Even with the autopilot he still didn't consider the airplane stable enough as a bomber. On the other hand, the Northrop test pilots felt that the stability problem had been overcome and, per Stanley, ". . . the aircraft was accepted by the Air Force as a satisfactory bombing platform . . ."

During the time of this third set of bombing tests, one of a number of incidents involving the J-35 jet engines occurred. On April 26th a fire broke out in one of the engine bays. The crew was able to get the fire out and land the plane but not before extensive damage was caused.

Air Force support for the flying wing was eroding with greater and greater speed. That past January Northrop was formally informed of the cancellation of the photo reconnaissance version production contract. In August the two XB-35s and two YB-35s were scrapped. By year's end, the Air Force ordered all remaining airframes scrapped save the sole flying YB-49 and the one YB-35 which was being converted into the YRB-49A.

Flight test activities continued at Edwards AFB until March 15, 1950 when Major Russ Schleeh and his crew were performing a taxi test in order to determine the elevator stick forces at liftoff. At some point during the run the nose wheel began to shimmy violently. Soon the nose gear collapsed and the nose of the gigantic wing came thundering down onto the desert floor and the craft broke in two. Fire erupted but the crew was evacuated safely, though there were a number of injuries. Major Schleeh suffered from a number of fractured vertebrae. Three flight engineers were aboard for this test; M/Sgt Bill Cunningham received serious head injuries, Capt. Phil French had a broken wrist, and M/Sgt Boone, like the others, received assorted cuts and bruises. Major Alan Warfield, pilot, also received cuts and bruises. The large flying wing program was all but over.

Opposite: On June 25, 1948, the second YB-49 crashed on its 25th flight. On board were Maj. Daniel H. Forbes, Jr. as pilot; Capt. Glen W. Edwards, copilot; Lt. Edward L. Swindell, flight engineer; and two Air Materiel Command civilians, Clare C. Lesser and C. C. La Fountain. Many details concerning the accident are still in question today, some 46 years later. (Edwards AFB History Office)

Opposite: Captain Glen W. Edwards. Muroc AFB was renamed Edwards AFB in honor of Captain Edwards on January 25, 1950. The previous June an Air Force Base near Topeka, Kansas, was renamed in Forbes' honor. (Edwards AFB History Office)

Hired by Northrop to test fly the XS-4, Charles Tucker was given the added job of spin testing the one remaining YB-49 in order to ascertain if it had any poor spin characteristics. (Northrop)

There was a lot of history occurring at the flight test base at Muroc. Here a Douglas XB-43 taxis across the ramp with a YB-49 and, to the right, one of the XB-35s in the background. (USAF)

The loss of the second YB-49 did not seem to disturb the flying wing program as much as one might think. The first YB-49 was sent back to Northrop soon after the accident of June 5th for further instrumentation, mostly strain gages, and then entered further contractor testing, including Chuck Tucker's spin test. (Northrop/ Western Museum of Flight)

The Air Force was not quite sure what it wanted to do with the majority of YB-35 airframes at the Northrop plant once it was certain that a B-35 derivative would not be produced and the B-49 jet flying wing was still in question. In this 1948 photo they are in temporary storage status. (Northrop/G. H. Balzer Historical Archives)

In early February 1949 the YB-49 made a flight from Muroc AFB to Andrews AFB near Washington, D.C. in 4 hours and 15 minutes. A very good time when compared to the official transcontinental record of 4 hours, 13 minutes, and 26 seconds held by Col. William H. Council in a Lockheed P-80 set on January 26, 1946. (Edwards AFB History Office)

Opposite: Aircrew on the February 9th trip to Andrews AFB were the right three in this photo: Major Robert Cardenas, Northrop's Max Stanley, and M/Sgt. William Cunningham as flight engineer. On the return flight on February 18th, Capt. Pete Seller, to Cardenas' right, took Stanley's place as copilot. (Edwards AFB History Office)

As good as the YB-49's time was to the east coast of the US, it was second best. The day before Major Russ Schleeh flew an XB-47 from Moses Lake, Washington, to Andrews (about the same distance as the YB-49 flew) in 3 hours and 46 minutes. (San Diego Aerospace Museum)

Aircraft on display at Andrews AFB in February 1949. The big flying wing and its competitors — the B-36 which had won out over the B-35 for the heavy bomber role and the XB-47 which was the YB-49's major competition. (Edwards AFB History Office)

The show of the most modern Air Force aircraft was put on at Andrews AFB in Maryland, just outside of Washington, D.C., at the request of the House Armed Services Committee, according to published reports of the time. It was described "as if a secret test base had been moved into the open and put under floodlights." The YB-49, with "no tail, no fuselage" was of great interest. (Edwards AFB History Office)

Opposite: About the only person to get a look inside the giant flying wing was President Harry S. Truman. His comments to the effect that some of these aircraft should be bought was music to Northrop's ears. (Northrop)

Major Robert Cardenas didn't take President Truman's remarks very seriously when the President suggested that the YB-49 should be flown down Pennsylvania Avenue. Major Cardenas was soon told that he was to do exactly that, carefully. Here he is caught in the lens of a civilian's camera as he comes over the Capitol dome. (Edwards AFB History Office)

The XB-47 besting the YB-49 put just another nail in the Flying Wing's coffin. As the design of the Boeing B-52 advanced, it not only sealed the fate of the B-49 as a bomber but, with plans of an RB-52A reconnaissance version, the B-52 ultimately killed the short lived RB-49A reconnaissance wing. (Boeing)

Below and following two pages: The end of the YB-49 program, and any hope of a B-49 of any variant, came on March 15, 1950. The Air Force crew was performing nose wheel lift-off speed tests at the time of the accident (their allotted flight time between inspections had expired and were therefore forbidden to fly the aircraft, though ground tests could be conducted. When the nose wheel touched down at the end of their first run violent oscillations began (which can be seen by the tracks in the desert floor in the first photo. The nose gear collapsed and the big wing nosed into the desert floor and the airplane separated into two parts (the crew compartment remaining with the right hand wing. (Photos 1 and 5, Edwards AFB History Office; Photos 2, 3, and 4, USAF via Phil French)

①

②

③

④

5

This photo was probably taken in the last quarter of 1948. Thirteen of the 15 XB/YB-35s purchased by the Air Force are present; only the two YB-49s are missing. All 13 aircraft are in a phase of conversion as shown in this photo (not being scrapped). The two XB-35s were programmed to become a ERB-35B and EB-35 while the 10 YB-35/35As were to be modified into jet-powered RB-35Bs (42-102369 was singled out to become the YRB-49A). (Northrop/G. H. Balzer Historical Archives)

Opposite: On April 26, 1951 the YRB-49A made its last flight, and reportedly the only flight by an Air Force crew. On that day General Al Boyd as pilot and Major Phil French as flight engineer, flew it for one hour going from Edwards AFB to Ontario Airport. (Northrop/San Diego Aerospace Museum)

Chapter 9
THE LAST HOPE
The RB-49 Project

Jack Northrop was always looking for improvements in his flying wing designs and for other applications. In late January 1948 he wrote the Air Force Director of Research and Development in Washington, D.C., suggesting range and speed improvements in the R-4360 variable discharge turbine (VDT) engine which was then scheduled for use in the B-36 and the replacement of the eight TG-180 engines with six General Electric TG-190 (J-47) engines in the B-49. With the troublesome dual-rotating propeller system in the XB-35s and loss of performance with the single eight-bladed propeller system soon to be incorporated in the experimental planes and scheduled for all the service test articles, it was soon realized that the piston-engined bombers were not going anywhere. Jet propulsion was the powerplant of the future. On March 2nd Northrop provided preliminary data for a

proposed B-49 photo reconnaissance program. Three versions were offered which differed in type and number of engines: (1) eight GE TG-190As, (2) six TG-190Hs, and (3) six TJT-7As.

A conference on reconnaissance aircraft was held at Air Materiel Command on April 12th. The possibilities of Northrop's FB-49 along with Republic's F-12, the Douglas FDC-6, and Boeing's B-50 and B-47 were considered. At the conclusion of the conference, their report stated that, ". . . in its interim stages of development [the FB-49] could most realistically accomplish a portion of the overall strategic reconnaissance mission . . ." and that procurement of such aircraft should be undertaken immediately. The aircraft was to be procured in three versions. The first was to be equipped with eight General Electric TG-190A (J47) engines and have a gross takeoff weight of 213,500 pounds. They estimated that the first of

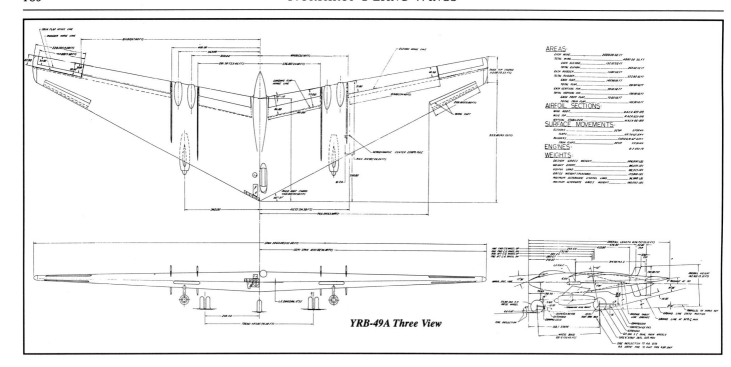

YRB-49A Three View

these aircraft would be available in January 1950. The second variant was to be equipped with six Westinghouse J-40 engines, when these engines became available. The third would have two T-37 Turbodyne turboprop engines and two TG-190A engines. It was anticipated that the Turbodyne engines would become available in October 1951. Version three was expected to have double the range of version one, but with a reduced cruise speed.

Action was taken immediately. On May 3, 1948, Northrop received a wire authorizing them to initiate engineering on the FB-49A with an anticipated order of 30 such aircraft, modification and flight test of the first YB-49 to incorporate FB-49A installations (it was then anticipated that this YB-49 would complete Phase II tests at Muroc on August 15, 1948), tool design, FB-49A mockup, FB-49B engineering, partial materials procurement, and static test jig design.

That same month a summary of the Strategic Reconnaissance Program for the Air Force was issued. It described the present plan "antiquated" for some time. One step called out to modernize the reconnaissance program was to re-equip five Strategic Reconnaissance Groups with RB-49s (the designation for photo reconnaissance aircraft changing from "F" to "R") beginning in March 1951.

Air Materiel Command requested permission from the Under Secretary of the Air Force, A. S. Borrows, to initiate negotiations with Northrop for the FB-49. They felt that Northrop should be the sole source for this plane because it's design was based on the YB-49. Maj. Gen. K. B. Wolfe, Director of Procurement and Industrial Mobilization Planning, recommended approval of this request. General Vandenberg's congratulations to Northrop for his work on the YB-49 and the results of its flight test program to date on May 12th seemed to emphasize that the flying wing was sure to enter military service at last. The following day the Under Secretary authorized that the negotiations proceed. The Under Secretary noted that with the millions already spent on developing Northrop's flying wing bomber these additional funds would insure benefits from the previous expenditures.

The crash of the second YB-49 on June 5th did not seem to adversely affect the reconnaissance flying wing program, for on the 12th Northrop received a letter contract for preliminary engineering. Northrop production capability for large flying wings, as experienced with the B-35/B-49 project, was quite limited and the Air Force desired to keep Consolidated Vultee's Fort Worth plant going as they did not intend to buy more than the 95 B-36s then on order. On June 30th Gen. Joseph T. McNarney, now commanding general of Air Materiel Command, wrote Northrop Aircraft advising them that the Air Force wanted to move RB-49 production to Fort Worth and requested that Northrop and Consolidated Vultee get together and work out an arrangement. He stated "an absolute minimum number" of the flying wings were to be produced by Northrop.

As a result of General McNarney's June 30th letter Northrop representatives met with their Consolidated Vultee counterparts at the latter's San Diego plant. The two concerns saw the General's directions differently, so Northrop wrote McNarney on July 9th requesting clarification. Meetings were set up for July 15th and 16th in Los Angeles where all concerned were to get together and work out a program.

The outcome of that meeting has led to controversy which is still with us today. The entire B/RB-49 project has been muddied up historically, factually, by what transpired over the following months as a result of that request. Personalities, egos, power plays, and hardball business gamesmanship all entered in. The result, which did not help to keep the large flying wing alive, embittered Jack Northrop and probably was a great factor in his eventual retreat from the aircraft industry, not to mention his perjuring himself during Congressional testimony in 1949.

The meeting of the 16th had Jack Northrop and Dick Millar representing Northrop Aircraft, Floyd Odlum and LaMotte Cohu from Consolidated Vultee, and Generals McNarney and Wolfe from Air Materiel Command. In this second meeting Secretary of the Air Force Stuart Symington, who was already in town for another meet-

Here the Turbodyne is coupled to an existing compressor and combustion system ready for a 50-hour qualification test in a Hawthorne test cell. (Northrop)

ing, joined the group. The suggestion arose that Northrop should merge with Consolidated Vultee.

Jack Northrop had bitter experiences in joint ventures with other companies. The fiasco with Martin on the B-35 project and problems with General Electric in the development of Heliarc welding and the Turbodyne jet engine were ingrained in his memory. And now the pressures to work with, and even merge with, Consolidated Vultee was almost too much.

Mr. Northrop asked Secretary Symington what the consequences would be if his company didn't merge. According to Northrop this conversation went as follows:

> Mr. Symington, was then Secretary of the Air Force. We didn't do something he wanted; he wanted us to merge with another company and we couldn't reach a satisfactory conclusion. In that merger with the company, we didn't feel that our values and their values were properly weighted, and we decided not to make the merger. In a previous meeting I asked him, 'What happens, Mr. Secretary, if we can't reach a conclusion on this?' And his statement was 'You will be God damn sorry if you don't!' Well, we didn't quite take it that way, perhaps we should have, but the whole thing [contract] viciously cancelled and they [the wings] were chopped up. They took away from us a big gas turbine; a turboprop development we had ready for one of the Flying Wings. He did his best, I guess, to wreck the company.

As July ended the RB-49 effort called for Northrop to be the prime contractor and Consolidated to fabricate a majority of the aircraft at the government-owned, Consolidated-operated plant, at

Fort Worth, Texas. Besides the 30 production aircraft, a mockup was also to be constructed. The surviving YB-49 was to be modified into the RB-49A configuration for flight testing. Maj. Gen. Kenneth B. Wolfe, Director of Procurement and Industrial Planning at AMC authorized the procurement of the reconnaissance flying wings on August 12th at a cost of nearly $83.5 million. On that date contract W33-038 ac-21721 calling for 29 RB-49As to be built by Consolidated Vultee and one by Northrop (plus a static test shell, spare parts, and data) was signed by Northrop Vice President C. N. Monson.

Turbodyne

Associated with the jet-propelled flying wing bombers, and highly dependent on their success, was Northrop's own jet engine development project known as Turbodyne. The original idea was that of Vladimir H. Pavlecka who, in the mid-1930s, tried to interest his then employer, Douglas Aircraft Company, in jet engine development. His idea was turned down. But when Jack Northrop left Douglas and started his own company in 1939, Pavlecka was given the opportunity of his life. Pavlecka and Northrop knew each other at Douglas and it wasn't long before he joined the little Northrop band in Hawthorne. He found a very receptive Jack Northrop and soon was heading up, albeit low budget, a jet engine project.

Funds were needed and trips to Washington were made where Northrop and Pavlecka visited the Bureau of Aeronautics and Bureau of Ships at the Navy Department and the Air Corps offices at

The Northrop-developed Turbodyne gas turbine engine. It was capable of delivering 10,000 horsepower. The genesis of this engine was the idea of Northrop research chief Vladimir Pavlecka at the beginning of Northrop Aircraft, Inc. Initially only a compressor contract was obtained from the US Navy. It was under an Army Air Forces contract that the XT-37 engine came about. (Northrop/ Western Museum of Flight)

the War Department. Trips were also made to the Materiel Division at Wright Field. Only lukewarm interest was shown by the Air Corps, but the Navy saw some use in the thing. A small contract for a compressor section was obtained from the Navy; the Air Corps would become involved a little later, though the Navy would remain the lead service on the project.

Like the flying wings, development was slow. Great Britain's Group Captain Frank Whittle, who felt that the centrifugal flow jet engine was the proper design, came to the US to assist on jet engine development. He and Pavlecka, who was in favor of the axial flow, vigorously disagreed on the path to take in the development process. Pavlecka also had disagreements with Cal Tech's von Karman

and soon he left Northrop. Art Phelan took over the project.

In time a complete engine was on contract, but it was a turboprop, designated XT-37. Three of these engines were completed in late 1947. Testing to date had demonstrated 5,150 horsepower with about twice that expected from the fully developed version. By coupling this engine to the large flying wing much greater speed could be obtained over the reciprocating engines of the XB-35 and greater range than that afforded by the turbojets in the YB-49.

The XT-37 was intended as a turboprop powerplant. Originally one unit was to be installed in an XB-35, but later it was decided that a YB-35 was to be modified to carry two of these units, though early flight tests were to be accomplished with only a single XT-37. The 18-foot counter-rotating propeller was manufactured by General Motors' Aeroproducts division. (Northrop/Western Museum of Flight)

What to do with the YB-35 Shells?

The Air Force had to do something with the YB-35s that were sitting around Northrop. Problems persisted with the needed government furnished equipment. The flight test program of the two XB-35s and the one YB-35 were abysmal. Besides, did the Air Force really want another propeller-driven bomber? A tanker version had been suggested and rejected. To decide on their fate, a conference was held on August 16th where Northrop and AMC representatives came up with four proposals.

1. Convert one of the YB-35s to jet engines with a XT-37 Turbodyne installation. Substitute a second YB-35 as a RB-49A prototype instead of the YB-49. Static test one XB-35 using equipment planned for the RB-49A static test. Convert nine YB-35s to jet engines and install APQ-24 radar and photo reconnaissance equipment.

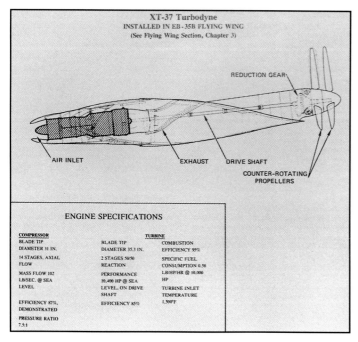

XT-37 Turbodyne
INSTALLED IN EB-35B FLYING WING
(See Flying Wing Section, Chapter 3)

REDUCTION GEAR

AIR INLET   EXHAUST   DRIVE SHAFT
                              COUNTER-ROTATING
                              PROPELLERS

ENGINE SPECIFICATIONS

COMPRESSOR	TURBINE	
BLADE TIP DIAMETER 31 IN.	BLADE TIP DIAMETER 35.3 IN.	COMBUSTION EFFICIENCY 95%
14 STAGES, AXIAL FLOW	2 STAGES 50/50 REACTION	SPECIFIC FUEL CONSUMPTION 0.58
MASS FLOW 102 LB/SEC. @ SEA LEVEL	PERFORMANCE 10,400 HP @ SEA LEVEL, ON DRIVE SHAFT	LB/HP/HR @ 10,000 HP
EFFICIENCY 87%, DEMONSTRATED	EFFICIENCY 85%	TURBINE INLET TEMPERATURE 1,500°F
PRESSURE RATIO 7.5:1		

Turbodyne Installation

2. Stop work on all planes, pickle and store them until Turbodyne installation was developed, then convert the YB-35s to Turbodyne-power.

3. Stop work on all planes, pickle and store. Complete test stand engineering to solve problems of propeller vibration, flexible mounted gear box, heat exchangers, and exhaust system.

4. Make jet conversions necessary in order to make prototype of Turbodyne modification. Static test one YB-35.

The answer came a month later when the Air Force agreed on a plan for the YB-35s. This plan called for two YB-35s to be modified to the YRB-49 configuration. One was to be a RB-49 prototype and the other to be a Turbodyne test bed. The remaining YB-49s were to be converted to YRB-49s, which included the installation of J-35-17 engines. Northrop received authorization to commence this modification effort on September 20, 1948.

Air Force evaluation of the eight J-47 jet engines proposed to power the RB-49A showed that this engine/airframe combination would not give sufficient range. It was felt that two J-40 and two T-37s would give the desired results.

In early October Northrop submitted a plan in which one YB-35 would become a static test article, one would be converted to jets and would be used as an XT-37-3 flying test bed, and the remaining nine would be modified into photo-reconnaissance aircraft with jet engines. The nine reconnaissance planes would be available to the Air Force in 15 to 18 months after contract award. This plan found favor within the Air Force but with a couple of changes. It was proposed that the number 1 XB-35 be used as the Turbodyne test bed (redesignated ERB-35B) and that the YB-35 Northrop had proposed as the Turbodyne test bed become a RB-49A prototype. The Director of Procurement and Industrial Planning recommended to the Secretary of the Air Force on November 1st that this plan be approved.

Photo Reconnaissance Wing Program

From the RB-49A contract signing on August 12th the project moved forward. On the 23rd a conference was held at Air Materiel Command with Northrop representatives. There proposed changes to the contract were discussed and a formal quote was requested covering RB-49 tooling program, conversion of one RB-49A to a B-49 bomber, contractor maintenance, and studies to increase mach number. On the 27th AMC sent a letter to Northrop discussing modifying nine of the YB-35 shells into YRB-49s. On the 16th of September the USAF Controller concurred with this conversion and AMC sent Northrop a wire on the 20th authorizing them to commence with the modification program.

The August 12th RB-49A contract was approved by the Secretary of the Air Force on September 20th. Now Northrop started organizing for the new program. On the 27th Northrop General Manager C. N. Monson issued a memo to all Administrative offices covering travel expenses between Hawthorne, California and Fort Worth, Texas. On October 15th Northrop Assistant General Manager B. G. Reed issued a memo stating that "Pending establishment of a Northrop administration office at Fort Worth, we will

temporarily handle transmission of engineering, tooling and materiel information through Manufacturing Control." This was followed on November 1st with a memo from Jack Northrop to all department heads announcing that effective November 16th W. G. Knieriem was appointed Fort Worth Division Manager of Northrop Aircraft.

Another blow to the prospects of the large flying wing entering the Air Force came on November 12th when General Cabell, Director of Intelligence, held a conference to review reconnaissance aircraft requirements. Air Materiel Command as well as Strategic Air Command representatives attended the conference. The conferees felt that the range of the RB-49 had been reduced by the additional requirements levied on Northrop to include selfsealing fuel tanks and two-gun remote control armament. The development of the RB-49 had been planned in three phases, extending over five to six years. The RB-49A, expected to be available in January 1950, was anticipated to have inadequate operating radius. The RB-49B, available in 1951, would be much slower than Boeing's B-47. It was believed that by the time the third version was available, in about 1953, that it would be in competition with Boeing's B-52. The B-52 was expected to be superior in range, speed, and altitude. From this the Air Staff recommended the elimination of the RB-49 from the reconnaissance plan.

With the RB-49 program now in question, Headquarters USAF approved the conversion program of the YB-35s to the photo reconnaissance mission. In late November a three day mockup inspection of the RB-49A was scheduled for December 7th. It was anticipated that the inspection effort would include discussions on weight reduction changes and the tail armament system.

YB-35 serial number 42-102378 being modified into the EB-35B. Four jet engines were also installed within the wing and two additional on pylons under the wing. (Northrop)

By December 1st Northrop's W. G. Knieriem was located at the Fort Worth plant. On the 22nd teletype services were set up between the Hawthorne and Fort Worth plants.

On December 29th the USAF Board of Senior Officers met, headed by Air Materiel Command's General McNarney. Their recommendation was for the termination of the RB-49 procurement. B-36s equipped with jet pods were to be substituted for the RB-49s. Northrop was directed on January 11, 1949, to stop all work concerning the production RB-49s pending formal notification; work on the YRB-49A was to continue. The formal notification of the termination came three days later.

Even though the RB-49 production had been terminated, the conversion of the YB-35s into photo reconnaissance aircraft continued. The aircraft designated YB-35 and YB-35A became RB-35B. XB-35 number one, which was to be modified as the Turbodyne test bed, changed from ERB-35B to EB-35B. Engines for the EB-35B were to consist of six J-35-A-19s and one T-37 (a second T-37 was planned to be added later).

As time went on, the configuration and disposition of the aircraft changed. In March the USAF decided to salvage the two XB-35s and two YB-35s. In place of the number one XB-35, the last YB-35A was selected for the Turbodyne modification. The B-35 Office at Air Materiel Command decided that no mockup or "689" inspections would be performed on the first YB-35B, EB-35B, or YRB-49A, only safety inspections. A flight test program for the EB-35B called for 30 hours of flight test with one Turbodyne engine and an additional 30 hours with two engines installed.

By the end of March, the seven RB-35s were scheduled for delivery January through May 1950. On March 30th, their designation was changed to YB-35B and they would be flying shells – jet engine conversion only, no tactical equipment. In mid-May Northrop was informed that there might be even further cutbacks in the jet

What to do with most of the YB-35 airframes seemed to be up in the air for years. When it looked as if the large flying wings had found a nitch in the Air Force as photo reconnaissance aircraft, it was decided to convert most of the YB-35 into photo-recon trainers for SAC (being designated RB-35Bs). But when the reconnaissance wing idea was axed and no operational mission for the flying wings could be found, the Air Force decided to make them into flying "shells" for flight testing only. Under this scenario they were once again redesignated, now YB-35Bs. In the foreground of this photo is one of the YB-35Bs followed by the YRB-49A in the making, and the EB-35B Turbodyne testbed. (Northrop/G. H. Balzer Historical Archives)

A nearly complete YB-35B. (Northrop/G. H. Balzer Historical Archives)

conversion program because of additional safety and engineering changes.

The demise of the large flying wing bomber got into high gear as 1949 was concluding. In November the government terminated the YB-35 jet conversion program and ordered the seven YB-35Bs that were undergoing conversion scrapped. The scrapping operations began on December 29, 1949, and was completed on February 4, 1950. Northrop personnel removed all useable parts and Bill Huffman of Mobile Smelting came onto Northrop Field and cut the Wings into smaller chunks with oxygen acetylene torches and melted them into ingots with his mobile smelters. (He had previously smeltered hundreds of F4U Corsairs and the Douglas XB-19.) Soon word came to dismantle the Turbodyne-powered EB-35B test bed. Northrop employees offered to complete this aircraft on their own time but Jack Northrop turned down their offer fearing that such action would not set well with the Air Force. On March 30th this aircraft too was scrapped. Ironically, on March 15th, the last flying YB-49 was destroyed when the nose gear collapsed during a taxi test.

Like the last gasp of a dying animal, the last and only flying wing, the YRB-49A, took to the air on May 4, 1950. The Northrop flight test crew included Fred C. Bretcher as pilot, Dale Johnson as co-pilot, and Frank Schroeder in the flight engineer's seat. Powered by six Allison J35-A-19 engines, the flight from Hawthorne to Edwards AFB was short and uneventful. It's flight test program was quite short; a total of 14 flights for a little over 18 hours flight time.

Not much has been noted of its flight testing at Edwards save its tenth flight on August 10th when the pilot's canopy came off while the aircraft was in a climb. It occurred at around the 35,000 foot mark and at a speed of about 225 mph. The pilot's oxygen mask was torn off his face and he sustained minor injuries. The alert flight engineer got the emergency oxygen to the pilot and the plane was brought down safely.

The plane was ferried to Northrop's facility at Ontario Airport, California, on April 26, 1951 by pilot Col. Albert Boyd, chief of flight test at Edwards, and Maj. Phil French as flight engineer; this is thought to be the only Air Force crew to fly this plane. It remained in storage status for about 18 months. On May 6, 1952, Air Materiel Command declared that there was no additional flying planned for the YRB-49A. On November 17, 1953, it was authorized to be scrapped. Reclamation (scrapping) was completed by December 1, 1953.

The Northrop factory in October 27, 1949. The following day it would be announced that eight of the aircraft were to be scrapped. This was not the first time that this occurred. Because of defense downsizing, greatly reduced funds, and the flying wing program overruns, four aircraft (the two XB-35s and two YB-35s) were ordered scrapped in March 1949; the scrapping took place that July and August. But this still was not the end of the Flying Wing program. The first YB-49 was still flying and modification of one YB-35 into the YRB-49A was to continue. (Northrop)

Left and below left: Between late December 1949 and March 30, 1950, the aircraft were stripped of useable parts, dismantled, and mobile smelters were brought in to make ingots out of them. To add insult to injury, the one remaining YB-49 was destroyed in an accident during taxi tests almost two weeks before the last plane, the EB-35B, was scrapped. (Edwards AFB History Office and USAF/Western Museum of Flight)

Northrop News

Issued Every Two Weeks at Northrop Field, Hawthorne, California   Wednesday, March 8, 1950

First Flight Due In April

In early March 1950 there was still hope for the large Flying Wing. The YRB-49A still had promise. (Northrop/Western Museum of Flight)

The YRB-49A included a number of lessons learned from the YB-49 experience. The copilot rode immediately behind the pilot in tandem configuration and the canopy was jettisonable for emergency purposes. The engines on pylons provided for more fuel space within the wing where four more engines were installed; it was also thought that the pylons would provide additional directional stability. (Northrop/Western Museum of Flight)

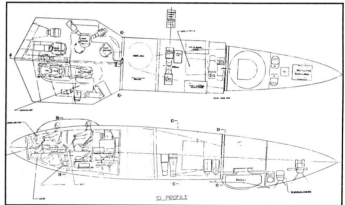

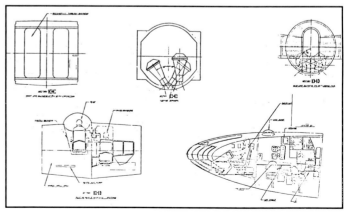

YRB-49A Inboard Profile

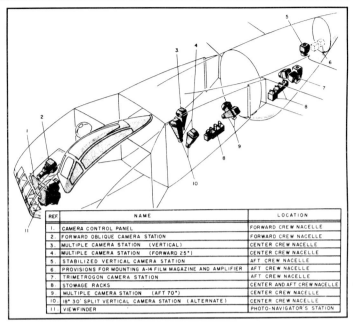

REF.	NAME	LOCATION
1.	CAMERA CONTROL PANEL	FORWARD CREW NACELLE
2.	FORWARD OBLIQUE CAMERA STATION	FORWARD CREW NACELLE
3.	MULTIPLE CAMERA STATION (VERTICAL)	CENTER CREW NACELLE
4.	MULTIPLE CAMERA STATION (FORWARD 25°)	CENTER CREW NACELLE
5.	STABILIZED VERTICAL CAMERA STATION	AFT CREW NACELLE
6.	PROVISIONS FOR MOUNTING A-14 FILM MAGAZINE AND AMPLIFIER	AFT CREW NACELLE
7.	TRIMETROGON CAMERA STATION	AFT CREW NACELLE
8.	STOWAGE RACKS	CENTER AND AFT CREW NACELLE
9.	MULTIPLE CAMERA STATION (AFT 70°)	CENTER CREW NACELLE
10.	18" 30' SPLIT VERTICAL CAMERA STATION (ALTERNATE)	CENTER CREW NACELLE
11.	VIEWFINDER	PHOTO-NAVIGATOR'S STATION

YRB-49A Photographic Equipment

Left: Flight test instrument station in the YRB-49A. (Northrop)

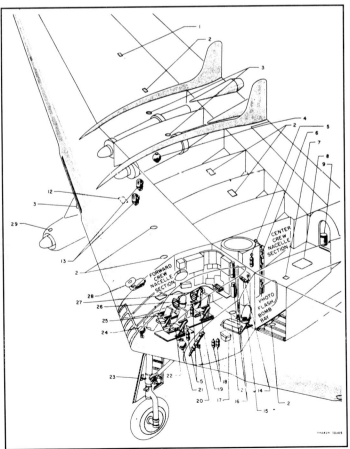

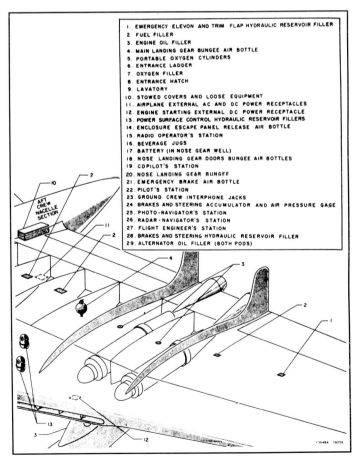

1. EMERGENCY ELEVON AND TRIM FLAP HYDRAULIC RESERVOIR FILLER
2. FUEL FILLER
3. ENGINE OIL FILLER
4. MAIN LANDING GEAR BUNGEE AIR BOTTLE
5. PORTABLE OXYGEN CYLINDERS
6. ENTRANCE LADDER
7. OXYGEN FILLER
8. ENTRANCE HATCH
9. LAVATORY
10. STOWED COVERS AND LOOSE EQUIPMENT
11. AIRPLANE EXTERNAL AC AND DC POWER RECEPTACLES
12. ENGINE STARTING EXTERNAL DC POWER RECEPTACLE
13. POWER SURFACE CONTROL HYDRAULIC RESERVOIR FILLERS
14. ENCLOSURE ESCAPE PANEL RELEASE AIR BOTTLE
15. RADIO OPERATOR'S STATION
16. BEVERAGE JUGS
17. BATTERY (IN NOSE GEAR WELL)
18. NOSE LANDING GEAR DOORS BUNGEE AIR BOTTLES
19. COPILOT'S STATION
20. NOSE LANDING GEAR BUNGEE
21. EMERGENCY BRAKE AIR BOTTLE
22. PILOT'S STATION
23. GROUND CREW INTERPHONE JACKS
24. BRAKES AND STEERING ACCUMULATOR AND AIR PRESSURE GAGE
25. PHOTO-NAVIGATOR'S STATION
26. RADAR-NAVIGATOR'S STATION
27. FLIGHT ENGINEER'S STATION
28. BRAKES AND STEERING HYDRAULIC RESERVOIR FILLER
29. ALTERNATOR OIL FILLER (BOTH PODS)

YRB-49A General Arrangement

First flight for the YRB-49A was on May 4, 1950. The crew consisted of Fred Bretcher, pilot; Dale Johnson, copilot; and Frank Schroeder was the flight engineer. (Edwards AFB History Office)

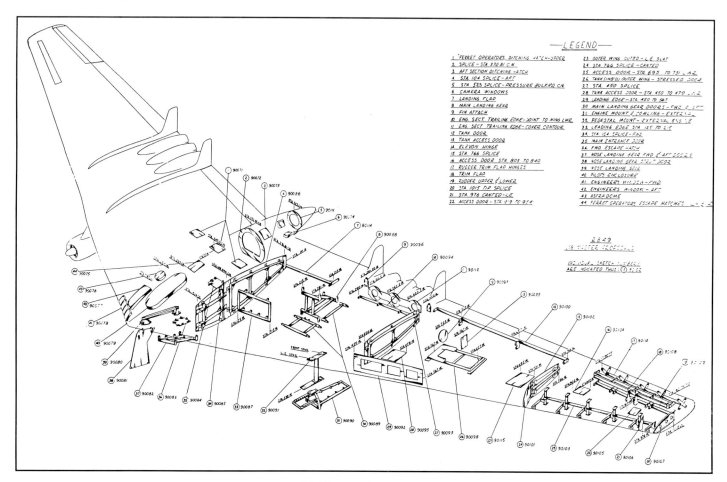

RB-49A General Arrangement

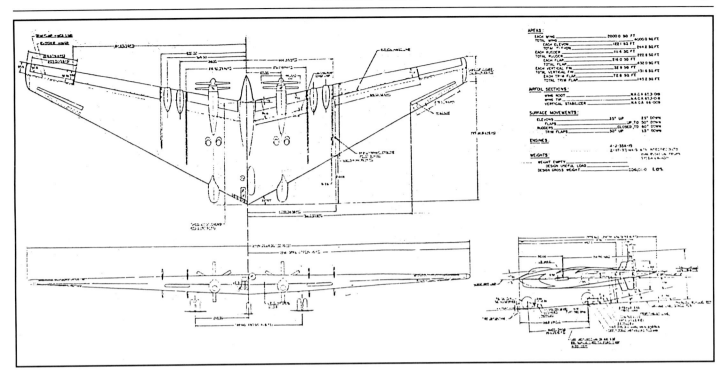

EB-35B Three View

Flight testing of the YRB-49A was apparently accomplished only by Northrop flight crews. Here a T-33 chase plane accompanies the Flying Wing. (Edwards AFB History Office)

An 188 lb. T-89 flash bomb is dropped by the YRB-49A. Six of these flash bombs could be carried. (Edwards AFB History Office)

Left and above: Proposed RB-49 Production Schedule

The YRB-49A in flight over the southern California Mojave Desert. (Northrop/Stu Luce)

Left: By early 1951 the YRB-49A was in semi-storage at Edwards AFB. Jack Northrop requested that it be flown to his company's facility in Ontario, California, so he could use it for further flying wing work. The Air Force, not having further interest in the flying wing, agreed to the request. (Northrop/Western Museum of Flight)

Below: YRB-49A at Ontario Airport, California. Here it would sit for about two and a half years before being scrapped. (Edwards AFB History Office)

Jack Northrop left his company and the aircraft industry in November 1952. The departure was not on the best of terms, and things Northrop and Flying Wing were to be eradicated. It is somewhat surprising that the YRB-49A lasted about a year after Jack Northrop's departure. (Northrop)

A F-89 director flies with a N-69D Snark off the coast of Florida. Note the Northrop Flight Dept. logo* on the Scorpion's tail. (Northrop) *Insert. (Western Museum of Flight.)

EPILOGUE

Development of other variants of the large flying wing were pursued by Jack Northrop and his designers into early 1950. The use of a B-49-type wing was envisioned for civilian airline use. An elaborate mockup of the passenger cabin was constructed and a Hollywood film company was hired to produce a promotional film. The airline industry showed no interest and the project was dropped.

There were a variety of medium and large flying wings that were also proposed for various military uses during those post war years. Besides these bomber and reconnaissance aircraft, Northrop proposed an updated version of the XP-79B for both the Army Air Forces penetration fighter and interceptor fighter competition in late 1945. The penetration fighter version was to be powered by a Westinghouse 24-C turbojet engine and the interceptor version was to be rocket powered (much like the original XP-79 design). Un-like the construction of the XP-79B, these aircraft were to be constructed out of 75S aluminum alloy. The outcome of these two types of fighters would be exemplified in the McDonnell XF-88 and Lockheed XF-90 in the penetration role and the Republic XF-91 and Convair XF-92 as the interceptors.

A third category of fighter was also called for, the all-weather fighter. The purpose of this type of aircraft was to be able to hit enemy targets under all weather conditions, day or night. Northrop's initial proposal included two designs, one conventional and one tailless, both with magnesium skins. Each design included two variations of engines. The tailless design showed its lineage from Northrop's XP-56 and XP-79B aircraft. Though the tailless configuration was not selected, the outcome was good for Northrop. This would be the last major design by Jack Northrop, the P-89 Scorpion.

In the fall of 1948 it looked as if Northrop's big flying wing had a future. The Air Force had ordered 30 RB-49As and the remaining YB-35 airframes finally found a purpose in life. They were to be modified into photo-reconnaissance aircraft and serve as trainers for RB-49A crews. At this time it seemed that a "Flying Wing Airliner of Tomorrow" was a possibility. Northrop spent a sizeable amount of company funds trying to promote such a project. The airlines were not interested. (Northrop)

The Flying Wing Airliner was envisioned as a spacious craft and would afford the passengers a forward-looking view. There were a number of designs contemplated which ranged from a B-49-type six jet engined aircraft to one powered by a pair of Turbodyne turboprops. (Northrop)

Northrop's X-4

Also shortly after the Second World War ended, a number of joint Army Air Forces, Navy, and National Advisory Committee for Aeronautics (NACA) research projects were begun. The outcome was the now famous X-series of aircraft flown by Air Force and NACA/NASA pilots as well as the Douglas/Navy D-558-1 and D-558-2 research aircraft.

With the end of hostilities in late 1945, much investigative research into German aviation technology was planned by the Army Air Forces. It was the merging of the AAF's interest in the Messerschmitt Me 163 Komet and Jack Northrop's passion for flying wing and tailless aircraft that produced Project MX-810. The purpose of this research vehicle was to investigate stability and control of tailless swept-wing aircraft at transonic velocities.

A proposal was offered the Army Air Forces by Northrop in early 1946. It probably was no surprise that Northrop, the unquestioned American expert in tailless aircraft design, received a contract for two of these craft in short order (April 5, 1946). Under the direction of Northrop engineer Arthur I. Lusk the XS-4 (later designated X-4) was designed. Northrop drew on their experience with the XP-56 and XP-79 projects. Wing controls included outboard elevons and large split flaps designed to serve as speed brakes and landing flaps. Power for the XS-4 came from two Westinghouse J30-WE-7-9 jet engines. Two of these tiny glossy white aircraft were built.

Northrop test pilot Charles Tucker took the first X-4 (46-676) into the air on December 15, 1948. At Muroc it was flown by Northrop and Air Force test pilots. It was soon found to be a maintenance nightmare, principally mechanical problems. During one six month period, the test team was able to get it airborne three times. On a number of occasions the Northrop/Air Force test team had to enlist the aide of the NACA maintenance organization there at Muroc. This aircraft would make only 10 flights, then was grounded and used as a source of spares for the second X-4.

It was up to the second X-4 (46-677) to provide the data expected from this research aircraft. Once again the first flight was accomplished by Northrop's Charles Tucker on June 7, 1949. In

the first 18 months the craft flew about 20 flights by Northrop and Air Force pilots. In November 1950 it (and the first X-4, to be used for spare parts) was turned over to NACA. Between that date and September 1953, an additional 82 flights were flown by Air Force and NACA pilots as part of the NACA research program. Such pilots as Yeager and Crossfield flew this sleek little craft.

The flight test program showed that above Mach 0.76 the aircraft experienced constant yawing and rolling motions. At the same time, elevon effectiveness decreased considerably. At higher Mach numbers, uncontrollable oscillations about the three axes were encountered. When Mach 0.9 was reached, an undamped porpoising motion was encountered. Looking back, the results were not too surprising as the much earlier Messerschmitt Me 163 and de Havilland D.H. 108 Swallow experienced much of the same difficulties. It was during the time that the XS-4 was being designed that one of Britain's most able test pilots, Geoffrey de Havilland, was killed when the Swallow he was flying entered into violent pitching at Mach .875 while in a dive in which it broke up from the severe air loads at the lower altitudes.

Snark

Though not always included when describing the Northrop family of flying wing and tailless aircraft, the SM-62 Snark program needs to be mentioned. A request for proposals was sent to numerous companies by the Army Air Forces in October 1945 for designs for a Guided Missile Research Program. Northrop's proposal was accepted and on March 28, 1946, a letter contract was received for Project MX-775. Under Northrop model number N-25, a swept-wing, tailless missile with a range of 1,500 to 5,000 statute miles was designed. The missile was to carry a 5,000 pound warhead and fly at speeds in excess of 600 mph. At the same time Northrop developed a daytime star tracking system which would help navigate the missile.

Requirements for the missile changed in 1951 which required a major redesign. Now designated by the company as the N-69, the missile needed to have a range of 5,500 nautical miles. The payload was increased to 7,000 pounds. Somewhat like the flying wing,

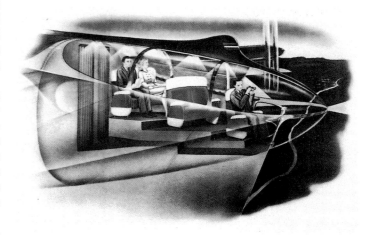

From a modified version of the B-49's stinger, passengers could watch from whence they came. (Northrop)

4-Engine Bomber Proposal

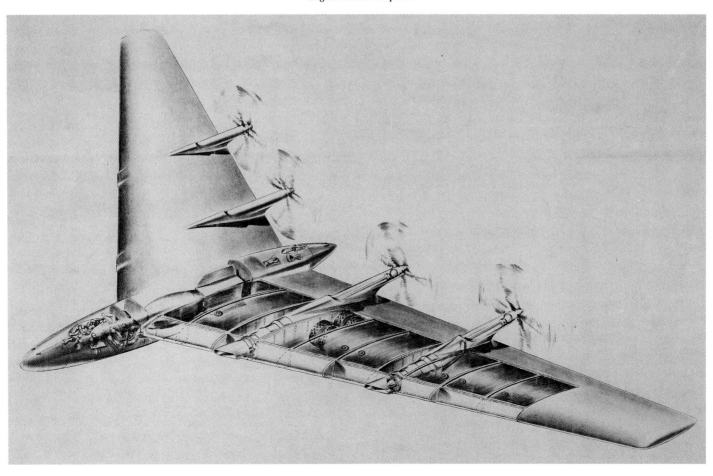

This January 1947 photo encompasses about all the projects that Northrop was contracted for at the time. Prominent in the center is the P-89 mockup. To the upper right is the XS-4 mockup. At the very top and center one of the big flying wings can be seen. (Northrop/G. H. Balzer Historical Archives)

the Snark was ahead of its time and the research and development program drew out much longer and cost a great deal more than what Northrop had promised. Also somewhat like the flying wing projects, it was Jack Northrop's relationship with the Air Forces'

Carl Spaatz and Joseph McNarney that helped keep the program alive.

The 702nd Strategic Missile Wing was activated at Presque Isle, Maine in January 1959. That May the first SM-62 Snark was

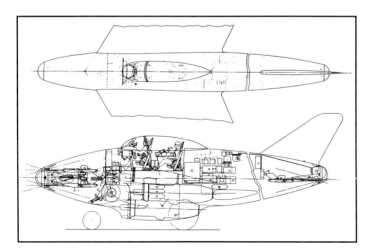

All Weather Fighter Proposal - Two TG-180 Engines (Offered in Tailless and Conventional Configurations) (Western Museum of Flight)

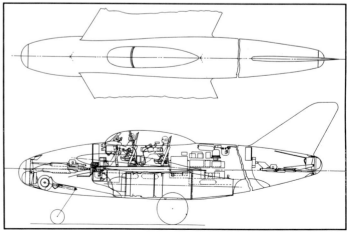

All Weather Fighter Proposal - Three Westinghouse 24-C Engines (Offered in Tailless And Conventional Configurations) (Western Museum of Flight)

received. Because of the Snark's limited capability, and the more promising Intercontinental Ballistic Missile coming of age, the air breathing Snark's career was short lived. On June 25, 1961 the 702nd was no longer in operations. A total (quantity requirements decreased throughout its long development cycle) of 51 SM-62s were produced.

A Sad Farewell

One might draw the conclusion that the flying wing and tailless aircraft produced by Northrop just didn't work. Looking at the record of the few – when compared to the "production" aircraft of World War II – that were produced, this would be correct. One of the four N-9Ms, one of the three MX-334/324s, one of the two XP-56s, and the sole XP-79B crashed in which two pilots were killed and one seriously hurt. The B-35/B-49 development program took much longer and cost a great deal more. Here too there was loss. Both flying YB-49s were lost, and the entire crew of one plane was killed.

But that was not all that unusual. At that time engineering was crude compared to today's standards. Flight testing was by "the seat of the pants." Planes that made great contributions to the war effort also suffered crashes and major technical problems. Just to

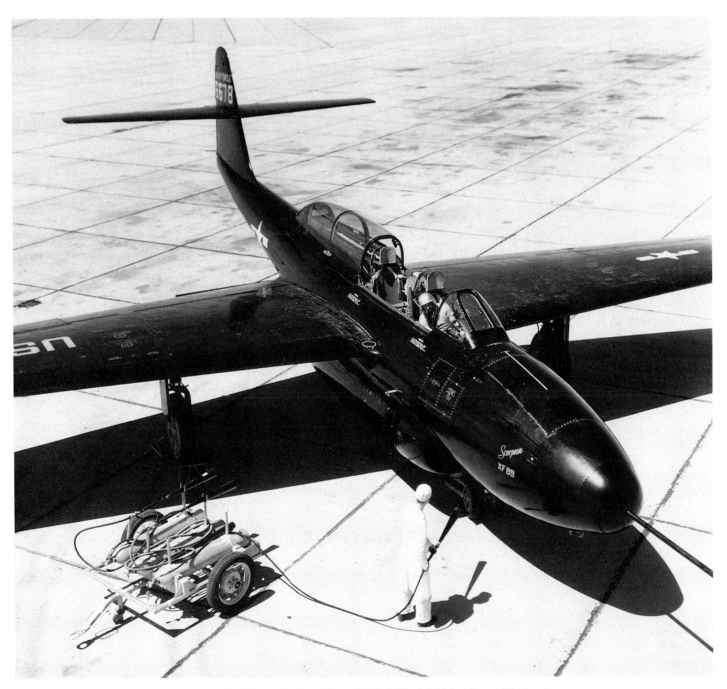

XP-89 at the flight test facility at Muroc AFB in California's Mojave Desert. (Northrop)

Number 1 X-4 (46-676) at Northrop Field in Hawthorne, California. First flight was on December 16, 1948. (Northrop)

name a few: Lockheed's P-38 Lightning, Boeing's B-17 Flying Fortress and B-29 Super Fortress, and North American's B-25 Mitchell. In the case of the XP-79B crash, it was neither a structural design nor an aerodynamic deficiency that caused it to crash. As for being on the verge of cancellation over a good part of its development effort, the B-35 project was no worse off than the B-36. Jack Northrop's large flying wings were ahead of the required technology; specifically, the stability and control augmentation and fly-by-wire systems that we have today. Besides, as the 1950s approached, speed and more speed was one of the prime requirements for bombers. The large chord wings of Northrop's, as aerodynamically clean as they were, were not built for speed.

Jack Northrop was an exceptional engineer. There has been much testimony to that fact by such peers of his as Ed Heinemann, Donald Douglas, Sr., and Claude Ryan. If anything, it was in the business environment that problems occurred. He seemed to always see the "potential" of his flying wing, but the actual realm was sometimes lost.

The scrapping of all but two of his beloved flying wings in late 1949 and early 1950 had to be a mighty blow to Jack Northrop. Those wings were what most of his adult life had been about. Then the accident that destroyed the last YB-49 in mid-March of that year had to seem just too much for one man to take. Jack Northrop continued work on such projects as the Snark and Scorpion, but the environment was changing at his company. Retired Air Force General Oliver Echols had become board chairman and general manager. Unlike his predecessors, Echols overrode Northrop in hiring and technical matters. The last straw was Echols' decision to hire Edgar Schmued over the person Jack Northrop wanted. Northrop's health suffered and according to those around him, he was not the same Jack Northrop – the vigor had gone out of him. In November 1952, he left his company and the aircraft industry for good.

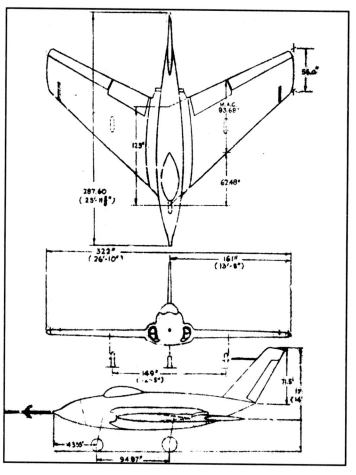

X-4 Three View

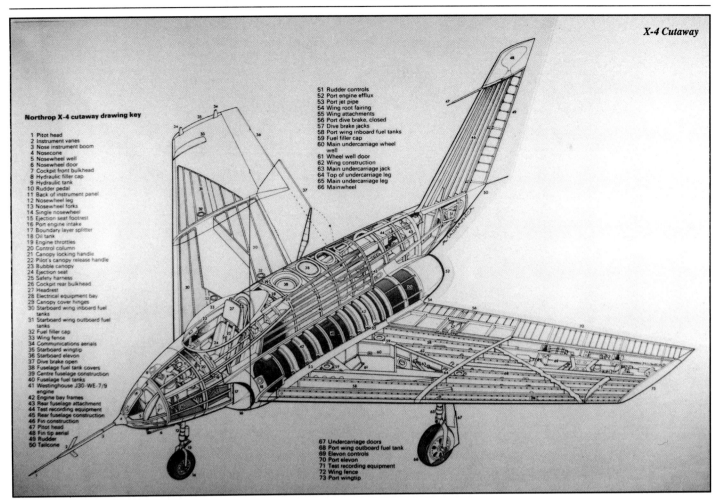

Northrop X-4 cutaway drawing key

1 Pitot head
2 Instrument vanes
3 Nose instrument boom
4 Nosecone
5 Nosewheel well
6 Nosewheel door
7 Cockpit front bulkhead
8 Hydraulic filler cap
9 Hydraulic tank
10 Rudder pedal
11 Back of instrument panel
12 Nosewheel leg
13 Nosewheel forks
14 Single nosewheel
15 Ejection seat footrest
16 Port engine intake
17 Boundary layer splitter
18 Oil tank
19 Engine throttles
20 Control column
21 Canopy locking handle
22 Pilot's canopy release handle
23 Bubble canopy
24 Ejection seat
25 Safety harness
26 Cockpit rear bulkhead
27 Headrest
28 Electrical equipment bay
29 Canopy cover hinges
30 Starboard wing inboard fuel tanks
31 Starboard wing outboard fuel tanks
32 Fuel filler cap
33 Wing fence
34 Communications aerials
35 Starboard wingtip
36 Starboard elevon
37 Dive brake open
38 Fuselage fuel tank covers
39 Centre fuselage construction
40 Fuselage fuel tanks
41 Westinghouse J30-WE-7/9 engine
42 Engine bay frames
43 Rear fuselage attachment
44 Test recording equipment
45 Rear fuselage construction
46 Fin construction
47 Pitot head
48 Fin tip aerial
49 Rudder
50 Tailcone

51 Rudder controls
52 Port engine efflux
53 Port jet pipe
54 Wing root fairing
55 Wing attachments
56 Port dive brake, closed
57 Dive brake jacks
58 Port wing inboard fuel tanks
59 Fuel filler cap
60 Main undercarriage wheel well
61 Wheel well door
62 Wing construction
63 Main undercarriage jack
64 Top of undercarriage leg
65 Main undercarriage leg
66 Mainwheel

67 Undercarriage doors
68 Port wing outboard fuel tank
69 Elevon controls
70 Port elevon
71 Test recording equipment
72 Wing fence
73 Port wingtip

Soon after Jack's departure, company policy seemed to be more like a Russian purge. Anything concerning Jack Northrop or flying wings were not to be mentioned. Apparently there was a cleaning out of files which included the destruction of drawings, photos, and much of what had to do with the wings.

Vindicated

As the old saying goes, "things change." And they certainly did. Avionics, electronics, stability and control augmentation, fly-by-wire – by the mid 1970s these were part of all aircraft. Technology had made great strides during the three or so decades after Jack Northrop left the industry. Speed was no longer the top priority. Jack Northrop would soon learn about one of the top priorities.

The need for a new bomber for the Strategic Air Command (SAC) was recognized in the mid-1960's. The XB-70 and short-lived B-58 left SAC with an aging – chronologically as well as technically – B-52 fleet. Bomber seemed to denote a negative connotation so the Advanced Manned Strategic Aircraft (AMSA) program was initiated, which would become the Rockwell B-1A. Like its predecessors, speed was a major requirement. But technology was overcoming speed as a major attribute. Deception, hiding from or fooling sensors was seen as the upcoming requirement. This is now commonly referred to as "stealth." Apparently in the mid-1970s a number of stealth aircraft technology programs were undertaken. One known outcome of these projects is the Lockheed F-117.

Competing with Lockheed for the F-117 was Northrop Corporation. Though not winning that contract, they had entered the world of stealth. At the 1991 Wright Brothers Lecture, American Institute of Aeronautics and Astronautics Aircraft Design and Operations Meeting on September 23, 1991, Northrop's Irving T. Waaland presented a paper titled "Technology in the Lives of an Aircraft Designer." In his paper he stated:

Northrop remained immersed in this new technology, convinced that its major impact on military effectiveness would make it the cornerstone of most new combat aircraft. In addition to advancing the low observables state-of-the-art, our technology efforts focused on enhancing the integration of stealth with aerodynamic efficiency and the integration of sensors, since the implementation of stealth beyond the world of demonstrators required the ability to perform all normal aircraft functions in a competitive manner. We developed a number of candidate configurations for different mission applications to broaden our understanding of stealth integration and its payoff. When we faced into the challenge of a stealthy, long range, heavy bomber, we started with a clean sheet of paper and an improved state-of-the-art in low observables technology.

Bomber was apparently still "verboten" and the stealth bomber program was, in AMSA-fashion, called the Advanced Strategic Penetrating Aircraft or ASPA. Very little is known of the early conceptual phase of this aircraft. Slightly more is known about what is

X-4 number 1 was trucked to Muroc AFB on November 15, 1948. This first example of the X-4 series was somewhat troublesome. A total of 10 flights were accomplished with this aircraft, all with Northrop test pilot Charles Tucker. (Northrop)

called the full scale development phase which started in late 1981. Air Force Major General Stephen B. Croker described the mission of this aircraft before the Committee on Appropriations, Subcommittee on Defense of the US Senate in April 1991:

> The original B-2 mission statement in the B-2 Weapon System Specification, dated 1 November 1981, stated that "the Advanced Strategic Penetrating Aircraft (ASPA) shall provide the capability to conduct missions across the spectrum of conflict, including general nuclear war, conventional conflict, and peacetime/crisis situations.

When the small group of engineers took on their assignment to design a stealth bomber did they start with the Northrop B-49 design? The answer is a resounding No! Both Irv Waaland and Dr. John Cashen, who along with Jim Kinnu and John Patierno formed the initial team in the late 1970s, have stated so. Apparently a number of the early "Stealth Bomber" team made trips to the east coast to see the National Air and Space Museum's Horten IX V-3 jet-powered flying wing. This fact takes nothing away from Jack Northrop. It gives more credence to his foresight.

Irv Waaland expounded on this during a public talk in January 1994:

> When we started the B-2, we started with a clean sheet of paper. What we were after first and foremost was low radar cross section.

We had done some work before we actually got started on the B-2. We looked at a large number of different ways of getting low radar cross section. Our conclusion was an all-wing platform really had a lot going for it. We had done studies on it some years before. When the Air Force asked us to look at developing a long-range penetrating bomber with low radar cross section, our first thought went to using the flying wing because it had the best chance of getting low radar cross section in a large size vehicle.

What we got from the YB-49 of course was a feasibility establishment. It had been done before; therefore, it could be done again. We had a lot more going for us because we already had fully powered controls. We had fully automatic control systems. So we had that leg up, a lot of confidence going in. The only thing we did not have full confidence in was could we operate completely without the vertical fins. Because we really didn't want to have vertical fins. Having these big broad area things up there makes it very difficult to get low radar cross section. We knew from all the readings of [Dr. William] Sears and [Jack] Northrop and Irv [Ashkenas] and so forth, that it was perfectly feasible to operate without the vertical fins. Our first configuration drawings actually had some verticals. They started at the center of the airplane, something like, what you see on the Stealth Fighter. We then moved down to little verticals at the wing tips. And we looked at using reaction controls at the wing tips, and finally went to the split flap as the primary method of going without any fins.

The B-2 is unique, I think, among most of the airplanes because it is unstable both in the pitch axis and the yaw axis. It has negative directional stability. It gets its directional stability by having good directional controls. In other words, when the wing starts to move, you hit the controls, get it back to where it belongs, and it just becomes keeping it where it wants to go. So we got the advantage of that, we did all the reading on the YB-49, made sure we understood it. We talked to Sears; we talked to Ashkenas; we talked to Max [Stanley] and got a lot of pointers from them – lessons learned.

One of the characteristics that you see in the B-2 when it flies is just like the YB-49. And that is, in normal flight, the rudders are open. You see them cracked open all the time. The reason for that is that the control effectiveness of those rudders is nonlinear. The first motion of them, at some conditions, you actually can get a reversal. When you first open them you reduce the drag and the wing wants to go the other way. When it's open, it already has some. It's ready to take a bite out of the air as soon as you start opening them. In all the movies you see of the YB-49, the rudders are open a little bit; all the films

Test pilot Chuck Tucker and a Northrop ground crew member with the X-4 at Muroc. Tucker was hired by Northrop specifically to fly the X-4, but because of design and manufacturing delays he was assigned to the YB-49 flight test program. (Northrop)

Preflight preparations at Muroc. (Northrop)

you see of the B-2, because you don't see it flying in a stealthy mode, the rudders are open a little bit, gives a little bit better control effectiveness for the same reason.

The other big thing we got out of the YB-49 was Max Stanley, who was accessed to the program, flew the simulator, and he saved us a bundle of money because our wind tunnel tests made our aerodynamicists and control system fearful that this ground effects of 'You'll never get the airplane down on the ground.' 'The characteristics are going to change.' 'We got this fantastic control system. All it is is a computer with a whole bunch of software, and we can just write a few more thousand lines of code and have a completely different program for when we're near the ground.' Money. Max flew the simulator and said 'Gee, it flies like a YB-49. They were afraid of the same thing; and the airplane just settled very gently, and I don't think you will have any problem.' So I was able to say let's just leave that stuff off the airplane and we'll find out. And sure enough, when Bruce Hinds flew the airplane it settled in just like Max said it would. He earned his money.

The fact that they are both 172 feet 6 inches is merely pure coincidence. We laid out an airplane, did all the calculations at one sweep to get stability and so forth and then we did an overlay with a YB-49 after we had it drawn. It turned out that they were identical. It wasn't a starting point.

First flight for the second X-4 (46-677) was on June 7, 1949 with Chuck Tucker at the controls. Twenty flights were accomplished under the contractor (Phase I) flight test program. (Northrop)

In 1980 Northrop Corporation was well into this project that very few would know about for many years to come. The company management had changed many times since Jack Northrop had left it; Thomas V. Jones was now its chief executive officer. It was through Jones' personal effort that the ailing Jack Northrop was to be informed of one of this nation's most secret projects. In April 1980 he was brought to one of the many buildings at the corporation's Aircraft Division in Hawthorne, California. Here he was ushered into a room where he met with the chief architects of what he was to see, John Cashen and Irv Waaland. A box was brought out and opened so he could see its contents. What he saw was then called the Advanced Technology Bomber or ATB; more commonly called the Stealth Bomber. With tears in his eyes, he said, "Now I know why God has kept me alive for the last 25 years." It pleased Northrop. There were no propeller shafts and housings as on the XB-35. And those fins and fences on the YB-49 – were also gone. The ATB was as pure a flying wing as John K. Northrop could have dreamed.

That following year, on February 18th, Jack Northrop passed away at the age of 85. Possibly one of the most fitting tributes paid to him came from fellow pioneer Donald W. Douglas, Sr., who passed only 17 days earlier. Douglas had once said, "Every major airplane in the skies today has some of Jack Northrop in it."

November 22, 1988 was rollout day for the B-2. As part of the ceremonies, Northrop's Thomas V. Jones stated:

> In closing, I'd like to express my thanks and my recognition to someone who can't be here today. But thanks to the Air Force, before he died, he learned in a very private, specially arranged briefing that the flying wing would eventually emerge from a legend of the past, and the secrecy of the present, to be recognized and to contribute to a safer America of the future. Jack Northrop, we salute you."

Where Are They Now

It is a shame that none of the big wings were sent to a museum rather than being scrapped. But there are examples of the smaller craft that have survived. The Smithsonian Institution's National Air and Space Museum has done a wonderful job of restoring the sole N-1M. It is today on display at their Silver Hill, Maryland, facility.

First flight under NACA control was on August 18, 1950. Chuck Yeager was the pilot on that date. The NACA would fly the little craft 82 times bringing total flights for the second X-4 to 102. On January 24, 1951 test pilot Scott Crossfield took the airplane to mach .92. (NASA)

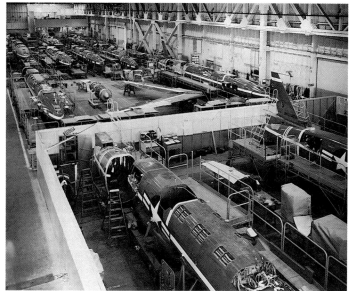

Northrop's Snark production line. (Northrop)

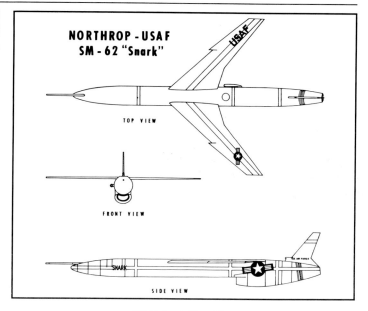

SM-62 Snark Three View

A Snark rockets off its launcher during flight test. (Northrop)

At that same facility, though not restored, lies the remains of the second XP-56. Traveling west across the country one can find both X-4s. The number two X-4 is hanging in the main building at the Air Force Museum located at Wright-Patterson Air Force Base near Dayton, Ohio, while the first X-4 is on display at the Air Force Academy in Colorado Springs, Colorado.

A couple of examples of Jack Northrop's flying wings can be found in California. At The Air Museum/Planes of Fame Museum in Chino is the N-9MB. Restoration work is nearly complete on this aircraft. On January 8, 1994, it made its first taxi test in decades followed by the first flight of this phoenix on November 8, 1994. At Hawthorne Municipal Airport, where Northrop Corporation's Aircraft Division is located, the Western Museum of Flight also resides. Among their collection is the glider version of the JB-1.

Could there be more? Three of the four little N-9s survived flight testing and pilot training. Besides the N-9MB at Chino, one of the other two was in a yard backing up to Compton, California, Airport around 1950 or 1951 according to local observers. Army Air Forces records also show that at least one of the two surviving MX-324/334s was sent to Freeman Field in Indiana to become part of the museum collection. Some references show that this aircraft ended up with the National Air and Space Museum but their records do not list it as one of their collection. Likewise, the 11th JB-10 was to be sent to Freeman. Will the years to come reveal where these or others are? We can only hope.

John K. Northrop's major designs. (Northrop)

John K. Northrop. (Northrop)

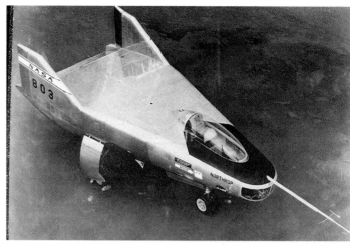

In April 1951 the last flight of a Northrop flying wing occurred. Nineteen months later Jack Northrop severed all relations with the company he formed and with the aircraft industry. About a year after Jack Northrop's departure the last flying wing was scrapped. Ten years later the Northrop Corporation once again had a flying wing, or sorts, called a "lifting body." (Northrop/Wolford Collection)

First of the Lifting Bodies to be built by Northrop Corporation's Norair Division in the mid-1960s was the M2-F2 (later to be modified into the M2-F3). This craft's design was based on NASA design criteria developed at the Ames Research Center in California. (Northrop)

Above and opposite: Another Northrop product of the mid-1960s was the HL-10 Lifting Body. This craft was based on designs laid out by NASA's Langley Research Center in Virginia. (Northrop/Wolford Collection)

For many years there was no contact between Jack Northrop and the company he founded. As time went on and the company's top management changed, Jack Northrop did return on special occasions. (Western Museum of Flight)

John K. Northrop, center, and his Stealth Bomber hosts. The two principal designers of Northrop's Stealth Bomber are Irv Waaland, to John Northrop's right; and John Cashen, to the far left of Northrop. (Northrop/Stu Luce)

The Air Force released this artist's rendering of the B-2 in April 1988. (USAF)

B-2 production at the Northrop-run final assembly facility at Air Force Plant 42 in Palmdale, California. (Northrop)

Rollout ceremony of Air Vehicle Number One (AV-1) at Palmdale, California, on November 22, 1988. This was the public's first look at the Stealth Bomber. (Northrop) Insert - Commemorative Rollout pin.

B-2 Test Team patch.

B-2 Combined Test Force patch.

From Air Force Plant 42 in Palmdale AV-1 (serial 82-1066) takes to the air for the first time on July 17, 1989. (Northrop) Insert - Commemorative First Flight pin.

Mission completed, this B-2A nears touchdown at Edwards AFB in California's Mojave Desert as the sun sets. (Northrop)

The B-2, named by the Air Force as the Spirit, flies over the Sierras. (Northrop)

USAF/NORTHROP B-2

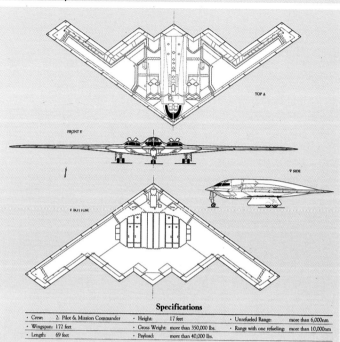

Specifications

Crew:	2; Pilot & Mission Commander	Height:	17 feet	Unrefueled Range:	more than 6,000nm
Wingspan:	172 feet	Gross Weight:	more than 350,000 lbs.	Range with one refueling:	more than 10,000nm
Length:	69 feet	Payload:	more than 40,000 lbs.		

AV-1 taxies by AV-2 at Edwards AFB. AV-2 first flew on October 19, 1990. (Northrop)

A closeup of AV-1 as it approaches a tanker for refuelling. (Northrop)

AV-3 is refueled by a KC-10 while AV-4, flying in formation, awaits its turn. (Northrop)

As a B-2 comes in for a landing, Northrop's entry into the Advanced Tactical Fighter contest, the YF-23, seems to be looking on. (Northrop)

One of the B-2s is caught silhouetted against some spectacular cloud formations. (Northrop)

Bomb drop tests with a MK. 84 "shape". (Northrop)

In this view the sawtoothed trailing edge of the B-2A is quite distinguishable. (Northrop)

Above and opposite page: The first B-2A to go to an operational USAF unit, 88-0329, is shown at Palmdale, California, awaiting the next day's flight to Whiteman AFB, Missouri. (Northrop)

Arrival at Whiteman AFB in December 1993. (Northrop)

Above and left: Each operational B-2A is being named "Spirit of _____." The first B-2A to arrive at Whiteman, 88-0329, was named Spirit of Missouri. The Aircraft's name can be seen on the outboard main landing gear door. (Northrop)

Above opposite:
A historic display in honor of the 509th Bomb Wing receiving its first B-2A at Whiteman AFB. (Northrop)

Below opposite:
Naming of the second B-2A destined for Whiteman AFB takes place at Northrop's Palmdale facility as one of the other B-2s makes a crowd pleasing flyby. (Northrop)

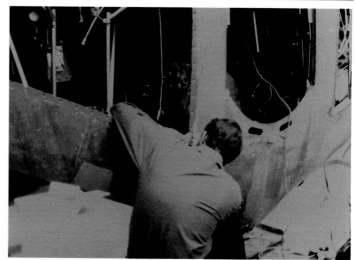

Above photos: Beginning restoration work on the Northrop N-1M by the Smithsonian Institution's National Air and Space Museum staff. (Wolford)

Above: The culmination of some 11,500 man hours of work in March 1983. (NASM)

On display at NASM's Silver Hill, Maryland, facility.

Another Northrop product in the National Air and Space Museum's collection is the second XP-56. It presently awaits restoration. (Vas)

Closeup of the nose and cockpit area of the XP-56. These photos were taken while the aircraft was in California awaiting restoration by a small museum. It turned out to be too difficult a job and was returned in late 1989 to the NASM. (San Diego Aerospace Museum)

The XP-56 cockpit as it appears today. (Vas)

The first X-4 on display at the Air Force Academy near Colorado Springs, Colorado. (Air Force Academy)

Left:
Rollout of a restored X-4 number two on January 20, 1988. Many present and past Northrop employees put in hours of labor and love in accomplishing this feat. (Vas)

Below
The second X-4 at the Air Force Museum at Wright-Patterson AFB near Dayton, Ohio, shortly after restoration. (Air Force Museum)

The fourth N-9M, designated N-9MB, as it appeared at The Air Museum near Ontario, California, in 1963. (Author)

The N-9MB at The Air Museum's Ontario, California, Airport facility a couple of years later. (Author)

Two photos above and below. Official rollout day for the public was held on May 8, 1994 at The Air Museum/Planes of Fame Museum at Chino Airport, California. (Author)

After some 12 years of restoration, the N-9MB is shown here going through its first engine runs on January 8, 1994. (Petry)

Among the dignitaries included at the N-9MB rollout, from left to right: Bruce
Hinds, Northrop's test pilot on the B-2A's first flight; retired Air Force Brig. Gen.
Robert Cardenas, who flew in both the N-9MA and B as well as many hours in the
YB-49; and Don Lykins, the museum's chairman of the board and designated pilot
for the N-9MB's first flight. (Author)

On June 11, 1994 John H. Northrop, son of John K. Northrop, and a successful
engineer in his own right, was given the opportunity to view the newly restored N-
9MB. (Author)

The engines rev up for a slow taxi for the many guests at the May 1994 rollout.
(Author)

Thanks to John H. Northrop's assistance, author Garry Pape also was given an
opportunity to try out the cockpit. (Author)

Inside the cockpit of the beautifully restored N-9MB. (Author)

Below: Taxiing back after a good test flight. As in all early test flights, all usually doesn't go as planned. On this flight some problem occurred at the end of the flight which prevented pilot Don Lykins from throttling back the engines. He had to shut off the power and make a dead stick landing and then restart the engines to taxi the little craft. Most of the large audience gathered to witness this historical occasion were not aware of the problem until it was reported on that evening's TV news. (Author)

There were a number of notables on hand for this milestone in flying wing history. To the far left of the picture is retired Air Force General Robert Cardenas. In the center, with the purple baseball cap, is Col. James H. "Jimmy" Doolittle III, grandson of the late General James H. "Jimmy" Doolittle (America's only 4-star Reserve Officer) of air racing fame and prominent World War II military leader. (Author)

Above: On Friday, November 11, 1994, the restored N-9MB took to the air at Chino Airport (home of the Planes of Fame Museum), California, in what was billed as its first flight (others at Chino Airport reported that it actually took to the air for an extended flight in the early afternoon of Tuesday, November 8th). (Author)

Post flight debrief for the flying wing enthusiasts and news media. From left to right are Ron Hackworth, restoration project manager; pilot of the N-9MB Don Lykins (he's also the chairman of the board of the Planes of Fame Museum); and museum president Edward Maloney. (Author)

The Planes of Fame "thank you" card was part of the display for the November 11 "first flight" program. Conspicuous by their absence from the list of donors was Northrop Corporation. (Author)

The JB-1 glider on display at the Western Museum of Flight at Hawthorne Airport, California. (Author)

The Northrop logo on the nose of the JB-1 glider. (Author)

Northrop Aircraft, Incorporated logo of 1940.

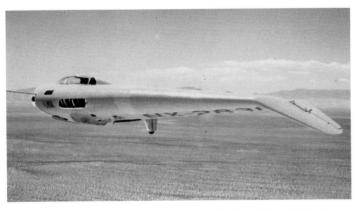

N-1M in flight over the southern Mojave Desert. (Northrop/Wolford Collection)

Northrop test pilot, and corporate secretary, Moye Stephens in the cockpit of the N-1M. (Northrop/Wolford Collection)

The minimum clearance between the canopy and the pilot's head in the N-1M is quite visible in this shot. (Northrop/Wolford Collection)

"Photo Day," December 4, 1941 in the Muroc area in the Mojave Desert. (Northrop/Wolford Collection)

N-1M in flight. (Northrop/Wolford Collection)

Jack Northrop congratulates Moye Stephens after the air show he put on for the newsreel and newspaper people on hand for the first public showing of the N-1M on December 4, 1941. (Northrop/Wolford Collection)

N-1M did much to prove Jack Northrop's belief that a flying wing could fly and perform as any other airplane. (Northrop/Wolford Collection)

An artist's conception of the P-56 interceptor. (Northrop/Wolford Collection)

The first XP-56 in its silver paint scheme. (Northrop/Wolford Collection)

Opposite above:
Second of the XP-56s had the extended vertical added before starting flight test. (Northrop)

Opposite below:
Three quarter rear view of XP-56 number two awaiting flight testing at one of the dry lakes in the Mojave Desert. (Northrop/Edwards AFB History Office)

Once a second N-9M was produced, this initial variant was popularly called the N-9M-1. (Northrop/Wolford Collection)

Northrop test pilot John Myers flies the first N-9M over southern California. (Northrop/Wolford Collection)

The fourth, and last, N-9M was designated N-9MB. (Northrop)

The only time that the three surviving N-9Ms flew in formation was in February 1946. The N-9MB is to the left, the N-9MA is in the upper right of the picture, and the N-9M-2 is in the lower right. At the time of this photo, both the N-9MA and B had identical paint schemes–yellow upper and blue lower surfaces. (Northrop)

An N-9M wings over the desert floor. (Northrop)

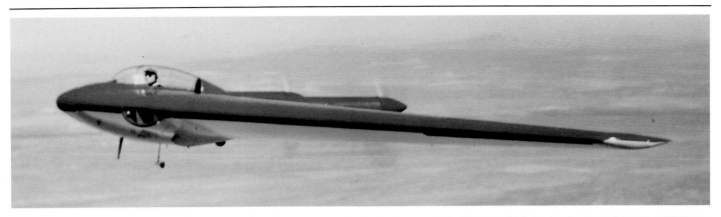

The N-9MA has reversed its colors in this photo; now the upper surface is painted blue and the lower yellow. (Northrop/Edwards AFB History Office)

Northrop test pilot Max Stanley checks out an Army pilot in this February 1947 photo taken at Muroc AFB. (Northrop)

Phantom model of the XB-35. (Western Museum of Flight)

An example of the R-4360 on display at the Planes of Fame Museum at Chino Airport, California. (Author)

The first XB-35 is rolled out of Northrop's Plant 3 in Hawthorne, California, in July 1945. Under the tarp to the right of the big wing is its one-third flying scale model, the N-9M. (Northrop)

Cutaway of the XB-35. (Northrop)

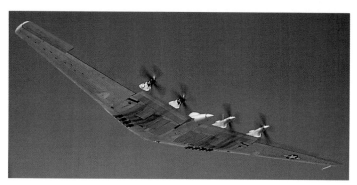

Above photos: This series of photos was taken by Northrop photographer Ray Wolford while flying in a P-61 Black Window chase plane during XB-35 number one's first flight. (Northrop/Wolford Collection)

In flight the XB-35 was a very sleek looking aircraft. (Northrop)

Above and three photos to the left:
XB-35 number one, serial 42-13603, and Muroc AFB. In place of the gun turrets this aircraft had aerodynamic shapes. Both the second XB-35 and the sole YB-35 to fly had turrets installed. (USAF/NASM)

The first XB-35 at Muroc AAB in mid-1946. (Northrop/Wolford Collection)

Northrop's XB-35 undergoing maintenance at Muroc AAB. (Northrop)

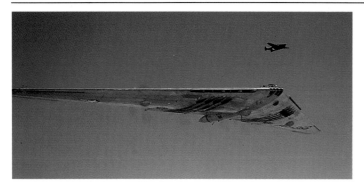

YB-35, serial 42-102366, with its P-61 chase plane during flight testing. (USAF/ NASM)

The YB-35 was the only one of the big wings to carry a buzz number. (USAF/ NASM)

The YB-35 flies over one of the many dry lake beds in the Mojave Desert. (USAF/ NASM)

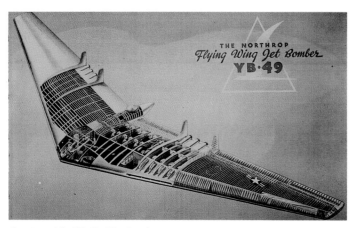

Cutaway of the YB-49. (Northrop)

The first YB-49, serial 42-102367, nearing completion at the Northrop plant. Because of the great amount of space required to build and later modify these gigantic flying wings, a good bit of work was accomplished in the outdoors. (Northrop)

Lining up on the runway at Northrop Field. (Northrop)

YB-49 number one being prepared for an upcoming test flight at Muroc AFB. (USAF/NASM)

Like a flying scimitar, the first YB-49 knives through the blue southern California skies. (USAF/NASM)

The YB-49 was as graceful looking on the ground as it was in the air. (USAF/NASM)

First YB-49 prepares for takeoff at Muroc AFB. (USAF/NASM)

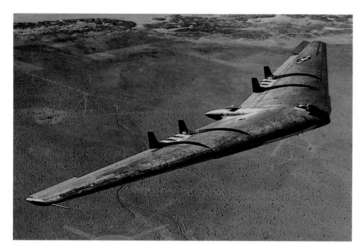

Jack Northrop's dream of a "clean" airplane was nearly realized in the YB-49. Reduced drag and increased lift is the basis of this sleek aircraft. (Northrop)

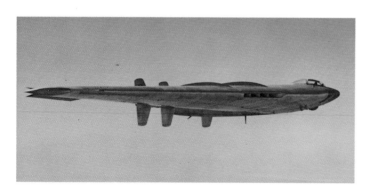

The flight test program of the second YB-49 was cut short with its crash on June 5, 1948, in which Major Danny Forbes, Capt. Glen Edwards, Lt. Edward Swindell, C. Leser, and C. LaFountain (the latter two being civilian employees of Air Materiel Command) were killed. (Northrop)

Above photos: Preparing for flight. (Northrop)

Bomb loading. (Northrop)

The only thing that marred the YB-49 was the vertical fins required for directional stability. They bothered Jack Northrop and he was always working towards finding a way to eliminate them. (Northrop)

The fences along the upper wing surface acted as a barrier to prevent spanwise flow of the boundary layer. The mechanical slots, which were sealed closed in high-speed flight, opened in the low-speed realm to delay stalls at higher angles of attack. (Northrop)

Second of the two YB-49s, serial 42-102368, in flight over the Mojave. (USAF/NASM)

Appendix A

WING CHRONOLOGY
OF NORTHROP AIRCRAFT, INC.

DATE	EVENT
March 7, 1939	Northrop Aircraft, Inc. is formed under California state laws.
June 1939	Company publicly financed through the sale of stock and warrants totaling $1.25 million.
August 1939	Temporary quarters set up in Hawthorne Hotel, Hawthorne, California.
Sept. 29, 1939	Official groundbreaking for Northrop Aircraft permanent facilities.
Late Jan. 1940	First contract received. Consolidated Aircraft of San Diego, $650,000.
Feb. 20, 1940	Main plant building ready for occupancy.
April 1940	First contract for a complete airplane. 24 N-3PBs for the Royal Norwegian Government.
June 22, 1940	XP-56 contract (W535 ac-15021) approved.
July 3, 1940	First flight of N-1M.
Sept. 1940	Wind tunnel construction.
Dec. 1940	Wind tunnel operational.

May 20, 1941	Assistant Secretary of War for Air Robert Lovett gets flying wing briefing at Northrop. Lovett suggested a bomber of the following specifications:
	    16,000 lb. bomb load
	    400 mph maximum speed
	    Margins go towards range

May 21, 1941	Letter from John Northrop to Col. Howard Bogert at Wright Field. Based on Secretary Lovett's suggested performance, Northrop estimated:
	    Based on four 2,000 hp engines
	    Range of approximately 5,000 miles
	    Operating speed of approximately 300 mph

May 24, 1941	General Oliver Echols, Materiel Division Chief, gets flying wing briefing at Northrop. Echols performance requirements for the bomber were:
	    400 mph high speed
	    5,000 lb. bomb load
	    All additional performance go towards range

May 25, 1941	Letter from John Northrop to Col. Howard Bogert at Wright Field. Based on General Echol's suggested performance, Northrop estimated:

	10,000 to 15,000 lb. bomb load 5,000 mile range 100,000 lb. aircraft gross weight
May 27, 1941	Materiel Division letter to Northrop requests Design Studies of Heavy Bombardment Type Aircraft.
July 2, 1941	John Northrop presented preliminary design during a conference at Wright Field.
July 13, 1941	Purchase Order 42-2552 called for a three-phase effort: I - Engineering data for evaluation of design and release for development, II - Tests of wind tunnel models and reports on N-1M progress, and III construction of N-9M with delivery in 360 days.
Aug. 6, 1941	Contract W535 ac-21920 for one XB-35 initiated.
Aug. 20, 1941	Telephone conversation between Lt. Col. F. O. Carroll, Experimental Engineering Section Chief at Wright Field with Northrop's Walt Cerny. Air Corps' desired specifications: 10,000 mile range 240 - 300 mph average cruising speed 350 - 450 mph high speed 35,000 ft. critical altitude 40,000 ft. service ceiling (with 2/3 fuel remaining)
Sept. 4, 1941	Contract W535 ac-21341 signed. N-9M contracted for N-1M data to be furnished to Wright Field
Sept. 9, 1941	Jack Northrop, Dr. Sears, et al meet in General Echols' office in Washington, D.C. Purchase of first plane authorized.
Sept. 30, 1941	Contract W535 ac-21341 approved.
Oct. 3, 1941	Purchase Order 42-2552, study phase of flying wing bomber, approved.
Nov. 22, 1941	Contract W535 ac-21920 approved (first XB-35).
Dec. 16, 1941	Northrop informed Wright Field that the Air Corps' Western District Supervisor issued a stop work on the flying wing contract so V-72/A-31 as well as Boeing and Consolidated subcontract work could be accomplished.
Jan. 2, 1942	Change Order No. 1 to Contract W535 ac-21920 (second XB-35) approved.
Feb. 13, 1942	Contract W535 ac-25060 for second XP-56 approved.
July 6-17, 1942	Mockup inspection.
Sept 10, 1942	Change Order No. 3 to Contract W535 ac-21920 for second N-9M and N-9MA.
Sept. 15, 1942	Northrop presents unsolicited proposal for P-999. This leads to XP-79 project.
Oct. 3, 1942	Original contractual first flight date of N-9M.
Nov. 2, 1942	Northrop and Pratt & Whitney representatives met at Wright Field to discuss engine development.
Nov. 25, 1942	Materiel Command issued Confidential Technical Instruction 1047 directing the cancellation of the B-33 project at the Glenn L. Martin Co. and replacing that effort with the B-35 project.

Dec. 9, 1942	Materiel Command issued Confidential Technical Instruction 1073 to cancel Martin's XB-33 contract and divert engineers to B-35 project.
Dec. 11, 1942	Materiel Command proposed purchasing 100 B-35s from both Northrop and Martin.
Dec. 12, 1942	Teletype PE-72 cancelled entire 402 B-33s.
Dec. 17, 1942	Contract W535 ac-33920 for 13 YB-35s approved.
Dec. 27, 1942	First flight of N-9M no. 1.
Dec. 28, 1942	Technical Executive at Wright Field informed Gen. Echols that Northrop stated they did not have the facilities to build any more that the two XB-35s and 13 YB-35s. It was recommended that Martin get the entire contract of 200 production B-35s.
Jan. 12, 1943	Authority to Purchase 217608 issued for 3 XP-79s.
Jan. 15, 1943	Original contractual first flight date for second N-9M.
March 15, 1943	Original contractual first flight date for N-9MA.
April 12, 1943	XP-56 no. 1 taxi tests begin.
May 19, 1943	First N-9M crashed, killing test pilot Max Constant.
May 21, 1943	Contract W535 ac-36997 approved for XP-79s.
June 24, 1943	First flight of second N-9M.
June 24, 1943	Supplemental Agreement No. 6 to Contract W535 ac-24555 was signed for Martin's production of 200 production B-35Bs.
June 30, 1943	Contract W535 ac-24595 approved (200 B-35Bs).
Aug. 27, 1943	First flight of JB-1 glider.
Sept. 4, 1943	First flight of MX-334 no. 2.
Sept. 6, 1943	First and second flight of XP-56 no. 1.
Sept. 21, 1943	First reliable drag data obtained from an N-9M type craft.
Oct. 2, 1943	First flight of MX-334 no. 3.
Oct. 6/7, 1943	First conference held to promote closer cooperation between all parties on the B-35 project (alleviate the problems with Martin).
Oct. 8, 1943	Flights 3 and 4 of no. 1 XP-56. Destroyed in high speed taxi accident following flight 4.
Oct. 25, 1943	At Jack Northrop's request another conference was held to discuss the problems he was having with Martin.
Nov. 22, 1943	Original contractual first flight date for XB-35 no. 1.
Nov. 30, 1943	First flight of MX-334 no. 1.

March 23, 1944	First flight of XP-56 no. 2.
April 22, 1944	Original contractual first flight date for XB-35 no. 2.
May 4, 1944	Deputy Assistant Chief of Air Staff, Maj. Gen. B. S. Meyers, recommended that Martin's B-35B production contract be cancelled and that Martin continue assisting on the XB-35 and YB-35 engineering.
May 18, 1944	Meeting of the Joint Aircraft Committee approved cancellation of B-35B production contract.
May 22, 1944	First flight of N-9MA.
May 26, 1944	Notice of Termination against production contract W535 ac-24555 issued to Martin against production effort.
June 28, 1944	Air Force performed acceptance flight tests on the N-9MA.
July 1, 1944	First flight of MX-334 no. 2.
July 5, 1944	First flight of MX-324.
July 30, 1944	Original contractual first flight date for YB-35.
Aug. 11, 1944	Last flight of XP-56 no. 2.
Nov. 9, 1944	Col. Putt and Gen. Echols telephone discussion about B-35 conversion to jet engines.
Dec. 1, 1944	First flight of JB-1.
Dec. 8, 1944	Contractual action initiated to produce six YB-35s in XB-35 configuration to expedite getting them into the air (these six YB-35s were initially going to be redesignated XB-35).
Jan. 26, 1945	First flight of N-9MB.
April 6, 1945	First flight of JB-10.
April 20, 1945	Delay in YB-35 effort authorized in order to expedite XB-35 and YB-49 effort.
June 1, 1945	Change Order No. 11 to Contract W535 ac-33920 to convert YB-35s no. 1 and 2 to YB-49s.
Sept. 12, 1945	First flight of XP-79B. Aircraft crashed, killing Harry Crosby.
June 13, 1946	XB-35 no. 1 taxi tests begin.
June 25, 1946	First flight of Number 1 XB-35.
Feb. 17, 1947	Decision to go to single rotation, 4-bladed propeller.
June 26, 1947	First flight of Number 2 XB-35.
Sept. 18, 1947	689 inspection of YB-49 no. 1 completed.
Oct. 21, 1947	First flight of YB-49 no. 1.
Dec. 22, 1947	Number 1 XB-35: 12 flights to date. Number 2 XB-35: 4 flights to date.

Jan. 13, 1948	First flight of YB-49 no. 2.
Feb. 6, 1948	Number 1 XB-35: conversion to single rotation propeller completed, propeller vibration ground and taxi tests in progress. Number 2 XB-35: conversion about 50% complete.
Feb. 12, 1948	First flight of XB-35 no. 1 with single rotation propeller.
Feb. 20, 1948	Number 1 XB-35 has 15 flights to date and about 16 hours flight time.
Mar. 2, 1948	Northrop Eastern Rep. sent memo to Chief of Recon. & Photo Branch, Wash., DC, with prelim data on 3 photo recon versions of B-49.
Mar. 12-22, 1948	First bomb drop tests. Max Stanley and Northrop aircrew with AMC bombardier. AF report: "7 satisfactory runs."
Apr. 12, 1948	Strategic Reconnaissance Aircraft conference.
Apr. 26, 1948	9.5 hour range test. Set record for jet-powered aircraft while flying round robin circuit.
May 3, 1948	Bomber Branch, Procurement Division, wires Northrop authorizing prelim work on RB-49.
May 12, 1948	First flight of YB-35.
May 13, 1948	Negotiations begin with Northrop for RB-49.
June 5, 1948	YB-49 No. 2 crashes and kills all aboard.
June 12, 1948	Letter Contract for 30 FB-49s issued.
June 17, 1948	Gen. McNarney suggests most RB-49s be produced at Fort Worth, Texas, to maintain facility operational.
June 30, 1948	McNarney letter instructing Northrop and Consolidated Vultee get together and work out RB-49 production arrangements.
July 8, 1948	Northrop and Consolidated Vultee reps meet in San Diego, Calif. Cannot come to consensus to meaning of Gen. McNarney's June 30 letter.
July 9, 1948	Jack Northrop letter to Gen. McNarney with results of July 8 meeting with Consolidated Vultee.
July 16, 1948	Northrop, Consolidated Vultee, and Air Force representatives meet in Los Angeles. Secretary Symington's tirade on Northrop merging with Consolidated Vultee.
Aug. 12, 1948	Maj. Gen. Wolfe, Dir. of Procurement and Industrial Planning, authorizes procurement of 30 RB-49s.
Aug. 12, 1948	Northrop Vice President C. N. Monson signs contract W33-038 ac-21721. One RB-49A to be built by Northrop-Hawthorne and 29 at Fort Worth.
Aug. 23, 1948	Conference at AMC with Northrop reps. Proposed contract changes and request for formal quote for tooling, conversion of 1 RB-49A to B-49 bomber, contractor maintenance, and studies to increase mach number of plane.
Aug. 27, 1948	AMC letter discussing modifying 9 YB-35s to YRB-49s.

Sept. 16, 1948	USAF Comptroller concurred in conversion of YB-35s to YRB-49s.
Sept. 16, 1948	Contract W33-038 ac-21721 for 30 RB-49As approved.
Sept. 17, 1948	Both XBs in "extended storage" status.
Sept. 18, 1948	Contract W33-038 ac-21721 for 30 RB-49As approved.
Sept. 20, 1948	Wire authorizing Northrop to modify YB-35A to RB-49A prototype.
Sept. 27, 1948	Northrop Gen. Mgr. C. N. Monson memo concerning travel expenses between Hawthorne, Calif., and Fort Worth, Texas.
Oct. 15, 1948	Northrop Asst. Gen. Mgr. B. G. Reed memo on Northrop-Convair coordination.
Oct. 26-29, 1948	YB-49 bombing test against B-29.
Nov. 1, 1948	Jack Northrop memo assigning W. G. Knieriem as Northrop Fort Worth Division manager effective Nov. 16, 1948.
Nov. 12, 1948	Board of reps. from Air Staff agencies meet. They feel B-52 promises better performance. Recommend RB-49 cancellation.
Nov. 22, 1948	Number 1 XB-35 accepted by Air Force at Northrop factory.
Nov. 24, 1948	RB-49 mockup inspection scheduled to start Dec. 7, 1948.
Dec. 15, 1948	First flight of X-4 no. 1.
Dec. 15, 1948	Gen. McNarney recommends Board of Senior Officers convene based on Nov. 12 meeting and recommendations.
Dec. 29, 1948	Board of Senior Officers meet. Northrop RB-49 (30 acft.), C-125 (30 acft.), North American B-45 (51 acft.) and F-93 (118 acft.), Kellet H-10 (10 acft.), and Convair YT-32 (1) programs cancelled. (Boeing would have their B/RB-54 (43 acft.) program terminated also.)
Jan. 7, 1949	Number 2 XB-35 accepted by Air Force at Northrop factory.
Jan. 11, 1949	Letter to Northrop to stop work on all RB-49 effort except YRB-49A.
Jan. 12, 1949	Procurement Directive 49-39 issued terminating RB-49 project (except YRB-49A).
Jan. 14, 1949	Northrop officially notified of termination.
Feb. 9, 1949	YB-49 transcontinental flight from Muroc to Andrews for air show.
Feb. 17, 1949	Because of Flying Wing overruns, DOD budget constraints and Air Force builddown, Gen. McNarney recommended stripping and salvaging 2 XB-35s and 2 YB-35s. Remaining funds would be used on EB-35B, YRB-49A, and RB-35B projects, as well as YB-49 flight test.
Feb. 25, 1949	Dir. of R&D advised Gen. Powers (Asst. Deputy Chief of Staff, Materiel) that only 2 in lieu of 9 YB-35s should be converted thus saving $7.5 million in research funds. The 7 YB-35s eliminated from the conversion program should be salvaged.
Mar. 7, 1949	HQ USAF had authorized AMC to salvage 2 XB-35s and 2 YB-35s. Northrop estimated the salvage operation would cost a little over $52,000.

May 7, 1949	Northrop was notified that the jet conversion program for the YB-35Bs might be cut back.
March 24, 1949	Contract Change Notice No. 3 (W33-038-ac-21721) changes from YB-49 to YB-35 for YRB-49A modification.
March 25, 1949	Contract Supplement to W33-038-ac-21721. 4 YB-35s and 3 YB-35As to be modified in the Jet Conversion (redesignated YB-35Bs). 2 XB-35s and 2 YB-35s to be scrapped and useable parts to be boxed and stored as spare parts.
June 7, 1949	First flight of X-4 no. 2.
July 20, 1949	YB-35, serial 42-102366 (sole flying YB) is scrapped.
Aug. 17, 1949	Jack Northrop testified before House Committe on Armed Services hearings on B-36, held in Los Angeles.
Aug. 19, 1949	XB-35 no. 2 (serial 42-38323) scrapped. YB-35 (serial 42-102369) scrapped.
Aug. 23, 1949	XB-35 no. 1 (serial 42-13603) scrapped.
Oct. 28, 1949	Northrop news release stated the Air Force announced this date that work would cease immediately on the seven YB-35 undergoing conversion and the sole ERB-35B (Turbodyne test bed) and "...consideration is being given to the possibility of ordering additional ... Scorpion ... interceptors."
Dec. 29, 1949	YB-35B (serial 42-102374) scrapped.
Dec. 30, 1949	YB-35B (serial 42-102373) scrapped.
Jan. 6, 1950	YB-35B (serial 42-102372) scrapped.
Jan. 16, 1950	YB-35B (serial 42-102371) scrapped.
Jan. 20, 1950	YB-35B (serial 42-102370) scrapped.
Jan. 23, 1950	YB-35B (serial 42-102375) scrapped.
Feb. 4, 1950	YB-35B (serial 42-102377) scrapped.
Mar. 15, 1950	YB-49 no. 1 destroyed in taxi test accident.
Mar. 30, 1950	EB-35B (serial 42-102378) scrapped.
May 4, 1950	YRB-49A first flight.
Apr. 26, 1951	Last flight of YRB-49A (Edwards AFB to Northrop facility at Ontario Airport, Calif.).
Nov. 1952	John K. "Jack" Northrop leaves Northrop Aircraft, Inc. and the aircraft industry.
Dec 1, 1953	YRB-49A (serial 42-102376) scrapped.

Appendix B

NORTHROP FLYING WING AND TAILLESS AIRCRAFT STATISTICS

Avion Model 1 (Modified to 1-A)

Northrop Specification:	Unknown
Wingspan:	30.5 ft.
Overall Length:	20 ft.
Overall Height	5 ft.
Wing Area:	184 sq. ft.
Maximum Wing Thickness:	34 in.
Wing Chord Taper:	45 in. (approx.) to 100 in.
Aspect Ratio:	5.1:1
Landing Gear Tread:	9 ft.
Empty Weight:	1,100 lb.
Gross Weight:	1,690 lb.
Fuel Capacity:	30 gal.
Speed - Maximum:	110 mph (pusher) and 99 mph (tractor)
Speed - Cruising:	92 mph (pusher) and 84 mph (tractor)
Endurance:	Unknown
Range:	Unknown
Service Ceiling:	Unknown
Engines (pusher):	1 Cirrus Mk. III (70 hp)
(tractor):	1 Menasco A4 Pirate (90 hp each)

N-1M

Northrop Specification:	Unknown
Wingspan:	38.72 ft. with droop (at 26º 46' sweep)
Overall Length:	17.95 ft.
Overall Height	
Top of Canopy:	4.92 (without "hat")
Wing Area:	302.5 sq. ft. (at 26º 46' sweep)
Airfoil Sections:	NACA 0025 Mod (root chord)
	NACA 0015 Mod (station 216 in. from root chord)
Maximum Wing Thickness:	25% at center line
Wing Chord Taper:	6.0:1.0
Aspect Ratio:	4.96:1 at 26º 46'
Landing Gear Tread:	8.33 ft.
Empty Weight:	3,425lb.
Gross Weight:	3,832 lb.
Takeoff Weight:	3,900 lb.
Speed - Maximum:	144 mph
Speed - Cruising:	120 mph
Endurance:	Unknown
Range:	300 miles
Service Ceiling:	6,160 ft.
Engines (original):	2 Lycoming O-146 (65 hp each)
(replacement):	2 Franklin 6AC264F2 (117 hp each)

N-9M, N-9MA, and N-9MB

Northrop Specification:	NS-99
Wingspan:	60.0 ft.
Overall Length:	17.79 ft.
Overall Height:	
Top of Canopy:	6.58 ft.
Top of Propeller:	8.65 ft.
Wing Area:	490 sq. ft.
Airfoil Sections:	NACA 65, 3-019 (root)
	NACA 65, 3-018 (tip)
Maximum Wing Thickness:	37.68"
Wing Chord Taper:	39 in. to 157 in.
Aspect Ratio:	7.4
Landing Gear Tread:	11.67 ft.
Empty Weight:	5,893 lb.
Gross Weight:	6,326 lb. (6,818 lb. for N-9MB)
Fuel Capacity:	100 gal. (2 tanks of 50 gal. each)
Speed - Maximum:	257 mph
Speed - Cruising:	208 mph
Endurance:	3.2 hours
Range:	500 miles
Service Ceiling:	21,500 ft
Engines:	2 Menasco C6S-4 (first 3 N-9Ms) (260hp each)
	2 Franklin XO-540-7 (N-9MB) (260hp each)

XP-56

Northrop Specification:	NS-2
Wingspan:	42.57 ft. (No. 1), 43.40 ft. (No. 2)
Overall Length:	23.58 ft.
Overall Height:	9.75 (No. 1 without extended fin),
	approx. 12.21 (No. 1 and 2 with extended fin)
Wing Area:	310 sq. ft.
Airoil Sections:	NACA 66, 2-0191 (root)
	NACA 66, 2-0167 (tip)
Maximum Wing Thickness:	24.83 in.
Wing Chord Taper:	43.33 in. to 130 in.
Aspect Ratio:	5.91
Landing Gear Tread:	12.57 ft.
Empty Weight:	8,699 lb. (No. 1), 9,879 lb. (No. 2)
Gross Weight:	11,350 lb.(No. 1), 12,588 lb.(No. 2)
Fuel Capacity:	215 gal. (Normal), 320 gal. (Max.)
Speed - Maximum:	467 mph (design goal, not attained)
Speed - Cruising:	375 mph (design goal, not attained)
Endurance:	1.5 hours
Range:	320 miles
Service Ceiling:	33,000 ft.
Engines:	1 Pratt&Whitney R-2800-29 Double Wasp (1625 hp each.)
Armament (Proposed):	4 - .50 cal. machine guns and
	2 - 20 mm cannon

MX-324/334

Northrop Specification:	NS-12
Wingspan:	36 ft
Overall Length:	14.25 ft.
Overall Height:	7 ft. (with added on vertical)
Wing Area:	252 sq. ft.

Airfoil Sections: NACA 66, 2-018 (Constant along the span)
Maximum Wing Thickness: 18%
Wing Chord Taper: 4:1
Aspect Ratio: 5:2
Vertical Fin: 5 ft.² to 15 ft.² (3 to 4 configurations)
Landing Gear Tread: Varied
Empty Weight: 2,960 lbs. (as glider)
Gross Weight: 3,656 lbs. (as glider)
Fuel Capacity: about 500 lbs.
Speed - Maximum: 300 mph (with rocket motor)
Endurance: Tow plus free flight – 14 to 29 minutes
Range: 20 miles
Service Ceiling: approx. 17,000 (max during flight test)
Engines: Aerojet XCAL-200 (MX-324) (200 lb. thrust)

XP-79 and XP-79B

	XP-79	XP-79B
Northrop Specification:	NS-14	NS-14B
Wingspan:	40 ft.	40 ft.
Overall Length:	13.22 ft.	14 ft.
Overall Height:	4.75ft.	7.5 ft.
Wing Area:	278 sq. ft.	278 sq. ft.
Airfoil Sections:	NACA 66, 2-018	NACA 66, 2-018
Maximum Wing Thickness:	18%	
Wing Chord Taper:	34 in. to 141.7 in.	
Aspect Ratio:	5.19	
Landing Gear Tread:	6.24 ft. (nose), 8.62 ft. (main)	6.28 ft. (nose), 8.33 ft. (main)
Empty Weight:	4,348 lb.	5,842 lb.
Gross Weight:	13,500 lb.	8,669 lb.
Fuel Capacity:		300 gal.
Speed - Maximum:	536 mph	547 mph
Speed - Cruising:	433 mph	480 mph
Endurance:	31.4 min at alt.	2.45 hours
Range:	454 miles	993 miles
Service Ceiling:		40,000 ft.
Engines:	XCAL-2000 (2,000 lb. thrust)	2 Westinghouse 19-B(1,200 lb. thrust each)
Armament:	Four .50 cal. machine guns	Four .50 cal. machine guns

JB-1 and JB-10

	JB-1	JB-10
Northrop Specification:	NS-16	NS 16A
Wingspan:	28.33 ft.	29.17 ft.
Overall Length:	10.54 ft.	11.97 ft.
Overall Height:	4.53 ft.	4.83 ft.
Wing Area:	155 sq ft	163 sq ft
Airfoil Sections:	NACA 66, 2-018 (root) NACA 66, 2-018 (tip)	NACA 66, 2-018 (root) NACA 66, 2-018 (tip)
Launch Weight:	7,084 lb	7,213 lb
Fuel Capacity:	236 gal.	235 gal.
Speed - Launch	160 mph	220 mph
Speed - Cruising:	452 mph	426 mph
Range:	670 miles	185 miles

	2 G.E.	1 Ford
Engines:	Type B1	PJ-31-1
	(400 lb. thrust ea.)	(900 lb. thrust)
Armament:	Two 2,000	Two 1,825
	lb bombs	lb warheads

XB/YB-35

Northrop Specification:	NS-9
Wingspan:	172 ft.
Overall Length:	53.08 ft.
Overall Height:	20.02 ft.
Airfoil Sections:	NACA 65, 3-019 (root)
	NACA 65, 3-018 (tip)
Sweepback:	26º 57' 48"
Wing Area:	4,500 sq. ft.
Maximum Wing Thickness:	85.5 in.
Wing Chord Taper:	9.33 ft. to 37.33 ft.
Aspect Ratio:	7.4
Landing Gear Tread:	41.4 ft.
Empty Weight:	91,000 lb. (with turrets)
Gross Weight:	154,000 lb. (with turrets)
Fuel Capacity:	5,000 gal. (XB), 10,000 gal. (YB),
	18,000 gal., (YB with Bomb Bay tanks)
Speed - Maximum:	391 mph
Speed - Cruising:	240 mph
Range:	7,500 miles
Service Ceiling:	40,000 ft. (restricted to 20,000 ft., not recommended above 15,000 ft.–due to APU problems)
Engines:	4 Pratt & Whitney R-4360 2 each of the -17 and the -21.
Bomb Load:	52,200 lb. max.
Armament:	Turrets with .50 cal. machine guns. One turret, upper and lower outboard wing with two guns each, one upper and lower center line turret with four guns each, and a tail stinger with four guns.

YB-49 and YRB-49A

Northrop Specification:	NS-9 (YB-49) and NS-41 (YRB-49A)
Wingspan:	172 ft.
Overall Length:	53.08 ft.
Overall Height:	14.98 ft. (YB-49)
Wing Area:	4,500 sq. ft.
Airfoil Sections:	NACA 65, 3-019 (root)
	NACA 65, 3-018 (tip)
Sweepback:	26º 57' 48"
Maximum Wing Thickness:	85.5 in.
Wing Chord Taper:	9.33 ft. to 37.33 ft.
Aspect Ratio:	7.4
Landing Gear Tread:	41.4 ft.
Empty Weight:	89,122 lbs. (YB-49), 84,000 (YRB-49A)
Takeoff Weight:	198,688 lb. (YB-49), 165,000 lb. (YRB-49A)
Gross Weight:	213,552 lb. (YB-49), 206,000 lb. (YRB-49A)
Fuel Capacity:	14,542 gal. (YB-49), 15,231 gal. (YRB-49A)
Speed - Maximum:	428 mph (YB-49), 381 mph (YRB-49A)
Speed - Cruising:	365 mph (YB-49), 340 mph (YRB-49A)
Endurance:(Basic Mission)	7.9 hrs. (YB-49), 6.7 hrs. (YRB-49A)

Range:(Basic Mission)   2,828 miles (YB-49), 2,250 miles (YRB-49A)
Service Ceiling:(Basic Mission)   45,200 ft. (YB-49), 45,500 ft. (YRB-49A)
Engines: 8 Allison J-35-A-15 (6 Allison J-35-A-19)
Bomb Load: 16,000 lb. max. (YB-49),
                                     six 188 lb. T-89 Flash Bombs (YRB-49A)
Armament: Tail stinger with four .50 cal. machine guns. (original design,
                                     later deleted) (None on YRB-49A)

X-4

Northrop Specification:	NS-26
Wingspan:	26.83 ft.
Airfoil Sections:	NACA 00010-64
Sweepback:	41° 34'
Overall Length:	23.25 ft.
Overall Height:	14.83 ft.
Wing Area:	200 sq. ft.
Maximum Wing Thickness:	10%
Wing Chord Taper:	56 in. to 123 in.
Aspect Ratio:	3.6
Landing Gear Tread:	12.42 ft.
Empty Weight:	4,940 lb. basic aircraft (5,601 with insturmentation)
Takeoff Weight:	7,550 lb.
Gross Weight:	7,820
Fuel Capacity:	240 gal.
Speed - Maximum:	643 mph
Speed - Cruising:	330 mph
Endurance:	44 min.
Range:	320 miles
Service Ceiling:	44,000 ft.
Engines:	2 Westinghouse XJ-30-WE-7/-9

N-25 and N-69

Northrop Specification:	Numerous	
	N-25	N-69 (data for N-69E)
Wingspan:	42.52 ft.	42.20 ft.
Overall Length:	51.91 ft	68.65 ft.
Overall Height:	12.42 ft.	14.84 ft.
Wing Area:	300 sq. ft.	326 sq. ft.
Takeoff Weight:	28,000 lb.	60,000 lb.
Speed - Maximum:	Mach 0.9	Mach 0.9
Speed - Cruising:	Mach 0.85	Mach 0.85
Range:	1,550 miles	6,000 miles
Service Ceiling:	45,000 ft.	50,000+ ft.
Engines:	1 Allison J-33-A-31	1 Pratt & Whitney J-57-P3
Armament:	None	5,000 lb. Warhead

MILITARY PROCUREMENT

CONTRACT	DATE	DATE APPROVED	AIRCRAFT	QUANTITY	SERIALS
P-56 PROJECT					
W535 ac-15021		Jun. 22, 1940	XP-56 Engineering		
AFP No. 165270	Aug. 5, 1940		XP-56	1	41-786
Change Order No. 1		Sep. 26, 1940	Same as above.		
AFP No. 179055 Sep. 5, 1941			XP-56	1	42-38353
W535 ac-25060		Feb. 13, 1942			
B-35/B-49 PROJECTS					
P.O. 42-2552	July 13, 1941	Oct. 3, 1941	Engineering and 1 .3 to .4 scale model (later designated N-9M)		
AFP 167172	Aug. 13, 1941		Design Study		
W535 ac-21341	Sep. 4, 1941	Oct. 30, 1941	N-9M (switched from P.O.)		
W535 ac-21920	Nov. 1, 1941	Nov. 22, 1941	XB-35	1	42-13603
Change No. 1	Dec. 12, 1941	Jan. 2, 1942	XB-35	1	42-38323
Change No. 3	Sep. 10, 1942		N-9M	2	(2nd N-9M and N-9MA)
Change No. 9	July 24, 1943		N-9MB	1	
LCSF	Sep. 30, 1942		YB-35	13	42-102366
W535 ac-33920	Dec. 2, 1942	Dec. 17, 1942			through
					42-102378
Change No. 11	June 1, 1945	June 22, 1945	YB-49	2 Mod.	
W535 ac-24555					
Supplemental Agreement No. 6		Jun. 30, 1943	B-35B	200	43-35126 through 43-35325
Letter Contract June 12, 1948			Engineering–FB-49A with 6 internal and 2 external J-47A engines; space provisions for J-40 and/or T-37 engines; partial materials procurement for 30 production FB-49A, engineering and materials procurement for YB-49 modification.		
W33-038-ac-21721	Aug. 12, 1948	Sep. 16, 1948	YRB-49A	1 Mod.	
			RB-49A	30	49-200 thru 49-229

CCN No. 3	Mar. 24, 1949		YRB-49A	YB-35 to be modified in lieu of YB-49.
Contract Sup.	Mar. 25, 1949		YB-35B 7	Modify 4 YB-35s and 3 YB-35As.
			Spare Parts	Strip (box and store spares) and scrap both XB-35s and 2 YB-35s (42-102366 and 102369).

TURBODYNE TEST BED

TWX MCPPXA34-10-26	Oct. 28, 1948	Modify XB-35, SN 42-13603, to Turbodyne test bed. Redesignate YRB-35.
AF33(038)-278	Dec. 7, 1948	Modify XB-35, SN 42-13603, to ERB-35B per Northrop spec. NS-45 dated Nov. 1, 1948.
Amendment No. 1	Feb. 17, 1949	YB-35, SN 42-102378, to be modified in lieu of XB-35.

BAILMENT CONTRACT

W33-038 ac-11000	May 23, 1945	June 2, 1945	Authorizes loan by Gov. of aircraft, engines, and equipment to Northrop.
RN-4241	Dec. 7, 1948, XB-35, SN 42-13603, Turbodyne Test Bed, redesignate ERB-35B		
RN-4537	Feb. 1, 1949, XB-35, SN 42-38323, Flex Mount Gear Boxes, redesignate EB-35.		
RN-4691	Feb. 21, 1949–YB-35A, SN 42-102378, replaces XB-35, SN 42-13603, as Turbodyne test bed.		
RN-4885	Mar. 28, 1949–4 YB-35s (SNs 42-102370 through 73) and 3 YB-35As (SNs 42-102374 through 76) to be converted to J-35-A-19 engines. Redesignated to YB-35Bs.		
RN-5238	May 4, 1949–YB-49, SN 42-102367, Contractor Phase III flight test.		

P-79 PROJECT

W535 ac-36137			MX324	3	
AFP No. 217608	Jan. 12, 1943		XP-79	3	
W535 ac-36997		May 26, 1945			
AFP No. 217623	Apr. 27, 1943		XP-79B	1 Mod.	43-52437
Change No. 1	May 21, 1943				

JB-1 AND JB-10 PROJECTS

W33-038 ac-4142		July 1, 1944	JB-1	13
		Feb. 19, 1945	JB-10	11 from JB-1 contract. One completed JB-1 modified.

X-4 PROJECT

W33(038) ac-14542	Apr. 5, 1946	June 11, 1946	XS-4	2	46-676 and 46-677

SNARK PROJECT

AF33(038)-1613			XSM-A-3		
AF33(038)-18414			XSM-62		
AF33(600)-32944			SM-62A		

Notes:

AFP - Authority for Purchase
CCN - Contract Change Notice
LCSF - Letter Contract Special Form
TWX - Teletype message
P.O. - Purchase Order

First Flights of Northrop Flying Wings and Tailless Aircraft

AIRCRAFT	DATE	CREW	LOCATION	FLIGHT TIME
Avion Model I	July 30, 1929	Edward A. Bellande	Mines Field, CA	about 1 min.
N-1M	July 3, 1940	Vance Breese	Baker Dry Lake, CA	"several hundred yards"
N-9M	Dec. 27, 1942	John W. Myers	Northrop Field Hawthorne, CA	55 minutes
N-9M-2	June 24, 1943	Harry Crosby	Northrop Field	5 min., lost canopy
JB-1 (glider)	Aug. 27, 1943	Harry Crosby	Rogers Dry Lake, CA	unknown (Muroc AAB)
XP-56 No. 1	Sept. 6, 1943	John W. Myers	Rogers Dry Lake, CA (Muroc AAB)	"about one mile"
MX-334 Glider No. 3	Oct. 2, 1943	John W. Myers	Rogers Dry Lake, CA	20 min (tow and free flight time) (Muroc AAB)
MX-334 Glider No. 1	Nov. 30, 1943	Harry Crosby	Rogers Dry Lake, CA	unknown (Muroc AAB)
XP-56 No. 2	March 23, 1944	Harry Crosby	Roach Dry Lake, NV	7 minutes
N-9MA	May 22, 1944	unknown	unknown	unknown
MX-334 Glider No. 2 [1]	July 1, 1944	Alex Papana	Harper Dry Lake, CA	unknown
MX-324 (Rocket Powered) [2]	July 5, 1944	Harry Crosby	Harper Dry Lake, CA	14 min towed flight 10 min free flight
JB-1	Dec. 7, 1944	pilotless	Eglin Fld, FL	about 5 sec.(about 400 ft.)
N-9MB	Jan 26, 1945	Harry Crosby	unknown	unknown
JB-10	Apr. 6, 1945	pilotless	Eglin Fld., FL	26 miles
XP-79B	Sept. 12, 1945	Harry Crosby	Rogers Dry Lake, CA (Muroc AAB)	14 minutes (crashed)

1 MX-334 No. 2 actually flew (if you wish to call it that) first when it lifted off the ground on several occasions on Sept. 14, 1943 while being towed behind an automobile. Harry Crosby was the pilot.

2 Glider No. 2 with XCAL-200 rocket motor installed.

XB-35 No. 1	June 25, 1946	Max R. Stanley Fred C. Bretcher Orva H. Douglas	Hawthrone to Muroc	44 minutes
XB-35 No. 2	June 26, 1947	Fred C. Bretcher Max R. Stanley Orva H. Douglas	Hawthorne to Muroc	26 minutes
YB-49 No. 1	Oct. 21, 1947	Max R. Stanley Fred C. Bretcher Orva H. Douglas	Hawthorne to Muroc	32 minutes
YB-49 No. 2	Jan. 13, 1948	Maj Robert L. Cardenas [3] Maj Daniel H. Forbes M/Sgt. William H. Cunningham	Hawthorne to Muroc	20 minutes
YB-35	May 12, 1948	Fred C. Bretcher Charles Tucker Orva H. Douglas	Hawthorne to Muroc	unknown
X-4 No. 1	Dec. 15, 1948	Charles Tucker	Muroc AFB, CA	unknown
X-4 No. 2	June 7, 1949	Charles Tucker	Muroc AFB, CA	unknown
YRB-49A	May 4, 1950	Fred C. Bretcher Dale Johnson Frank Schroeder	Hawthorne to Edwards AFB	30 minutes

3 The "Northrop News" January 28, 1948 issue lists the Northrop crew of Fred C. Bretcher, Latham "Slim" Perrett and O.H. Douglas as performing this flight.

Appendix E

NORTHROP PROJECT DESIGNS

	Northrop			Government		
Project Number	Description or Type	Model Spec.	Northrop Designation	Contract Number	Project No.	Model No.
		Flying Wing/Tailless Designs				
N-1	2 Eng. Medium Bomber 2 Eng. Flying Mockup	N-1M				
N-2	1 Eng. Pursuit	NS-2		W535 ac-15021 W535 ac-25060	MX-14	XP-56
N-9	4 Eng. Bomber 2 Eng. Flying Mockup	NS-9 NS-99 N-9M		W535 ac-21920	MX-140	XB-35
				W535 ac-33920	MP-13	YB-35
				W535 ac-33920	MX-51	YB-49
		NS-9A		W535 ac-33920		YB-35A
N-12	Glider	NS-12		W535 ac-336137	MX-324/ MX-334	
N-14	Interceptor Pursuit	NS-14		W535 ac-36997	MX-365	XP-79
		NS-14A				XP-79A
		NS-14B				XP-79B
N-16	1 & 2 Eng. Missiles	NS-16		W33-038-ac-4142	MX-543	JB-1/ JB-10
N-18	1 Eng. Missile	NS-18				JB-1B
N-25	Guided Missile	NS-25A		AF33(038)-1613	MX-775	XSM-A-3
N-26	Research Aircraft	NS-26		W33(038)-14542	MX-810	X-4
N-31	Flying Wing Medium Bomber (6 Turbojet Eng) Flying Wing Medium Bomber (4 Turbprop Eng)	NS-31A NS-31B				

N-37	Photo Recon.	NS-37	W33-038-ac-21721		RB-49A
N-38	Photo Recon				
N-39	YB-35 Conversion	NS-39	W535 ac-33920		RB-35B
N-40	B-49 Bomber Prototype	NS-40			
N-41	Photo-Reconn. Prototype	NS-41	W33-038-ac-21721	MP-55	YRB-49
N-45	Turbodyne Test Bed	NS-45	AF33(038)-278		ERB-35
N-46	Photo-Reconn.				RB-49
N-47	Photo-Reconn.				RB-49
N-48	Gear Box Test				EB-35
N-50	Jet Bomber	NS-50		MP-56	YB-49
N-51	YB-35 Conversion	NS-51	W535 ac-33920	MP-48	YB-35B
N-52	Photo-Reconn.	NS-52	W33-038 ac-21721	MP-55	YRB-49
N-69	Guided Missile	Various	AF33(038)-18141	MX-775	XSM-62
N-72	SM-62A Weapon	NS-114	AF33(600)-32944	MX-775	SM-62A

Turbodyne Project

N-10	Turbodyne Compressor (Navy)		NOa(S)-1321		
N-19	Turbodyne (Army)	NS-19	W33-038-ac-6218	MX-562	XT-37
N-45	Turbodyne Test Bed	NS-45	W33(038)-ac-21721		

Other Associated Projects

N-6	Zap Wing Conversion	NS-6	USN		OS2U-1 Mod.
N-16	Missile Sleds			MX-544	

BOMBER COMPARISON DATA

LONG RANGE BOMBERS

	XB-35	XB-36	B-36A	B-36D	XB-52	B-52B
Top Speed	391 mph @35,000 ft.	346 mph @35,000 ft.	338 mph @31,600 ft.	383 mph @34,800 ft.	600+ mph	629 mph @19,800 ft.
Cruising Speed	183 mph	216 mph	217 mph	225 mph	525 mph	522 mph
Service Ceiling	39,700 ft.	36,000 ft.	42,000 ft	45,200 ft.	50,000 ft.	47,300 mi.
Range (with payload of)	720 mi. 51,070 lb.	3,850 mi. 77,784 lb.	10,000 mi. 10,000 lb.	7,500 mi. 10,000 lb.	7,000 mi. 10,000 lb.	6,200 mi. 10,000 lb.
First Flight	6/25/46	8/8/46	8/30/47	7/11/49	10/2/52	12/ /54
Enters Service.	N/A	N/A	6/26/48	12/ /50	N/A	6/29/55

MEDIUM RANGE BOMBERS

	YB-49	XB-47	B-47A
Top Speed	495 mph @20,000 ft.	578 mph @15,000 ft.	564 mph @35,000 ft.
Cruising Speed	430 mph	466 mph	486 mph
Service Ceiling	42,000ft.	37,500ft.	46,100 ft.
Range (with payload of)	4,000 mi. 10,000 lb.	2,650 mi. 10,000 lb.	3,050 mi. 10,000 lb.
First Flight	10/21/47	12/17/47	6/25/50
Enters Service.	N/A	N/A	5/ /51

Appendix G

DESIGNATION CHANGES OF B-35-TYPE AIRCRAFT PRODUCED

USAF SERIAL NO.	ORIGINAL DESIGNATION	REDESIGNATIONS				DATE ACCEPTED	DISPOSITION OF AIRCRAFT
42-13603	XB-35	ERB-35B Jan. 14, 1949	XB-35 Jun. 30, 1949			Dec. 3, 1948	Scrapped Aug. 23, 1949
42-38323	XB-35	EB-35 Feb. 19, 1949	XB-35 Jun. 30, 1949			Jan. 1, 1949	Scrapped Aug. 19, 1949
42-102366	YB-35	XB-35* Nov. 18, 1944	YB-35 late 1945	RB-35B Oct. 1948	YB-35 Mar. 30, 1949	Mar. 31, 1949	Scrapped Jul. 20, 1949
42-102367	YB-35	XB-35* Nov. 18, 1944	YB-49 Jun. 12, 1945			May 25, 1949	Accident, Destroyed Mar. 15, 1950
42-102368	YB-35	XB-35* Nov. 18, 1944	YB-49 Jun. 12, 1945			Jun. 16, 1948	Crashed Jun. 5, 1948
42-102369	YB-35	XB-35* Nov. 18, 1944	YB-35 late 1945	YRB-49A Jan. 14, 1949	YB-35 Jun. 30, 1949	Sep. 30, 1948	Scrapped Aug. 19, 1949
42-102370	YB-35	XB-35* Nov. 18, 1944	YB-35 late 1945	RB-35B Oct. 1948	YB-35B Mar. 30, 1949	Mar. 14, 1949	Scrapped Jan. 20, 1950
42-102371	YB-35	XB-35* Nov. 18, 1944	YB-35 late 1945	RB-35B Oct. 1948	YB-35B Mar. 30, 1949	Mar. 14, 1949	Scrapped Jan. 16, 1950
42-102372	YB-35	XB-35* mid 1945	YB-35 late 1945	RB-35B Oct. 1948	YB-35B Mar. 30, 1949	Mar. 14, 1949	Scrapped Jan. 6, 1950
42-102373	YB-35	XB-35* mid 1945	YB-35 late 1946	RB-35B Oct. 1948	YB-35B Mar. 30, 1949	Mar. 14, 1949	Scrapped Dec. 30, 1949
42-102374	YB-35		YB-35A Oct. 10, 1946	RB-35B Oct. 1948	YB-35B Mar. 30, 1949	Mar. 14, 1949	Scrapped Dec. 29, 1949
42-102375	YB-35		YB-35A Oct. 10, 1946	RB-35B Oct. 1948	YB-35B Mar. 30, 1949	Mar. 14, 1949	Scrapped Jan. 25, 1950
42-102376	YB-35		YB-35A Oct. 10, 1946	RB-35B Oct. 1948	YRB-49A Jun. 30, 1949	Feb. 21, 1949	Scrapped Dec.1, 1953
42-102377	YB-35		YB-35A Oct. 10, 1946	RB-35B Oct. 1948	YB-35B Mar. 30, 1949	Mar. 14, 1949	Scrapped Feb. 4, 1950
42-102378	YB-35		YB-35A Oct. 10, 1946	EB-35B Jun. 30, 1949	YB-35B Mar. 30, 1949	Feb. 21, 1949	Scrapped Mar. 30, 1950

*It is unclear if these YB-35s were actually redesignated XB-35 or if correspondence only referenced to them as such because they were to be built to XB-35 specifications.

263

B-35 AND B-49 SERIES AIRCRAFT FLIGHT LOGS

Note: Following is best estimate based on records available.

Flight record of XB-35 Number 1, serial number 42-13603 (C/N 1484)

DATE	FLIGHT	DURATION	CUM. TIME	PURPOSE/REMARKS
Jun. 25, 1946	1	0:44	0:44	First flight. Northrop flight crew. "...reached altitude 10,000 feet.No trouble." Phase I testing begins.
Jul. 3, 1946	2			Max speed of 250 mph reached. Trouble with governors.
Sept. 11, 1946	3		3:04	Grounded after flight for propeller oil leaks and gear box troubles.
Mar. 26, 1947	4	0:27	3:11	Right outboard tire blew out on landing. No. 3 gear box repaced.
April 12, 1947	5	3:15	6:26	
April 1947	6			
April 1947	7			
April 1947	8			
Apr. 30, 1947	9			One gear box failure. Spark plugs, ignition harness and landing gear doors needed to be replaced after the five flights in April.
May 2, 1947	10		12:48	2 propellers malfunctioned on same side
By end of July	11			(2 APU failures to date)
Feb. 12, 1948	12	1:24		Purpose: engineering checks and propeller vibration runs. Flight was "highly satisfactory" and only minor irregularities reported. First flight with single rotation, 4-bladed propellers.
Feb. 16, 1948	13	0:21		Purpose: continuation of prop vibration runs. Flight terminated due to failure of RH main gear I.B. forward door acturation rod—door failed to close after gear retraction.
Feb. 17, 1948	14 13	0:07		Purpose: continuation of prop vibration runs. A repetition of flight failure occurred.
Feb. 18, 1948	15		15:47	Purpose: prop vibration, cooling, and speed run tests. After 55 min. flight time, during speed runs, LH landing gear fwd doors opened approx. 4 inches. Failed to get doors to close, flight terminated.
	16			

Mar. 10, 1948	17	2:20		Purpose: continuation of prop vibration survey and fuel consumption test. Flight satisfactorily accomplished. Crew reported irregulatities: RH pilot's foot brake failed during taxi run, nose wheel steering did not operate properly, nose wheel shimmied on take-off, and excessive hydraulic lead in no. 2 prop shaft housing.
	18			
Oct. 7, 1948	19		24:0	Revoved from storage at Muroc and flown to Hawthorne. (Final Flight)

Scrapped: Aug. 23, 1949

All flights by contractor
Total Flights: 19
Total Flight Time: 24:0

Flight record of XB-35 Number 2, serial number 42-38323 (C/N 1485)

DATE	FLIGHT	DURATION	CUM. TIME	PURPOSE/REMARKS
June 26, 1947	1	0:26	0:26	First flight. Northrop flight crew. Phase I testing begins.
July 9, 1947	2	0:20	0:46	APU failure.
Aug. 6, 1947	3	2:56	3:44	APU failure.
Dec. 11, 1947	4			APU failure.
	5			
	6			
	7			
Aug. 14, 1948	8			Muroc to Hawthorne (Final Flight)

Scrapped: Aug. 19, 1949

All flights by contractor
Total Flights: 8
Total Flight Time: 12:00

Flight record of YB-35, serial number 42-162366 (C/N 1482)

DATE	FLIGHT	DURATION	CUM. TIME	PURPOSE/REMARKS
May 12, 1948				First Flight
Aug. 14, 1948				Last flight, Muroc to Hawthorne

Scrapped: July 20, 1049

Total Flights: Unknown
Total Flight Hours: Unknown

Flight record of YB-49 Number 1, serial number 42-102367 (C/N 1487)

DATE	FLIGHT	DURATION	CUM. TIME	PURPOSE/REMARKS
Oct. 21, 1947	1	0:34	0:34	First flight. Northrop flight crew. Phase I testing begins.
Oct. 23, 1947	2	1:31	2:05	Purpose: Obtain speed power points at different altitudes. P-80 escort. The rear nose wheel door blew off at 280 IAS. Pilot attempted to lower main gear but it remained up and locked. Lowered gear by emergency system and landed normally.
	3			Unknown
	4			Unknown
	5			Unknown
Dec. 2, 1947	6	1:25		Maj. Cardenas checked out.
Dec. 9, 1947	7	1:18		Purpose: Determine rate of climb, check operation of emergency elevon electrical system, and perform speed vs. power runs. At 300 mph IAS, time to climb from 6,000 ft. to 13,000 feet was 3 min. 19.5 sec.
Dec. 11, 1947	8	2:02		Unknown
Dec. 11, 1947	9	2:00		Returned aircraft to Northrop plant.
Dec. 22, 1947	10			Fourth APU failure. The plane could not be landed in a normal condition after such failures because of the lack of flaps.
	11			Unknown
	12			Unknown
Jan. 13, 1948	13			Unknown
Jan. 13, 1948	14			Jack Northrop was along on this flight.
	15			Unknown
	16			Unknown
	17			Unknown
	18			Unknown
	19			Unknown
	20			Unknown
	21			Unknown
	22			Unknown
Feb. 19, 1948	23	2:00		Familiarize AF pilots

Feb. 20, 1948	24	1:00		Familiarize AF pilots During flights 23 and 24 Maj. Cardenas made 5 landings, Lt. Col. F. J. Ascani made 2, and Maj. D. Forbes made 2.
Feb. 26, 1948	25	2:30		Unknown
Mar. 10, 1948	26	1:45		Purpose: Fuel tank vent pressure determination and control force bellows test. All tests satisfactory.
Mar. 17, 1948	27	1:27		Purpose: Fuel vent pressure tests. No. 4 engine wouldn't start. Took off and then air-started no. 4 successfully at 8,000 ft. All tests satisfactory.
	28			Unknown
	29			Unknown
	30			Unknown
May 11, 1948	31			Landing was made with half-flap almost in a stall. No.1 8 engine quit after landing.
	32			Unknown
May 17, 1948	33		47:44	Phase I completed. Northrop turned plane over to AF for Phase II testing.
May 20, 1948	34	0:45		Phase II testing begins. Familiarization and checkout of Capt. Edwards.
May 21, 1948	35	1:45		Unknown
	36			Unknown
May 25, 1948	37			Final checkout of Capt. Edwards
May 28, 1948	38			Unknown
June 3, 1948	39			Unknown
	40		63:29	Plane returned to Northrop to perform Interim Phase I tests in order to investigate stability, control, and stalling characteristics that the AF pilots in Phase II testing to date felt were unacceptable.
Early June 1948				Grounded to investigate No. 2 crash.
Jul. 21, 1948	41	0:52		First flight since crash of YB-49 No. 1. Commenced Northrop's Interim Phase I flight test. Purpose: shake-down and conduct tests on control forces. Flight terminated due to left hand rudder had tendency to stay partially open.
July 22, 1948	42	2:53		Purpose: Unknown. Only minor discrepancies were noted.
July 23, 1948	43	1:04	67:17	Purpose: Unknown. During flight had to shut down no. 1 engine. Plane grounded for engine change after flight.

	44			Unknown
	45			Unknown
	46			Unknown
August 1948	47			Maj. Gen. Roger M. Ramey, 8th Air Force Commander flys YB-49 (exact date and flight number unknown).
	48			Unknown
	49			Unknown
	50			Unknown
Sept. 18, 1948	51			Flown for "Air Force Day" to Lockheed Air Terminal in Burbank, CA (exact flight number unknown)
	52			Unknown
	53			Unknown
	54			Unknown
	55			Unknown
Oct. 23, 1948	56		102:14	End of Interim Phase I. Interim Phase I: 16 flights and 38:45 hours.
Oct. 26, 1948	57	2:30		Purpose: Bombing tests. Cardenas pilot. Practice mission with 10 M-38A2 (100 lb. practice) bombs.
Oct. 27, 1948	58	1:55		Purpose: Bombing tests. 10 AN-M64A1 (500 lb. general purpose inert) bombs dropped from 10,000 ft. alt. at 200 knots AIS.
Oct. 28, 1948	59	2:05		Purpose: Bombing tests. 10 AN-M64A1 bombs dropped from 20,000 ft. alt. at 187 knots AIS.
Oct. 29, 1948	60	2:40	112:12	Purpose: Bombing tests. 6 AM-M64A1 bombs dropped from 30,000 ft. alt. at 174 knots AIS. Total of 4 tests, 9:58 hrs.
	61			Contractor Interim Phase I resumes.
	62			Unknown
	63			Unknown
Nov. 12, 1948	64	2:33		Purpose: Flap vibration and control tests. Test revealed present landing flap vibration not hazardous to flight but corrective action required before condition becomes aggravated.
Nov. 18, 1948	65	0:55		Purpose: Record effectiveness of the air separators installed on rib walls of bomb bays no. 2 and 7. Controls tests also accomplished. Buffeting condition greatly reduced.

Nov. 18, 1948	66	3:01	119:29	Same as above.
Dec. 1948	67			Unknown
	68			Unknown
	69			Unknown
	70			Unknown
	71			Unknown
	72			Unknown
	73			Unknown
	74			Unknown
Jan. 1949	75			Unknown
Feb. 9, 1949	76	4:30		Muroc AFB to Andrews AFB, D.C.
Feb. 15, 1949	77	1:10		Andrews local.
Feb. 17, 1949	78	1:15		Flight down Pennsylvania Ave. in Washington, D.C.
Feb. 18, 1949	79	1:40		Andrews AFB to Wright-Patterson AFB, Ohio
Feb. 23, 1949	80			Wright-Patterson to Winslow, Arizona.
Mar. 2, 1949	81	1:15	153:19	Winslow to Muroc AFB
Mar. 6, 1949	82	1:20		High altitude and high attitude to check possibility of pressure venting of oil from tanks (investigation of Feb. 18 incident).
Mar. 7, 1949	83	2:00		Stability and control tests.
Apr. 5, 1949	84			Contractor Interim Phase I continued. Houde system checked, Edison system data obtained at t/o, yaw stabilizer checked at 180 and 265 mph AIS, 12,000 and 20,000 ft. alt., automatic slot switch checked, flap vibration with bomb bay 4 open checked, and control and attitude data obtained during landing.
Apr.7, 1949	85			Edison system data and rear spar temp. data were obtained during t/o, yaw stabilizer checked at 200 and 265 mph AIS at 30,000 ft. alt., Col. Gerrity, Capt. Wethe, and Capt. Masden flew plane from pilot's cockpit, Col. Gerrity and Capt. Wethe flew under the hood, control and attitude data obtained during landing.
Apr. 15, 1949	86	1:00		Indoctrination flight for Maj. Russell Schleeh.
Apr. 16, 1949	87	1:30		Unknown
Apr. 21, 1949	88	1:15		Unknown
Apr. 22, 1949	89	5:30		Unknown

	90		Unknown
	91		Unknown
	92	167:26	Interim Phase I completed.
Apr. 1949	93		Special AF Project
Apr/early May 1949	94	170:00	Special AF Project The two Special Project flights were for a total of about 2:34.
May 4, 1949	95		Northrop flight testing (Phase III testing).
	96		Unknown
	97		Unknown
	98		Unknown
	99		Unknown
	100		Unknown
	101		Unknown
	102		Unknown
June 7, 1949	103		
June 7, 1949	104		
June 8, 1949	105		
June 15, 1949	106		Exact match between dates (June 7-20) with flight number unknown. Maj. Russ Schleeh performed bombing tests in this period.
June 16, 1949	107		
June 17, 1949	108		
June 20, 1949	109		
	110		Unknown
	111		Unknown
	112		Unknown
	113		Unknown
	114		Unknown
	115		Unknown
	116		Unknown
	117		Unknown

	118			Unknown
	119			Unknown
	120			Unknown
	121			Unknown
	122			Unknown
	123			Unknown
	124			Unknown
	125			Unknown
	126			Unknown
	127			Unknown
	128			Unknown
Aug. 15, 1949	129			Unknown
	130			Unknown
	131			Unknown
	132			Unknown
	133			Unknown
	134			Unknown
	135			Unknown
	136			Unknown
	137			Unknown
	138			Unknown
Feb. 23, 1950	139		250:33	End Northrop testing Phase III time: 80:33.
Mar. 2, 1950	140	2:30		AF to perform limited stability and control tests (Phase II continued).
Mar. 3, 1940	141	3:20		Same as 140
Mar. 8, 1950	142	2:45		Same as 140
Mar. 10, 1950	143	3:30		Same as 140
Mar. 14, 1950	144	3:45	265:53	Same as 140 Flights 140 - 141 totaled 15:20 hrs.

Mar. 15, 1950	N/A			While Maj. Schleeh was putting the plane through a high speed taxi run, the nose wheel collapsed and the airplane was destroyed.
July 21, 1950				Salvage and reclamation completed.

Total Northrop flight time: 194:26 (121 flights)
Total Air Force flight time: 71:27 (23 flights)
Aircraft Total: 265:53 (144 flights)

Flight record of YB-49 Number 2, serial number 42-102368 (C/N 1488)

DATE	FLIGHT	DURATION	CUM. TIME	PURPOSE/REMARKS
Jan. 13, 1948	1	0:36	0:36	First flight. Northrop Field to Muroc AAB. Phase I testing begins.
Feb. 3, 1948	2	2:37	3:13	Purpose: Functional check. Check operation of bomb bay doors for later bomb runs.
Feb. 22, 1948	3	1:14	4:27	Purpose: Check flight and fuel consumption data. Nose wheel door did not lock closed when gear was retracted. Two more gear retractions were made at 120 IAS in an effort to lock the door.
Feb. 23, 1948	4	0:36	5:03	Purpose: Check flight and fuel consumption data. Bracket on forward nose wheel door between the door and actuator failed at 160-170 IAS, allowing the nose wheel to hit the door before the wheel was fully retracted. The main gear were lowered normally and the nose wheel lowered by emergency drop.
Feb. 25, 1948	5	2:15	7:18	Unknown
Feb. 27, 1948	6	1:22	8:40	Purpose: Fuel consumption runs at 35,000 feet.
Mar. 12, 1948	7	1:35	10:15	Purpose: Bomb drop test. Bombs were not released due to bad weather. Dry runs made over bombing range.
Mar. 15, 1948	8	2:07	12:22	Purpose: Bomb drop test. No. 2 bomb bay door would not completely open and no. 7 door failed to function properly. Dry runs made over bombing range.
Mar. 18, 1948	9	1:57	14:19	Purpose: Bomb drop test. Flight was considered "highly successful by the crew." Noise level check made.
Mar. 22, 1948	10	1:52	16:11	Purpose: Bomb drop test. This ended the series of bombing tests. With this successful flight, a total of "7 satisfactory runs" had been accomplished during this testing period. Grounded for engine change prior to special project (Project CAMEL) and Phase II tests.
Apr. 3, 1948	11	2:36	18:47	Purpose: Functional check; noise level check; fuel consumption run. During a turn at 250 IAS at 35,000 ft. the aft cabin bubble canopy blew out resulting in immediate cabin decompression.
Apr. 16, 1948	12	1:45	20:32	Unknown

Apr. 19, 1948	13	Unknown	Unknown	Unknown
Apr. 20, 1948	14	Unknown	Unknown	Unknown
Apr. 21, 1948	15	Unknown	27:28	Unknown NOTE: Total flight hours for Flights 13, 14, and 15 are 6:56.
Apr. 23, 1948	16	5:05	32:33	Purpose: Range Test. Long range demonstration attempt (round robin, Muroc-San Francisco-Phoenix-Muroc). Flight was termiated after one complete circuit due to failure of a valve in the cabin pressurization system and breakdown of right hand APU. Cruise portion of flight at optimum altitude was impossible be cause high altitude resulted in misfiring of left hand APU. Right main gear failed to fully extend when attempting to land. Landing delayed 45 min. while emergency system used to lower gear.
Apr. 26, 1948	17	9:30	42:03	Purpose: Range Test. Long range demonstration. No 5 engine was lost due to fuel nozzle failure after 8:10 hours into the flight and one APU failed 5 min. before landing. The 9:30 duration was a record for jet-powered aircraft. Made 2 circuits of round robin (Muroc-Bakers Field-Fresno-Oakland-Fresno-Bakers Field-Muroc-Riverside-Blythe-Phoenix-Blythe-Riverside-Muroc) plus an additional trip from Muroc-Oackland-Muroc was flown. Aircraft was in "photo reconnaissance configuration" (no bombs or armament)-6,000 lbs. of equipment or ballast was carried.
May 10, 1948	18	1:02	43:05	Purpose: Functional test flight prior to Phase II. Aft nose wheel door was not closed after takeoff. Plane was slowed down and the landing gear handle moved to close the door properly. Cabin pressurization system did not operate properly during flight. Plane's climb was discontinued at 27,000 ft. to keep APUs from stalling.
May 12, 1948	19	Unknown	Unknown	Unknown
May ??, 1948	20	Unknown	44:54	Phase I concluded. Total flight hours for Flights 19 and 20 are 1:49.
May 28, 1948	21	4:06	49:00	Phase II flight test begins. Purpose: Performance test.
Jun. 2, 1948	22	1:10	50:10	Purpose: Familiarization and demonstration flight for USAF officers.
Jun. 3, 1948	23	2:49	52:59	Purpose: Performance test. Gear door trouble was experienced during the climb on this flight.
Jun. 4, 1948	24	3:53	56:52	Purpose: Performance test.
Jun. 5, 1948	25	1:19	58:11	Purpose: Performance test—checking service ceiling (40,000 ft.), low power stalls, speed power calibration, and power points. Airplane crashed and burned.
July 1948				Salvage and reclamation completed.

Total Northrop flight time:	44:54 (20 flights)			
Total Air Force flight time:	13:17 (5 flights)			
Aircraft Total:	58:11 (25 flights)			

Flight record of YRB-49A serial number 42-102369 (C/N 1489)

DATE	FLIGHT	DURATION	CUM. TIME	PURPOSE/REMARKS
May 4, 1950	1	0:30	0:30	First Flight
May 10, 1950	2	1:30	2:00	
May 16, 1950	3	1:00	3:00	
June 3, 1950	4	1:05	4:05	
June 6, 1950	5	1:35	5:40	
June 8, 1950	6	0:15	5:55	
	7			
	8			
	9			Demonstration and test flight.
Aug. 10, 1950	10			Pilots canopy came off at about 35,000 ft. alt., speed about 225 mph.
	11			Flights 10-13: stability tests, yaw stabilizer tests, bomb drop ping (flare bombs) and bonb bay evaluation. Flight 8-13: Total flight time 10:45
	12			
Sep. 10, 1950	13			Last test flight recorded.
Apr. 26, 1951	14	1:00		Removed from storage at Edwards AFB and flown to Northrop's facility at Ontario Airport, Calif. for storage. This was possibly the only flight by an Air Force crew.

Air Materiel Command - "no future flying time scheduled" for YRB-49A: May 6, 1952

Scrapped: Nov. 1953

Total flights:	14
Total flight time:	17:40 (plus flight no. 7 hours).

NORTHROP FLYING WING AND TAILLESS AIRCRAFT NAMES

AIRCRAFT	NAME(S) ATTRIBUTED
Avion Model I	Avion Model I Experimental Number 1 EX-1 Avion Flying Wing 1929 Flying Wing 1929 All Wing
N-1M	Jeep
XP-56	Black Bullet Silver Bullet Dumbo
N-9M	none
B-35 series	Flying Wing
B-49 series	Flying Wing
MX-324	Rocket Wing
XP-79B	Flying Ram
JB-1	Power Bomb
JB-1 Glider	Bat
JB-10	Jet Bomb
X-4	Skylancer Bantam
N-25/N-69	Boojum Snark

REGISTRATION AND SERIAL NUMBERS ASSIGNED

AIRCRAFT DESIGNATION	CONTRACTORS NUMBER	CIVILIAIAN REGISTRY	MILITARY SERIAL	CO. PROJ. NO.	MIL. PROJECT NUMBER
Avion Model I		X-216H			
N-1M		NX-28311		N-1	
XP-56	325		42-1786	N-2	MX-14
XP-56	326		42-238353	N-2	MX-14
N-9M-1				N-9	
N-9M- 2				N-9	
N-9MA				N-9	
N-9MB				N-9	
XB-35	1484		42-13603	N-9	MX-140
XB-35	1485		42-38323	N-9	MX-140
YB-35	1486 through 1498		42-102366 through 42-102378	N-9	MP-13
B-35B	Martin Production Contract		43-35126 through 43-35325		
YB-49	1487		42-102367	N-9	MX-51
YB-49	1488		42-102368	N-9	MX-51
RB-49A(Ordered then cancelled)	3000 through 3030		49-200 through 49-229	N-37	
YRB-49A	1496		42-102376	N-41	MP-55
MX-324				N-12	MX-324
MX-324				N-12	MX-324
MX-324/MX-334				N-12	MX-324 MX-334
XP-79				N-14	MX-365
XP-79A				N-14	MX-365
XP-79B			43-52437	N-14	MX-365
JB-1 (piloted glider)				N-16	MX-543
JB-1 (powered)				N-16	MX-543
JB-10				N-16	MX-543
JB-1A					
JB-1B				N-18	
X-4	3237		46-676	N-26	MX-810
X4	3238		46-677	N-26	MX-810

Bibliography

Government Studies

Air Materiel Command Staff. <u>Case History of XB-35 Airplane Project</u>, Historical Office, Air Materiel Command, Wright Field; c. late 1946

Air Materiel Command Staff. <u>Case History of XP-56 Airplane</u>, Historical Division, Air Materiel Command, Wright Field; January 1946

Air Materiel Command Staff. <u>Flight Test, Incident, and Accident Data on Selected Multi-Engine Bombers</u>, Historical Division, Air Materiel Command,Wright-Patterson Air Force Base; April 1959

Air Technical Service Command Staff. <u>History of the MX-324, MX-334</u>, Memorandum Report No. TSEAL-2-4302-20-5, 31 January 1945

Brewer, Gerald W. <u>Tests of the Northrop MX-334 Glider Airplane in the NACA Full-Scale Tunnel</u>, National Advisory Committee for Aeronautics, Memorandum Report January 1944

Hallion, Richard P. <u>A Synopsis of Flying Wing Development, 1908 -1953</u>, History Office, Air Flight Test Center, Edwards Air Force Base, 9 January 1986

Marrow, Ardath M. <u>Case History of the YB-35, YB-49 Airplanes (Supplement to Case History of the XB-35 Airplane)</u>, Historical Office, Executive Secretariat, Air Materiel Command, Wright-Patterson Air Force Base; February 1950

Robinson, Robert C. <u>High-Speed Aerodynamic Characteristics of a 1/7-Scale Model of the Northrop YB-49 Airplane</u>, National Advisory Committee for Aeronautics, Research Memorandum, RM-A7C13, March 24, 1947

Thornton, O. B., Capt. <u>Final Report of Development, Procurement and Acceptance of the XP-56 Airplane</u>, AAF Technical Report No. 5714, Air Materiel Command, July 30, 1948

Tuttle, D. T., Capt. <u>Final Report on the Development of the Northrop XP-79B Airplane</u>, AAF Technical Report No. 5509, Air Materiel Command, July 11, 1946

Werrell, Kenneth P. <u>The Evaluation of the Cruise Missile</u>, Air University, September 1985

Military Documents

<u>Aircraft Model Designation</u>, Report No. TSEST-A7, 1 June 1946

AN 01-15EAB-1, <u>Pilot's Handbook for Model YB-49 Airplane,</u>

AN 01-15EAB-2, <u>Erection and Maintenance Instructions for Model YB-49 Airplane</u>, 1 April, 1948

AN 01-15EBB-1, <u>Flight Operating Instructions, USAF Series YRB-49A Aircraft</u>, 15 September 1950

Characteristics Summary, Service Test, YB-49

Individual Aircraft Record Card, Form No. RR 1103 (B-35 and B-49 series aircraft)

Memorandum Report, <u>JB-1, Jet Propelled Bomb</u>, Moorman, E. W., 1st Lt., 21 December 1944

Memorandum Report, <u>Jet Propelled Bomb, Type JB-10, Project MX-543</u>, Moorman, Edward W., Capt., 3 August 1945

Memorandum Report, <u>Phase II Tests of the YB-49 Airplane, USAF No. 42-102368</u>, Amann, John R., Capt. MR No. MCRFT-2156, Air Materiel Command, September 1, 1948

Progress Report of Army Air Forces Pilotless Aircraft as Guided Missiles, Development Status and Availability, Report No. AAF-MD-E98, 1 June 1945, 1 July 1945, 1 August 1945, 1 September 1945, and 1 January 1946

Report of Serial Numbers Assigned to Aircraft on Active Air Force Contracts, AFPI Form 41

Standard Aircraft Characteristics, YB-49 Flying Wing

Northrop Documents

An Analysis of Northrop Aircraft, Inc., H. Paiss, May 23, 1956

Annual report, Fiscal Year Ending July 31, 1949

Pilot's Handbook for the XB-35 Heavy Bombardment Airplane, Serial Number AAF 42-38323 (Northrop Number 1485), Northrop Report No. HB-21

Erection and Maintenance Instructions for Army Model XB-35 Heavy Bombardment Airplane, Serial Number AAF 42-38323 (Northrop Number 1485, Northrop Report No. HB-22

Handbook of Erection and Manintenance Instructions for X-4 Airplane, Northrop Report No. HB-26

Internal Northrop Aircraft, Incorporated Correspondence:

From:	To:	Date:	Subject Matter:
Dale Armstrong	AAF Public Relations Office, Los Angeles	1/9/47	MX-334 and XP-79 Projects
C. N. Monson	All Personnel	7/23/48	In negotiations with Convair to subcontract FB-49A production in Texas.
A. F. Thompson	All Departments	7/28/48	Warren L. Sparks becomes Manufacturing Control Co-ordinator for FB-49A Project effective Aug. 1.
C. N. Monson	All Admin. Officers	9/27/48	Travel expenses between Hawthorne, CA and Fort Worth, Tx.
B. G. Reed	All Admin. Officers	10/15/48	Northrop-Convair Coordination.
J. K. Northrop	All Dept. Heads	11/1/48	Effective Nov. 16, 1948 W. G. Knieriem appointed Fort Worth Division Manager of NAI.
J. G. Macdonnell Messrs Burke, et al		11/19/48	Personnel and Area Requirements for C-125, RB-49, MX775, and B-35 conversion.
C. N. Monson	All Admin. Officers	12/1/48	W. G. Knieriem at Fort Worth at NAI Operations Manager. All correspondence to Fort Worth operations personnel to be routed through Knieriem.
J. G. Macdonnell	All Dept. Heads	12/22/48	Teletype equipment now set up in RB-49A Project office on Engineering mezzanine at Hawthorne, CA plant for communication with Fort Worth.

John Knudsen Northrop, 1895 - 1981, A Giant of the Golden Age of Aviation, Northrop Corporation, c. 1981

Letter, John K. Northrop to General H. H. Arnold, May 13, 1941

Model Specification, XP-56 Interceptor Pursuit, Single Engine, Report No. NS-2

Model Specification, XP-79 Interceptor Pursuit, Report No. NS-14

Model Specification, XB-79B Interceptor Pursuit, Report No. NS-14B

Model Specification, JB-1, Report No. NS-16

Model Specification, Prototype - YRB-49A (Conversion of YB-35), NS-41A

Model Specification, Flying Scale Model Airplane, Northrop N-9M, Report No. NS-99

Model Specification, Long Range Reconnaisance Airplane (Conversion of YB-35), Air Force Model RB-35 B, Report No. NS-39

Model Specification, Airplane, Flying Test Bed EB-35-B, Northrop Model N-45, Report No. NS-45

NEWS releases:
      Northrop's "Flying Ram" Unveiled by Army, June 24, 1946
      Northrop "Rocket Wing" First to Fly in U. S., January 28, 1947
      Air Force Reduces Flying Wing Program, October 28, 1949
      New Northrop Wing Makes First Flight, May 4, 1950

NORAIR Project Designations, August 26, 1959

The Norcrafter (originally The Aircrafter)
      March 1940 (Vol. 1, No. 1)
      July 1940
      October-November 1940
      December 1940
      March-April 1941
      December 1941

The Northrop Flying Wing of 1929-30, Prepared by: Northrop Aircraft Group History Office, 1981

Northrop Model/Project Numbers, June 14, 1980

The Northrop News
      "Last Rites Held For Test Pilot Max Constant," May 25, 1943 – September 14, 1943
      "Her Pilots–," August 16, 1944
      "The Flying Wing Bomber," May 1, 1946
      "Special Issue on the Northrop Flying Wing XB-35 Bomber," May 1, 1946
      "Northrop Design – the First True 'Flying Wing'," May 1, 1946
      "Evolution of the Flying Wing," May 1, 1946
      "Wing Makes Flight Test," July 10, 1946
      "XB-35 Flight Successful," July 10, 1946
      "Northrop Flying Wing Dawn Flight," April 23, 1947
      "New XB-35 at Muroc on Second Test Hop," July 16, 1947
      "YB-49 Embarks On Muroc Air Tests," November 5, 1947
      "Northrop YB-49 Flying Wings Are World's Longest Ranging Jets," January 28, 1948
      "New Flying Wing Makes Muroc Hop," May 19, 1948
      "AF To Buy 30 Jet Wings," June 16, 1948
      "Northrop To Subcontract Jets," July 28, 1948
      "Gen. Ramey Gives YB-49 High Praise," August 25, 1948
      "Into The Future .. With the Northrop Flying Wing," September 22, 1948
      "Convert B 35s To Jet," November 17, 1948
      "Knieriem To Fort Worth On RB-49s," November 17, 1948
      "Air Park," February 9, 1949
      "Northrop Jet Wing Spans Continent at Record Pace," February 23, 1949
      "Wing Jet Conversion," Jult 13, 1949
      "First Flight Due In April," March 8, 1950
      "Northrop Developed, Flew First Manned Rocket-Powered Vehicle 25 Years Ago," September 10, 1969
      "Former test pilot Max Stanley tells about . . . Flying the Wing," July 10, 1981
      "Scorpion's View of Ontario," June 20, 1951
      "Northrop Missile Pilots Write Air History," June 4, 1952
      "The X-4 research Aircraft," October 8, 1952
      "John K. Northrop Retires, Echols Elected President," December 3, 1952
      "Former Test Pilot Recalls Early Days," February 25, 1983

Northrop Organizational Charts
As of July 5, 1949
As of April 1, 1950

Preliminary Estimated Weight and Balance, XP-79Z, Report No. W-60, October 26, 1945

Second Annual Report, Fiscal Year to July 31, 1941

State of the Company speech by C. N. Monson, General Manager, on April 12, 1948

The Story of Jack Northrop and the Flying Wings, c. 1949

Weight Data, YB-49 Flying Wing Bomber, W-55.13, November 7, 1949

Miscellaneous Documents

Baker, Francis J. The Death of the Flying Wing: The Real Reasons Behind the 1949 Cancellation of Northrop Aircraft's RB-49, Draft Dissertation, Claremont Graduate School, 1984

Begin, Lee. The Northrop Flying Wing Prototypes, American Institute of Aeronautics and Astronautics, Aircraft Prototype and Technology Demonstrator Symposium, Dayton, Ohio, March 23 - 24, 1983

Bellande, Edward. Flight Log: January 1, 1929 through December 21, 1929

Luce, Stewart. Jack Northrop's Life and Aircraft Designs

Northrop Aircraft Corporation, Models 1, 1-A, 2 and 3; United Technologies Archives

Sears, W. R. Flying-Wing Airplanes: The XB-35/YB-49 Program, American Institute of Aeronautics and Astronautics, The Evolution of Aircraft Wing Design Symposium, Dayton, March 18-19, 1980

Stanley, Max. The Flying Wings, The Society of Experimental Test Pilots, Twenty-Fourth Symposium Proceedings, September 24-27, 1980

Newspapers

"Aircraft Pioneer Jack Northrop Dies at Age 85." Los Angeles Times, February 20, 1981

"Congressman To See Air Force Planes." Corddry, Charles, Dayton Daily News, February 19, 1949

"Edward Bellande, Pioneer Aviator, Businessman, Dies." Los Angeles Times, November 18, 1976

"Firm Still Grows in 40th Year." Dore, Richard, The Daily Breeze, September 30, 1979

"49-Year-Old Design Resurrected as Stealth." Antelope Valley Press, November 4, 1988

"Founder Created a Family Atmosphere at Northrop." Dore, Richard, The Daily Breeze, September 30, 1979

"New Jets Provide Thrill Here For Graying Air Force Research Head." Dayton Daily News, February 19, 1949

"Northrop: A Pioneer of Aviation." Dore, The Daily Breeze, September 30, 1979

"Northrop's 'Flying Wing' Makes Debut on the Front Page, But Mystery Remains About This Mystery Plane," American Aviation, October 15, 1941

Periodicals

"A Gathering of Giants," <u>Northrop Institute of Technology Alumni Journal</u>, April 1968

Editor's Corner, <u>Naval Aviation News</u>, June 1978

"Flying Wing Has Novel Cockpit Layout," <u>Aviation Week</u>, October 13, 1947

"John K. Northrop: Aviation Pioneer Designer of Wings, 1895-1981," <u>Nuance</u>, Winter 1981

"Northrop Flying Wing," <u>Aero Digest</u>, March 1930

"Northrop Flying Wing Tested," <u>Aviation Engineering</u>, June 1930

Allen Francis J. "Northrop's Flying Wing," <u>Wings</u>, February 1986

Balzer, Gerald. "The Aircraft of Jack Northrop," <u>American Aviation Historical Society Journal</u>, Spring 1981

Bangs, Scholer. "Design Details of the Northrop XB-35," <u>Aviation</u>, April 1947

Gunston, Bill. "The All-Wing Northrops, Part 1," <u>Aeroplane Monthly</u>, January 1974

Gunston, Bill. "The All-Wing Northrops, Part 2," <u>Aeroplane Monthly</u>, February 1974

Gunston, Bill. "Prototype Pursuits," <u>Aeroplane Monthly</u>, December 1979

Hoffman, M. L. "The Northrop 'Flying Wing'", <u>Air Transportation</u>, March 1, 1930

Jay, W. K. "The Development of Northrop," <u>Western Flying</u>, August 1934

McLarren, Robert. "Low-Drag Accented In All-Wing," <u>Aviation Week</u>, December 20, 1948

McRuer, D. T. "The Flying Wing's Electronic Tail," Honeywell <u>Flight Lines</u>, November 1950

Mizrahi, Joe. "Sizing Up the Stealth," <u>Wings</u>, February 1990

Northrop, John K. "The All-Wing Type Airplane," <u>Aviation</u>, March 29, 1930

Northrop, John K. "The Flying Wing," <u>Western Flying</u>, March 1930

Northrop, John K. "The Northrop 'All-Wing'", <u>Aviation</u>, December 1941

Northrop, John K. "The Northrop XB-35 Flying Wing Superbomber," <u>Aviation</u>, August 1946

Northrop, J. K. "All-Wing Aircraft," <u>Flight</u>, June 5, 1947 (Part I) and June 12, 1947 (Part II)

"Northrop XB-35 Flying Wing Set for Flight Tests," <u>Aviation</u>, May 1946

"Northrop's Flying Wing," <u>Aero Digest</u>, November 1941

"Northrop's Flying Wing Bombers," <u>Aerophile</u>, May 1978

"Northrop's XB-35 and the F-15," <u>Aero Digest</u>, June 1946

Seifert, Howard S. "Twenty-Five Years of Rocket Development," <u>Jet Propulsion</u>, November 1955

Wagner, Ray. "U.S. Pusher Fighters of World War II," <u>Air Pictorial</u>, May 1975

Walton, Rus. "Jack Northrop And His Wonderful Wing," Flying, February 1948

Werrell, Kenneth P. "Northrop Snark, The Case Study of Failure," American Aviation Historical Society Journal, Fall 1988

Young, Bill and Gerald Balzer. "Northrop N-9M Flying Wing, Part I Description," American Aviation Historical Society Journal, Winter 1993

Young, Bill and Gerald Balzer. "Northrop N-9M Flying Wing, Part II Flight Test," American Aviation Historical Society Journal, Spring 1994

Books

Allen, Richard Sanders. The Northrop Story, 1929 - 1939. New York: Orion Books, 1990

Anderson, Fred. Northrop: An Aeronautical History. Century City: Northrop Corp., 1976

Biddle, Wayne. Barons of the Sky. New York: Simon & Schuster, 1991

Brown, K. S. et al, comp. United States Army and Air Force Fighters 1916 - 1961. Ed. Bruce Robertson. Letchworth: Harleyford, 1961

Brown, Michael E. Flying Blind, The Politics of the U.S. Strategic Bomber Program. Ithaca: Cornell University Press, 1992

Coleman, Ted. Jack Northrop and the Flying Wing. New York: Paragon, 1988

Craven, Wesley Frank and James Lea Cate, eds. The Army Air Forces In World War II, Volume Six, Men and Planes. U.S. Government Printing Office, 1983

Hallion, Richard P. On The Frontier, Flight Research at Dryden, 1946 - 1981. Washington: National Aeronautics and Space Administration, 1984

Hallion, Richard P. Test Pilots, The Frontiersmen of Flight. Washington: Smithsonian Institution Press, 1988

Heinemann, Edward H. and Rosario Rausa. Ed Heinemann, Combat Aircraft Designer. Annapolis: Naval Institute Press, 1980

Jones, Lloyd S. U.S. Bombers Fallbrook: Aero Publishers, 1974

Jones, Lloyd S. U.S. Fighters. Fallbrook: Aero Publishers, 1975

Kohn, Leo J. The Flying Wings of Northrop. Milwaukee: Aviation Publications, 1974

Knaack, Marcelle Size. Encyclopedia of U.S. Air Force Aircraft and Missile Systems, Volume II, Post-World War II Bombers, 1945 - 1973. Washington: US Government Publishing Office, 1988

Maloney, Edward T. Northrop Flying Wings. Corona Del Mar: World War II Publications, 1988

Miller, Jay. The X-Planes. Arlington: Aerofax, Inc, 1988

Schoneberger, William A. California Wings, A History of Aviation in the Golden State. Woodland Hills: Windsor Publications, 1984

Scott, Bill. Inside the Stealth Bomber, The B-2 Story. Blue Ridge Summit: Tab/Aero Books, 1991

Underwood, John. Madcaps, Millionaires and "Mose". Glendale: Heritage Press, 1984

Wagner, Ray. American Combat Planes. Garden City: Hanover House, 1960

Wooldridge, E. T. Wing Wonders, The Story of the Flying Wing. Washington: Smithsonian Institution Press, 1985

Public Programs, Television Programs, and Video Tapes

"An Evening with Jack Northrop and His Associates," American Institute of Aeronautics and Astronautics, Los Angeles, CA, September 1974

"Night in Aviation History" banquet, sponsored by Northrop Institute of Technology, February 8, 1968

"The Northrop Story," Northrop Corp., 1990

"Northrop's First Flights," Northrop Corp., 1990

"Reminiscences On-The-Wing," Northrop Vintage Aircraft Boosters Club, January 26, 1994

"Those Wonderful Wings!," Flight Test Historical Foundation, May 19, 1990

"Welcome Back Tucker," Northrop Vintage Aircraft Boosters Club, October 27, 1993

"The Wing Will Fly," The Discovery Channel, 1991

Gen. Robert Cardenas remarks at Planes of Fame Museum's N-9MB program, May 7, 1994

Interviews (in person, telephone, and tape)

Phil French, March 31, 1994

Herbert DeCenzo, October 10, 1972

Bill Huffman, March 29, 1994

John W. Myers, June 13, 1974

John K. Northrop, Sept. 27, 1972

John H. Northrop, June 11, 18, and 26, 1994

Max Stanley, July 9, 1994

Willis D. (Bill) Vinson, August 14 and 17, 1993

Vladimir Pavlecka, April 15, 1973

Charles Tucker, September 13, 1993

Index